Chandragupta Maurya

Chandragupta Maurya

The creation of a national hero in India

Sushma Jansari

UCLPRESS

First published in 2023 by
UCL Press
University College London
Gower Street
London WC1E 6BT

Available to download free: www.uclpress.co.uk

A CIP catalogue record for this book is available from The British Library.

ISBN: 978-1-80008-390-5 (Hbk)
ISBN: 978-1-80008-389-9 (Pbk)
ISBN: 978-1-80008-388-2 (PDF)
ISBN: 978-1-80008-391-2 (epub)
DOI: https://doi.org/10.14324/111.9781800083882

Contents

List of figures and tables vii
Abbreviations xi
Acknowledgements xiii

Introduction 1

Part I Setting the scene in antiquity 13

1 Chandragupta and Seleucus: a clash by the banks of the Indus 15

2 Megasthenes: travelling between empires 40

Part II Establishing the narrative 67

3 Sir William Jones and James Mill: synchronising histories and creating a divide 69

4 Embedding the divide: competing accounts during the British Raj 85

5 Reaction and transformation: reshaping history for a new era 103

Part III Antiquity, art and contemporary popular culture 127

6 A national project of a different sort: representations of Chandragupta in the Birla Mandirs 129

7 Wimbledon to New Delhi: a statue of Chandragupta in the Indian Parliament 159

List of figures and tables

1.1 Chandragupta Basadi on Chandragiri at Śravaṇa Beḷgoḷa, Karnataka is believed to have been erected by Chandragupta. © Nicholas Barnard. 20

1.2 Bhadrabāhu Cave on Chandragiri at Śravaṇa Beḷgoḷa, Karnataka is associated with Chandragupta's ritual suicide. © Nicholas Barnard. 21

1.3 A detail from the carved screen inside Chandragupta Basadi which depicts events from the lives of Chandragupta and the Jain monk Bhadrabāhu. © Nicholas Barnard. 22

2.1 Wooden palisade revealed during excavations by J. A. Page and M. Ghosh at Bulandi Bagh, Patna in 1926–27. Source: Archaeological Survey of India 1926–1927, Wikimedia Commons, bit.ly/3BMVWei. 56

4.1 The Pataliputra stone capital found during L. A. Waddell's excavations at Bulandi Bagh, Patna in 1895. It is on display at Patna Museum, Bihar. Source: Nalanda001 and Gary Todd. Shared under a Creative Commons Attribution-ShareAlike 4.0 International licence (CC BY-SA 4.0), Wikimedia Commons, bit.ly/3DV7BL4. 92

6.1 Exterior of the Lakshmi Narayan temple, New Delhi designed by Sris Chandra Chatterjee. This temple was completed in 1939 and was the first Birla Mandir to be conceived and constructed. Source: Dan Lundberg. Shared under a Creative Commons Attribution-ShareAlike 2.0 International licence (CC BY-SA 2.0), Wikimedia Commons, bit.ly/3R9mFr7. 131

6.2 Statue of Chandragupta Maurya in the grounds of the Lakshmi Narayan temple, New Delhi. Source: Ashish Bhatnagar, Wikimedia Commons, bit.ly/3flJzhK. 138

6.3 The wedding maṇḍapa in the grounds of the Lakshmi Narayan temple, New Delhi. © Agnieszka Staszczyk. 144
6.4 Frieze inside the wedding maṇḍapa depicting the marriage of Chandragupta and Helena. The maṇḍapa is in the grounds of the Lakshmi Narayan temple, New Delhi. © Agnieszka Staszczyk. 144
6.5 Painting of Chandragupta and Cāṇakya in the main temple hall of the Lakshmi Narayan temple, New Delhi. © Agnieszka Staszczyk. 147
6.6 Rajasthan School painting of Yaśodā holding the infant Kṛṣṇa, attended by a woman. Registration Number 1880,0.2372. © The Trustees of the British Museum. Shared under a Creative Commons Attribution-NonCommercial-ShareAlike 4.0 International (CC BY-NC-SA 4.0) licence. 149
6.7 Painting of Chandragupta and Cāṇakya in the central hall of the New Vishwanath temple, Varanasi. © Agnieszka Staszczyk. 151
6.8 Painting of Chandragupta and Cāṇakya in the central hall of the Srimadbhagavadgita temple, Mathura. © Agnieszka Staszczyk. 153
6.9 Painting of Chandragupta and Cāṇakya in the central hall of the Lakshmi Narayan temple, Bhopal. © Agnieszka Staszczyk. 154
6.10 Painting of Chandragupta and Cāṇakya in the upper gallery, main hall of the Deva temple, Patna. © Agnieszka Staszczyk. 155
7.1 Bronze statue of Chandragupta by Hilda Seligman. Source: Parliament of India. Shared under a Creative Commons Attribution-ShareAlike 4.0 International licence (CC BY-SA 4.0), Wikimedia Commons, bit.ly/3SAl6DI. 169
7.2 Postage stamp illustrating Chandragupta, designed by Sankha Samanta. © Government of India, licensed under the Government Open Data License – India (GODL). Photograph: Ali Mackie. 175
8.1 Scene from the Gazi Scroll, probably depicting the Muslim saint Gazi Pir. Registration Number 1955,1008,0.95. © The Trustees of the British Museum. Shared under a Creative Commons Attribution-NonCommercial-ShareAlike 4.0 International (CC BY-NC-SA 4.0) licence. 185

Table

Abbreviations

ABC	A. K. Grayson, *Assyrian and Babylonian Chronicles*
BCHP	*Babylonian Chronicles of the Hellenistic Period*, published online: https://www.livius.org/sources/about/mesopotamian-chronicles/ (last accessed: 8 December 2022)
BNJ	Brill's New Jacoby
CHI	E. J. Rapson (ed.) *The Cambridge History of India*, Vol. I
FGrH	F. Jacoby, *Die Fragmente der griechischen Historiker*
FHG	K. Müller, *Fragmenta Historicorum Graecorum*
IG	*Inscriptionem Graecorum*
LGPN	*Lexicon of Greek Personal Names*
MDAI (A)	*Mitteilungen des deutschen archäologischen Instituts* (A): Athenische Abteilung (1876–)
ODNB	*Oxford Dictionary of National Biography*
OHI	V. A. Smith, *The Oxford History of India*
RC	C.B. Welles, *Royal Correspondence*
Dip.	*Dīpavaṃsa*
Mah.	*Mahāvaṃsa*
Mil.	*Milindapañha*
Sth.	*Sthavirāvalīcaritra*
TiP	Yativṛṣabha, *Tiloya-paṇṇatti*
App. *Syr.*	Appian, *Syrian Wars*
Arist. *Pol.*	Aristotle, *Politics*
Arr. *Anab.*	Arrian, *Anabasis*
Arr. *Ind.*	Arrian, *Indike*
Arr. *Succ.*	Arrian, *Ta met'Alexandron*
Ath. *Deip.*	Athenaeus, *Deipnosophists*
Clem. Al. *Strom.*	Clement of Alexandria, *Stromateis*

Curt.	Quintus Curtius Rufus, *Historiarum Alexandri Magni Macedonis Libri Qui Supersunt*
Diod.	Diodorus Siculus, *Bibliotheca historica*
Euseb. *Chron.*	Eusebius, *Chronica*
Euseb. *Hist. Ec.*	Eusebius, *Historia ecclesiastica*
Euseb. *Praep. Evang.*	Eusebius, *Praeparatio evangelica*
Hdt.	Herodotus, *The Histories*
Joseph. *AJ*	Josephus, *Antiquitates Judaicae*
Joseph. *Ap.*	Josephus, *Contra Apionem*
Just. *Epit.*	Justinus, *Epitome* (of Trogus)
Luc. *Macr.*	Lucian, *Macrobii*
Oro. *Hist.*	Orosius, *Historiae Adversus Paganos*
Philost. *Ap.*	Philostratus, *Vita Apollonii*
Phot. *Bibl.*	Photius, *Bibliotheca*
Plut. *Alex.*	Plutarch, *Vitae Alexander*
Plut. *Dem.*	Plutarch, *Vitae Demetrius*
Plut. *Eum.*	Plutarch, *Vitae Eumenes*
Plin. *NH*	Pliny the Elder, *Naturalis historia*
Polyaen. *Strat.*	Polyaenus, *Strategemata*
Strab.	Strabo, *Geographica*
AIWC	All India Women's Committee
ASI	Archaeological Survey of India
BM	British Museum
EIC	East India Company
ICS	Indian Civil Service

Acknowledgements

Since I was a child, my Nanima shared her love of India's history and many mythological stories with me. As I got older, we spoke about our family's fascinating albeit difficult lives and journeys across India, Burma (Myanmar), Tanzania and Kenya before settling here in the UK in the 1970s. This history of movement and transformation and yet with this long thread extending back to India has always intrigued me. The underlying idea finds expression in this book through Chandragupta's story which was itself shaped by colonialism and its aftermath and, through popular culture, still resonates today not only in India but among the global Indian diaspora.

There are so many people I would like to thank profusely for their help and guidance as I've been writing this book. I received the contract to write my book towards the end of 2020, and we all know what a year that was. My research plans were kyboshed as travel was off the table and libraries and archives were closed. Home schooling (what a euphemism) while working on an intense, time-consuming project at work and attempting to find time to write is a hell that I don't wish to revisit. Somehow, amid these challenges, this book gradually took shape and the kindness and generosity of my family, friends and colleagues during such difficult times made all the difference.

Accessing documents and books at this time was made easier by scholarly openness, and I'd particularly like to thank Prathama Banerjee, Shirin Rai, Richard Stoneman and Archana Venkatesh. It's always helpful and interesting to speak to people about their work, and conversations and email exchanges with Nasreen Munni Kabir, Adity Kay, Arani Ilankuberan, and Isabel, Lincoln and Dominic Seligman, have fed into and enriched the book. Kapil Gogri and Richard Morel helped put me in touch with Sankha Samanta, who shared information about his research and artistic vision in creating the artwork for the Chandragupta stamp. Tathagata Neogi kindly translated into English the inscriptions associated with Chandragupta in the Birla Mandirs. Nicholas Barnard, Agnieszka

Staszczyk and Ali Mackie generously permitted me to reproduce their photographs in this book, and I was able to use the Hotung Research Fund to cover the cost of additional images from the British Museum.

A supportive head of department makes all the difference, and Jane Portal helped me prioritise writing on the home straight. Margot Finn helped and encouraged me in getting this project off the ground and across the finish line, while answering numerous questions along the way. Jagjeet Lally read through and commented on numerous chapters of the book in their various incarnations, thereby immeasurably improving them. Rachel Mairs and Phiroze Vasunia were wonderful examiners for my thesis and continued to support me through the process of transforming the work into a book. Eleanor Robson has been a stalwart mentor to me over the years. She stepped in as my PhD supervisor when I had a 3-month-old baby and times were tough. Without her enduring support and belief in me – and the pep talk to end all pep talks in December 2015! – there would have been no thesis nor this book.

I save my final thanks for my dearest husband Edward and our beloved daughter Anuradha. There are no words to express my profound love for them both.

I dedicate this book to Edward, Anuradha and my Nanima.

Introduction

We take it for granted that some ancient figures become heroes, and others do not. When we consider the question at all, it is usually assumed that such transformations are largely a matter of chance. And while there may be cases in which sheer luck is involved, this book shows that heroes can also be shaped by the tide and pull of historical forces and determined personalities. Here, the journey that Chandragupta Maurya took from obscure ruler to national Indian hero is traced from fragmentary texts to historical textbooks, through sculptures, films and comic books.

The origins of this book lie in a conundrum I faced when first embarking on some reading for my thesis in 2014. I naively hoped to balance the equation, as far as possible, in looking at Seleucid-Mauryan relations through the eyes of both Western and South Asian scholars. As I did so, I became increasingly aware of a significant and striking discrepancy between the interpretation and presentation of the Seleucid-Mauryan encounter and its outcome of each group of historians.

I found that a number of prominent Indian historians, such as P. L. Bhargava and N. S. Kalota, stated in strongly emotive language not only that Chandragupta 'conquered and subdued Seleukos'[1] and was thereby the 'emancipator'[2] of his country. They also wrote that the terms of the treaty demonstrated Seleucus' recognition of Chandragupta's superiority, because Seleucus was obliged to 'conclude a humiliating treaty' with Chandragupta.[3] Even in works where the language was more moderate, the consensus remained that Chandragupta emerged victorious from his clash with Seleucus, as noted by Romila Thapar, for example.[4] There was no suggestion of any other possible outcome.

In contrast, while Western historians tended to present a wider range of opinions on the military interaction between Seleucus and Chandragupta, the terms of the treaty were viewed as a positive result for Seleucus. In relation to the battle, for example, Richard Billows suggested that Seleucus was 'reasonably successful' in the war against Chandragupta.[5] John D. Grainger, in contrast, stated that Seleucus 'clearly lost' the battle.'[6] While discussing the treaty, Frank Holt wrote that Seleucus accepted a token submission from Chandragupta, while Susan Sherwin-White and Amélie Kuhrt agreed with F. W. Walbank that the elephants Seleucus received constituted a major prize.[7]

At this point I wondered what was going on, because one could be forgiven for assuming that all of these scholars were drawing on different sources, that presented the encounter and its outcome in two diverging and incompatible ways. But they weren't. There are no South Asian sources for any aspect of their interaction, so they were all reliant on exactly the same Graeco-Roman texts, written by a select group of authors. Strabo, Appian, Plutarch and Justin are the only ancient authors known to have written about the clash between Seleucus and Chandragupta and the treaty they agreed in its aftermath (see Chapter 1).

None of these texts revealed which, if either, of the rulers emerged victorious from the military encounter, or even what this conflict entailed. Similarly, the evidence does not show what Seleucus or Chandragupta thought of the terms of the treaty that they had agreed, nor whether one of them came out of it better off than the other. In fact, only three parts of it have come down to us: Seleucus transferred land to Chandragupta; Chandragupta gave 500 elephants to Seleucus; and there was a marriage alliance, although it is not clear who or what this involved. This lack of detail turned out to be crucial.

The limited information in the ancient sources makes the later scholarly inferences and conclusions so interesting because the evidence is wide open to interpretation. In this instance, each of the two groups of modern historians is viewing and assessing this historical moment through a very different filter, that is, the way that best fits their preconceptions of the power relationships between Seleucus and Chandragupta. The result is that their conclusions differ substantially.

Knowledge is not objective, nor is the way in which we understand ancient history. Historians come at the source material in their own individual ways, from different regional, historical and cultural contexts. In the case of Seleucus and Chandragupta, they attributed meaning to the remaining ancient fragments in very different ways. At this point, some questions posed by James Secord, historian of science, are pertinent. How and why does knowledge circulate? How does it cease to be the exclusive property of a single individual or group and become part of the taken-for-granted understanding of much wider groups of people?[8] These questions helped shape the arrangement of this book into three parts, which sequentially move the story from antiquity to the present day.

Until recently, the study of the reception of ancient history, and particularly Graeco-Roman history, has tended to focus on the West. This situation is gradually changing, and Phiroze Vasunia's book *The Classics and Colonial India* (2013) played a significant role in this development. In his work, Vasunia drew attention not only to how the inheritance of Graeco-Roman history influenced the British colonial outlook on India, but also to the wide-ranging Indian reception of Graeco-Roman antiquity during the colonial period. Vasunia's work provided a model for the central section of this book, including the wider socio-political contextualisation of the historians I discuss. While Vasunia touches on the importance of Chandragupta to Indian nationalism, his primary focus is on Alexander the Great. This book is, therefore, the first to address in detail the British and Indian reception of the founding of Seleucid-Mauryan relations and, in this way, aims to fill a lacuna in scholarship.

The evolving relationship between Britain and India turned out to be crucial in the academic transformation of Chandragupta from little-known ruler to empire-building hero. Well-known scholars writing during the heyday of the East India Company were integral to the story. Sir William Jones, a judge and the founder of the Asiatic Society of Bengal, sparked the process in 1793. This was the year in which he shared his discovery with fellow Society members that the 'Sandrocottus' of Graeco-Roman literature was the very same 'Chandragupta' found in Sanskrit texts. What he couldn't have known was how James Mill, economist and historian, would twist this information to accord with his perception of India in *The History of British India* (1817) published some 24 years later (see Chapter 3).

Although widely accepted as the first – and for a long time only – history of India available to an English-speaking audience, Mill's work makes deeply uncomfortable reading today. He wrote it as a vehicle for getting a job with the East India Company, and it is filled with his own deeply held prejudices against India and its people. Wherever there was an opportunity to denigrate an aspect of Indian history or culture, he grasped it with both hands. The meeting between Seleucus and Chandragupta, and its outcome, was no exception. In this case, Mill chose to transform the sources in such a way that they became, for him and much of his readership, a comfortable fiction: Seleucus was accorded victory over Chandragupta. For Mill, there was a strong correlation between this ancient relationship and his ideas about contemporary British-Indian relations.

Mill's interpretation caused a chain reaction in the scholarship that came after him. If his image of Seleucus versus Chandragupta formed the early consensus, then British and Indian historians writing at the height of the British Raj and in the years leading up to independence dismantled and then reshaped it in ways that accorded with their own perceptions of British-Indian relations. Somewhat surprisingly, it was Vincent A. Smith, of the Indian Civil Service and a historian of ancient India, who switched victory from Seleucus to Chandragupta. Meanwhile, R. C. Dutt, one of the first professional Indian historians of ancient India, linked Chandragupta's triumph over Seleucus with the unification of northern India.

While Smith is often held up as an arch-orientalist, in this case the label doesn't quite fit. And, as the power relations between Britain and India shifted and the balance began to change, so, too, did Chandragupta's position rise in relation to Seleucus. At hardly any point did the scales even out: instead, they swung violently in the other direction.

The second generation of Indian historians, including R. C. Majumdar and R. K. Mookerji, went beyond Dutt's interpretation and transformed Chandragupta into a ruler who not only repulsed European incursions into India but unified India into a major power. Their Chandragupta – and he was very much their creation – was the ancient hero par excellence. This interpretation, like Mill's before them, was based not on the sources but on the historians' own ideas about the changing power relationship between Britain and India. As their politics and close association with Indian nationalist movements had an impact on their work, so too did their work on the Mauryans influence politicians, and even guide the choice of symbols for the Indian Republic.

Jawaharlal Nehru, the first Prime Minister of the Republic of India, for example, wholeheartedly adopted this potent image of Chandragupta, and, indeed, the Mauryan dynasty as a whole. His support for and interest in Chandragupta found expression in letters he wrote between 1930 and 1933 to his ten-year-old daughter, Indira, which were later published in a volume titled *Glimpses of World History* (1934), as well as his history book *The Discovery of India* (1946). In a letter dated 1931, Nehru focuses on Chandragupta, writing:

> During Chandragupta's reign Seleucus, the general of Alexander who had inherited the countries from Asia Minor to India, crossed the Indus with an army and invaded India. He repented very soon of his rashness. Chandragupta defeated him badly and Seleucus went back the way he had come.[9]

This sentiment is echoed in his later history. The words he employs in relation to Chandragupta's reaction to the death of Alexander, and also his description of Cāṇakya, are telling. After receiving news of Alexander's death,

> immediately Chandragupta and Chanakya raised the old and ever-new cry of nationalism and roused the people against the foreign invader. The Greek garrison was driven away and Taxila captured. The appeal to nationalism had brought allies to Chandragupta and he marched with them across north India to Pataliputra. Within two years of Alexander's death, he was in possession of that city and kingdom and the Maurya Empire had been established.[10]

This book was written in 1944 while Nehru and others were in prison for their participation in the Quit India Movement. These words, and many others in the book, draw on the past for comfort and inspiration at a difficult moment in the struggle for independence. Here, past and present come together and the excitement and energy of that earlier struggle is palpable. Interestingly, there are echoes of Gandhi's life in Nehru's description of Cāṇakya in the following section:

> a man who played a dominating part in the establishment, growth and preservation of the empire. ... He was no mere follower of a king, a humble adviser of an all-powerful emperor .... [A]vailing himself of every device to delude and defeat the enemy, he sat with the reins of empire in his hands and looked upon the emperor more as a loved pupil than as a master. Simple and austere in his life, uninterested in the pomp and pageantry of high position, when he had redeemed his pledge and accomplished his purpose, he wanted to retire, Brahmin-like, to a life of contemplation.[11]

If Nehru saw Chandragupta as his ancient antecedent in their similarity of purpose, then Cāṇakya/Gandhi played a similar role in the achievement of their shared aims. One wonders how aware Nehru was of these likenesses when he was writing his books, or how striking the comparisons would be to his readers more than 70 years later.

The elevation of the Mauryans as the ancient dynasty par excellence was not confined to the written word, but found expression in the symbols adopted for the new Republic. H. P. Ray has written in detail about the use of Aśoka's Sarnath lion capital as India's state emblem and his *chakra* at the centre of India's national flag.[12] What is generally less well known is Nehru's role in the installation of the Aśokan bull capital from Rampurva between the central pillars of Rashtrapati Bhavan's forecourt. He did not want this important artwork and piece of history confined within the walls of a museum but on open display for the public to see.[13]

So it is not enough to look at historians and their literary output, because history is not confined to history books but has manifold implications and outcomes in the world. Another outlet for their work is popular culture. Looking at Chandragupta, we can see that his star began to rise from the end of the nineteenth century. The narrative that had been fashioned for him by Indian historians writing during this period found its fullest expression in Indian popular culture in the decades that followed. It was also in the popular arena that Chandragupta's life and achievements were codified. Just as in the history books, fact and fiction were merged. The key difference, however, is audience and influence. While the history books inevitably had quite a small audience, the films, television series, historical novels and comic books produced reached many millions of people, not only in South Asia but globally. This is impact on a different scale.

In modernity, the first playwrights and filmmakers to take up the story of Chandragupta and present it to a general audience did so with a specific agenda in mind. This agenda very much echoed and expanded on the core narrative found in history books. In Dwijendralal Ray's play *Chandragupta* (1911) and H. M. Reddy's adaptation of this play into the film *Mathru Bhoomi* (1939), for example, the story of Chandragupta versus Seleucus stood in for Indians versus the British (see Chapter 8). In this way, Chandragupta moved from history books onto the stage and then to the silver screen, but the message with which the historians had imbued him remained the same: he was the hero that Indian nationalists could look to for inspiration as they agitated for freedom from colonial rule. After all, if he had managed it to glorious effect in the past, then surely those such as Nehru could recreate the outcome and expel the British from contemporary India. One can imagine Mill turning in his grave at this use of the relationship of Seleucus and Chandragupta.

There is a darker side to this story of Indian versus European, and although it has come to prominence through more recent popular culture, its roots are older. In the television series *Chandra Nandini* (2016–17), for example, Chandragupta's Indian wives are presented as virtuous and good. In contrast, his Greek wife Helena, daughter of Seleucus, is a jealous and scheming woman whom Chandragupta eventually sends back to Greece with their children of mixed heritage (see Chapter 8). This idea is echoed in Adity Kay's historical novel *Emperor Chandragupta* (2016). Here, Durdhara is the dutiful and loyal Indian wife, while Helen is the childish and selfish foreign one (see Chapter 9). This storyline has come a long way from the original sources and does not reflect well on what contemporary Indian society can and will accept in terms of foreigners in their midst, particularly within their families.

For a high-profile example, one only needs to look at the vitriol directed towards Sonia Gandhi, the Italian-born wife of Rajiv Gandhi (Indira Gandhi's son and Jawaharlal Nehru's grandson), and their children, because of their perceived 'foreignness'. This is not a recent phenomenon: an aversion to Hindus marrying non-Hindus, or even other Hindus but of different castes, is caught up in much older ideas about caste. While some have moved on from this way of thinking, it is still deeply ingrained in society, not only in the subcontinent but among the global diaspora. The difference in the case of Chandragupta is that while some historians chose to overlook his possible marriage to a Greek woman because it did not accord with their perception of how a Hindu ruler ought to behave, contemporary writers of scripts and historical fiction chose another tack. They filled in the gaps of the storyline with a narrative that they knew would not impede consumption by – and therefore profits from – the public at large. They presented Helena as they did because they could: the audience would not be up in arms about her depiction and boycott the series or the book. In fact, the representations went mostly unnoticed and reviewers didn't even comment on the way Helena and her children with Chandragupta were presented.

Another worrying outcome of more recent retellings of Chandragupta's story can be seen in comic books aimed at children. *Amar Chitra Katha* (ACK) comics are aimed at children and sell in their millions. They regale their readers with mythological stories about the gods as well as narratives about important historical figures. The ACK motto is 'the route to your roots' and in relation to the people of the past they present their comics as historically accurate. This aspiration is all well and good until one looks at the *Chandragupta* comic. Apart from Chandragupta's overthrow of the Nanda dynasty, and his connection with Cāṇakya, there is nothing here that reflects evidence from the available sources. The result is that generations of young readers grow up believing that the version of Chandragupta's story they read in this comic is simplified but accurate. Unfortunately, in this case their trust is misplaced (see Chapter 9).

The writing and reception of history has important ramifications for how we engage with the past during different periods, and across a range of media and platforms. The outcomes of particular presentations of the past and changes in interpretation can only be guessed at. This is because we do not know how ideas about and engagement with the past will shift, change and manifest in new environments. Jones and Mill, for example, could have had no conception of what their work would go on to trigger in colonial-era Indian scholarship. Similarly, Indian historians writing around the time of independence could have little idea that their work would be adopted and changed over the decades to find expression across such a wide range of popular culture channels, including television, and through storylines they might baulk at.

The interpretations presented by most of the British and Indian historians discussed in this book deviate significantly from the available evidence. The result is that they essentially produce fictional accounts of the past that accord with their own ideas about historical and contemporary events, including political relations. The result of leaving the sources at the wayside and substituting one's own perceptions is that history becomes fictionalised to the point where it is difficult to separate historical works from costume dramas. This is what happened in the case of Chandragupta, and it is the story that is told in this book.

Chapter overviews

Chapter 1 provides a discussion of the full range of available Graeco-Roman and South Asian literary sources to reconstruct Chandragupta's rise to power. On this evidence it is argued that the traditional date ascribed to the start of his reign – *c.*320/319 BC – cannot continue to be uncritically accepted and repeated in scholarship. Nor, therefore, can the dates of his successors, and therefore the Buddha and Mahāvīra, be based on this Mauryan start date. Following this analysis, sources that deal with Chandragupta's clash with Seleucus by the banks of the Indus, and their subsequent treaty, are assessed. This examination is important because later British and Indian scholars, discussed in Chapters 3, 4 and 5, presented wildly diverging interpretations of the clash and the treaty.

Megasthenes and his *Indica* are the focus of Chapter 2. This ancient ambassador, traveller and author provides the only eyewitness account of Mauryan India that survives from the time of Chandragupta's rule. He may also have been involved in the establishment of diplomatic relations between Seleucus and Chandragupta. For these reasons, Megasthenes is an important source for the region and period. In this chapter, Megasthenes is historically and geographically contextualised, in terms of his relations with Sibyrtius, Porus, Seleucus and Chandragupta, and of his travels in the subcontinent. The chapter also includes a proposed reconstruction of the *Indica*'s original structure.

Chapter 3 begins with the important link that Sir William Jones made in the late eighteenth century between the 'Chandragupta' of Sanskrit literature and the 'Sandracottus' of Graeco-Roman sources. This was a vital historical development because it meant, for the first time, that Indian and Graeco-Roman history could be synchronised and dates assigned to this period of ancient Indian history. The chapter moves on to discuss Mill's *The History of British India* (1817). Mill was one of the earliest adopters of the link made by Jones, and he imposed his own moralistic interpretation on the Seleucid-Mauryan encounter. He chose to construe the available sources in such a way as to present Seleucus as victorious over Chandragupta, even though the evidence does not state that either ruler conquered the other or emerged more successful from the treaty. This interpretation was to prove influential for almost a century.

There were profound changes in the British relationship with India between when Mill was writing in the early nineteenth century, and when the prominent historians of ancient India, Vincent A. Smith and Edward J. Rapson, were working, during the late nineteenth and early twentieth centuries. Chapter 4 investigates the impact that the move from East India Company to British Raj had on the selection and education of the administrators sent out to India, including Smith. The chapter explores the influence this experience and the new political circumstances had on the research and writing of ancient histories of India. It also moves forward the story of Mauryan archaeological, epigraphic and literary discoveries. In this way, a framework is provided for Smith and Rapson's interpretations of the Seleucid-Mauryan clash and subsequent treaty, including in the Oxford and Cambridge histories of India with which they were involved.

From the early twentieth century onwards, Indian historians reacted against the narrative established by Mill and perpetuated in the work of some later British scholars. In their work, beginning with R. C. Dutt's *The Civilization of India* (1900), the tables were turned in favour of Chandragupta: he was accorded victory over Seleucus. This is despite the fact that they were using the same sources as British scholars. Chapter 5 goes into the reasons behind this change in emphasis, including the rise of Indian nationalism, the involvement of many historians in the independence movement, and eventual independence from colonial rule. Notably, the only ancient references to the contact between Seleucus and Chandragupta are found in Graeco-Roman sources. The chapter therefore also examines the ways in which Indian scholars had access to this material, specifically through John W. McCrindle's late nineteenth-century translations, which remain influential to the present day.

A series of representations of Chandragupta are found in a rather unexpected setting: five Birla Mandirs in Delhi, Patna, Mathura, Bhopal and Varanasi. Chapter 6 focuses on the first Birla Mandir, the Lakshmi Narayan temple in Delhi completed in 1939, to explore the reasons behind Chandragupta's inclusion in these religious complexes. There is a detailed discussion of the imagery and associated text of the statue, mural and paintings that depict Chandragupta at all of the sites. Sris Chandra Chatterjee, the architect of the Birla Mandir in Delhi, was inspired by ancient Indian architecture, including that of Magadha, the heartland of the Mauryan Empire. His Modern Indian Architecture and design for the temple are examined in the chapter, as are his links with Indian nationalism and *swadeshi*, both of which influenced his architectural style. Taking a holistic approach to understanding the decoration of the Birla Mandirs, and especially the way in which Chandragupta is represented, enables us to understand more clearly the messages that the Birla family hoped to share with the worshippers and visitors to their temples.

The first sculpture to be installed in the Indian Parliament complex after independence was Hilda Seligman's bronze of Chandragupta as a shepherd boy. The background to this story is told for the first time in Chapter 7, which includes a discussion of the inspiration behind such an unusual depiction of this ruler. Seligman's literary output, and her charitable work in India, enabled her to develop a wide network of influential contacts there, including Rabindranath Tagore, the Princess of Berar, and many others. It is suggested that these connections were influential in the transfer of the statue from Seligman's garden in Wimbledon to its new home in such a prominent position in New Delhi. This story is set in the wider context of the high-profile post-independence discussions that took place about the decoration of the parliament.

Chapter 8 focuses on the numerous plays, films and television series produced between the fifth century AD and the present day. In late to mid-nineteenth-century India, it was not prudent to criticise the colonial government directly, so playwrights and filmmakers turned to the past and substituted the British with historical invaders of India, including Alexander's, and later Seleucus', Macedonian forces. Chandragupta's popularity reached its peak during this period and swiftly declined thereafter. It was only in the 2010s, through historical television series, that public interest in Chandragupta resumed. There was a distinct change in emphasis in the modern storylines: Chandragupta's interaction with Seleucus and the Greeks was relegated to the background, and the primary focus was now on his rise to power within India.

The final chapter explores the development and function of Chandragupta's story in historical novels written for adults, and in comics produced for children. A. S. Panchapakesa Ayyar's *Three Men of Destiny* (1939) and Qurratulain Hyder's *Aag Ka Darya* ('River of fire'; Urdu 1959 and English 1998) were published on either side of independence and Partition. The books reflect the aspirations and concerns each author felt about these seismic events in the subcontinent's history, with Chandragupta's story woven through the narratives. In the later twentieth century, three popular historical novels by Rajat Pillai (2012), Adity Kay (2016) and Indrayani Sawkar (2019) centred on Chandragupta. These three books rode the wave of interest in Chandragupta sparked by the multiple television series released during this period. The storylines echoed what had come before in terms of their broad narrative arc, but with a key difference: for a modern audience, the Chandragupta versus Seleucus clash no longer needed to represent the India versus Britain fight for independence. Lastly, the way the story of Chandragupta's life and achievements has been reshaped and repackaged for children is discussed through three *Amar Chitra Katha* comic books: *Chanakya* (1971), *Chandragupta* (1978) and *Megasthenes* (1987). Despite purporting to provide a 'route to your roots', the story contained in *Chandragupta* leads to an ahistorical past, a story devoid of history.

Notes

1 Kalota 1978, 97.
2 Bhargava 1935, 101.
3 Bhargava 1935, 38.
4 Thapar 1990, 70.
5 Billows 1994, 89.
6 Grainger 2007, 130.
7 Holt 1988, 101; Walbank 1981, 54; Sherwin-White and Kuhrt 1993, 11–12.
8 Secord 2004, 655.
9 Nehru 1934, 52.
10 Nehru 1946, 123.
11 Nehru 1946, 123.
12 Ray 2014.
13 President of India's website, 'The main building & central lawn: circuit 1'. https://rashtrapatisachivalaya.gov.in/rbtour/circuit-1/rampurva-bull (accessed 19 October 2022).

Part I
Setting the scene in antiquity

The two chapters in Part I of this book look at the evidence for Chandragupta's reign and his interactions with Seleucus. This source-based analysis is vital because it is the foundation on which all later interpretations rest. A detailed exploration of the Graeco-Roman sources reveals that little information remains about the encounter and treaty between the rulers and that neither Seleucus nor Chandragupta is depicted as the clear victor. In addition, it is not even clear in which work(s) the details originated. Megasthenes' *Indica* is a possibility. Megasthenes is likely to have been Seleucus' ambassador to Chandragupta's court and the surviving fragments of his *Indica* are the most important literary source for early Mauryan India. For this reason, he gets a chapter to himself, which contextualises him temporally and geographically.

Few surviving South Asian sources mention the founder of the Mauryan dynasty, and none at all have anything to say about Chandragupta's meeting with his counterpart in the west, Seleucus. Viśākadatta's fifth-century play *Mudrārākṣasa*, for example, which tells the story of Chandragupta's rise to power, does not mention his encounter with Seleucus. The limited literary material, contemporary or otherwise, concerning Chandragupta's reign and kingdom makes it impossible to corroborate the details given in Megasthenes' *Indica*. Instead, most of the sources focus on Chandragupta's grandson Aśoka, the Mauryan emperor famous for his conversion and adherence to Buddhism. This is because, in contrast to the Graeco-Roman sources, the South Asian texts relevant here are religious in nature. Buddhist literature is the best represented because of Aśoka's religious affiliation, followed by that of the Jains and Brāhamaṇas. For instance, the Buddhist Sri Lankan chronicle and its commentary, the *Mahāvaṃsa* and the *Mahāvaṃsa-ṭīkā*, provide information primarily about Aśoka but also, because of their association with him, some details concerning his father and grandfather (see Chapter 1).

An exploration of the two groups of sources – Graeco-Roman and South Asian – makes it clear that ancient authors had their own particular agendas and interests, which shaped the ways in which they thought and wrote about the rulers of the Hellenistic/Mauryan period. These differences created significant disparities between the types of literary evidence that survive, what sort of information is preserved, and how it is presented. These disparities did not disappear in modernity; on the contrary, they were reinforced and became part of the canon. These differences and the underlying reasons for them are investigated in Part II.

1
Chandragupta and Seleucus: a clash by the banks of the Indus

Exit Alexander

Alexander III ('the Great') of Macedon defeated Darius III, king of the Achaemenid Empire, at the Battle of Gaugamela in 331 BC. Following his victory, Alexander moved towards the eastern Achaemenid possessions, arriving first in Bactria and Sogdiana before reaching the Punjab in *c.*327–326 BC.[1] Alexander was accompanied by his officers Aristobulus, Nearchus, Ptolemy I and Onesicritus, each of whom went on to write influential accounts of Alexander's campaigns which also included information about India. Seleucus, formerly one of Alexander's *paides*, was also present as commander of the Royal Hypaspists.[2]

As Alexander crossed the Indus into the Punjab with his army, he encountered a region described by the Graeco-Roman authors as prosperous, well ordered, and divided into a number of realms, each of which comprised multiple cities. Alexander aimed to extend and consolidate his rule over the Punjab, while local Indian rulers wanted to maintain control over their own kingdoms and spheres of influence. Unsurprisingly, Alexander's entry into this region at the head of an army precipitated a series of embassies from local rulers who were, with good cause, concerned about his military intentions. Alexander also sent out his own ambassadors to rulers in the region. These embassies represent the very first instances of official Graeco-Macedonian and Indian ambassadorial contact and exchange.

While most of the embassies exchanged served to avert violence, Cleochares was unsuccessful in his attempt to gain Porus' submission to Alexander and this failure led to one of the bloodiest, albeit ultimately victorious, campaigns of Alexander's career.[3] Alexander's success in battle provided him with a useful example of the violence that he could unleash if his authority was not accepted by other regional rulers. However, information found in Arrian reveals there was more to this particular story than a simple case of ambassadorial failure, specifically that Alexander undertook military action against Porus in collaboration with recently made Indian allies. On receiving Alexander into his kingdom as a friend, the Indian ruler Taxiles appears to have orchestrated a combined Graeco-Macedonian and Indian military response against his neighbour and enemy Porus.[4] The political exchange and military engagement was therefore not entirely one-sided: Alexander exploited pre-existing tensions between neighbouring rulers, and Indian rulers engaged in realpolitik to achieve their own aims.

On defeating Porus, Alexander returned his original kingdom to him and added additional territory to his overall control.[5] The victory over Porus, perhaps aided by Alexander's treatment of him, provoked a second flurry of ambassadorial activity in the region. Some rulers sent high-ranking envoys and gifts to Alexander; one such ruler was Abisares, who had sent an embassy to Alexander when he first arrived in the Punjab, and was now permitted to retain his kingdom as a satrap.[6] Other rulers had a different approach. When Alexander approached the cities under Sophytes' rule with the intention of campaigning against them, Sophytes came out of his capital and voluntarily surrendered to Alexander. By means of his pre-emptive action, Sophytes too was permitted to retain control of his realms.[7]

In the Punjab, as elsewhere, Alexander reappointed some local rulers to their original realms as satraps, and in so doing brought, however superficially, an Achaemenid system of administration and authority to the region. Alexander also added additional, competing layers of control to Indian kingdoms through the appointment of his own Graeco-Macedonian administrators. For example, in Taxila, he appointed Philip, son of Machatas, as satrap of the Indians. How control over this satrapy was organised or divided between Taxiles and Philip, is not known.[8]

Despite Alexander's exhortations to travel beyond the Hyphasis into India, his troops refused to continue any further east. The Punjab, therefore, formed the eastern extremity of his empire.[9] Arrian reported Alexander's last action at the Hydaspes, before travelling south and leaving the region:

> He [Alexander] himself convened his Companions and all the Indian envoys who had come to visit him, and proclaimed Porus king of the Indian land so far acquired, seven nations in all, including more than two thousand cities.[10]

As Alexander left this region, so too did the focus of our available literary sources. The result being that little is known about the Punjab in the period between Alexander's departure in *c.*326 BC and Seleucus' arrival in the east in *c.*307 BC.

Alexander left behind him a significant degree of instability that was likely to have been compounded by his final proclamation pertaining to the extension of Porus' authority. This is not least because there was pre-existing enmity between some of the regional rulers, notably Taxiles and Porus. By appointing Porus 'king of the Indian land so far acquired', Alexander was hardly encouraging good relations between Porus and his neighbours – especially when Alexander had already agreed that local rulers such as Taxiles, Abisares and Sophytes should retain control over their respective kingdoms.

Alexander's Graeco-Macedonian satraps and garrisons also remained in the region, providing yet more competing, uneasy layers of authority. As previously noted, Alexander had appointed Philip, son of Machatas, satrap of the Indians in the region of Taxila, but he also gave him control of Gandhara and the regions between the Acesines and the Indus as far as their confluence.[11] Whereas Alexander had longer-term aspirations for the region, as indicated by his desire that cities and dockyards be founded at places such as the juncture of the Acesines and the Indus, it was not to remain under Graeco-Macedonian authority for long.

The instability Alexander engendered through his actions and appointments in this region was soon apparent. In 325 BC, Philip was assassinated by the mercenaries Alexander had left with him, and they, in turn, were killed by Philip's bodyguards.[12] Alexander ordered the Macedonian general Eudamus and Taxiles to take charge until Philip's replacement was appointed. This joint appointment eventually, perhaps inevitably, led to further insecurity: in *c.*317 BC Eudamus murdered Porus and travelled west, taking away 120 elephants from Porus' kingdom. Taxiles' role in these actions is unknown, but given his previous enmity towards Porus, it is not beyond the realms of imagination that he encouraged Eudamus' actions. Within eight years of Alexander's departure, the area was left without a layer of Graeco-Macedonian authority.[13]

According to Justin's *Epitome of Pompeius Trogus*, it was around this time that Chandragupta, the founder of the Mauryan dynasty, entered this region, which lay on the geographical periphery of the Mauryan empire.[14] Most scholars assert that Chandragupta's arrival here came after his overthrow of the Nanda dynasty and his establishment of his own dynasty in its place. This timing, however, like many other aspects of Chandragupta's reign, remains uncertain, and some scholars have also suggested that Chandragupta's activities in the region preceded the foundation of the Mauryan empire.[15] The inconclusive and problematic evidence for Chandragupta's life and events means that either interpretation is possible.

In order to understand Chandragupta's arrival in the Punjab and his later encounter with Seleucus within the overall context of his reign it is necessary to evaluate the available sources for his life and activities.

Generally, modern historians of ancient India and the Hellenistic period accept that Chandragupta carved out his empire by harassing the outlying regions of the Nanda empire. After this, he gradually worked his way to the centre of Nanda power in the Ganges basin and wrested power from this dynasty. It is also widely, and casually, accepted that Chandragupta came to power in *c.*320/319 BC. However, all of the information concerning Chandragupta's rise to power and the dates of his reign must be treated with caution: the evidence, such as it is, is based on limited and problematic Graeco-Roman and South Asian sources, little of the content of which is contemporary with the events they report.

Below, I give a brief overview of the surviving sources alongside a discussion of the information they provide about Chandragupta's life and reign. This dual approach is important: limited cross-disciplinary research has meant that knowledge concerning the nature, purpose and even the dating of many of these sources has tended to remain within the bounds of narrow fields of scholarship. Many of the South Asian sources discussed here, for example, remain little known beyond Indological studies, while Graeco-Roman sources are little known within the sphere of Indology. This situation has meant that material from otherwise unfamiliar textual traditions has been repeatedly, and uncritically, cited in support of arguments for particular chronologies or sequences of events. An unfortunate result of this repetition is that the constructed chronological patterns have become accepted 'fact', despite standing on extremely shaky foundations, as seen below.

Chandragupta's rise to power

One of the key sources for the story of Chandragupta's rise to power is a Sanskrit text, the *Sthavirāvalīcaritra* ('The lives of the Jain elders'), which is also known as the *Pariśiṣṭaparvan* ('The appendix'). This work is a self-contained sequel to the *Triṣaṣṭhiśalākapuruṣacaritra* ('The lives of the sixty-three illustrious people'). The *Sthavirāvalīcaritra* relates the lives of some of the early leaders of the Jain community, such as Mahāvīra, the twenty-fourth *jina*, who was contemporary with the Buddha.[16] The lives contained within this work are written as hagiographies with significant moments defined by legend rather than historical fact.

Several chapters in this work also relate the Jain version of the ancient history of northern India, with a particular focus on the Nanda and Mauryan dynasties. It is in this section that Chandragupta's rise to power, with the help of his minister Cāṇakya, is described. Cāṇakya, impressed by the regal behaviour and wisdom of the youthful Chandragupta, decided to make him a king. They hired soldiers using Cāṇakya's gold and unsuccessfully besieged Pataliputra.[17] While on the run from Nanda's forces, they encountered a woman serving porridge to her children and so begins the famous story: one child burned his fingers by putting them in the middle of the hot porridge instead of eating from the cooler edges. She berates her child using Cāṇakya as an example, saying, 'Dim-witted Cāṇakya rendered himself defenceless when he began to besiege Nanda's capital, without securing the outlying districts.'[18] Learning this lesson, Cāṇakya and Chandragupta proceeded to conquer the outlying districts of Nanda's kingdom, eventually overcoming its heartlands and taking power. As seen later in this section, there are similarities between Hemacandra's story and that found in the *Mahāvaṃsa-ṭīkā*.

According to a late Jain tradition, which is included in the text, Chandragupta converted to this religion.[19] This point is important, and relevant here: the *Sthavirāvalīcaritra* was one of three texts written in western India by the Jain Śvetāmbara ('white-clad')[20] monk and polymath Hemacandra (1089–1172). His purpose in writing them was to explain the essentials of the Jain faith to his patron, the Caulukya emperor Kumārapāla, who also converted to Jainism.[21] Hemacandra drew on a range of written works, as well as Jain tradition and popular stories transmitted orally, for his information.[22] However, the date and origin of Hemacandra's information concerning Chandragupta's conversion and his ascent to power remain unclear and cannot, therefore, be verified. Furthermore, recent analysis of a wide range of Jain literary and epigraphic sources – all of which are many hundreds of years later in date than the events they claim to report – contests a verifiable, historical link between Chandragupta and Jainism.[23]

According to Digambara ('sky-clad') Jain tradition, the Jain monk Bhadrabāhu converted Chandragupta to this religion. The story continues that Chandragupta later renounced his throne, and when a famine struck Ujjain Chandragupta and the monk led a migration to southern India. On arriving at Śravaṇa Beḷgoḷa, they undertook the *sallekhanā* (ritual suicide by starvation). The story has found expression through inscriptions, sculpture and the founding of a temple at this site.

Digambara Jains are particularly associated with southern India, where they historically enjoyed royal patronage and where their most important religious sites are located. Śravaṇa Beḷgoḷa in Karnataka is one of the most important sacred places for them. It comprises numerous sites spread across two hills, Chandragiri and Vindyagiri. Chandragupta Basadi ('temple'), located on Chandragiri, is believed to have been erected by Chandragupta; Bhadrabāhu Cave is linked with Bhadrabāhu and Chandragupta's ritual suicide and, according to tradition, is the place where Chandragupta died (Figures 1.1 and 1.2).[24] The date of the foundation of the temple is unknown, although a two-part screen depicting events from Chandragupta and Bhadrabāhu's lives may date from the twelfth century (Figure 1.3).[25]

A closer look at the evidence for Chandragupta's conversion to Jainism and his and Bhadrabāhu's association with Śravaṇa Beḷgoḷa reveals that it is both late and problematic. In addition, except for Jain sources, there is no evidence to support the view of Chandragupta's

Figure 1.1 Chandragupta Basadi on Chandragiri at Śravaṇa Beḷgoḷa, Karnataka is believed to have been erected by Chandragupta. © Nicholas Barnard.

Figure 1.2 Bhadrabāhu Cave on Chandragiri at Śravaṇa Beḷgoḷa, Karnataka is associated with Chandragupta's ritual suicide. © Nicholas Barnard.

conversion and migration. For example, the earliest literary source for Chandragupta's conversion to Jainism is Yativṛṣabha's *Tiloya-paṇṇatti*, a Jain cosmological text written in Prakrit during the early seventh century.[26] An inscription dating from *c.*600 AD found at Chandragiri in Śravaṇa Beḷgoḷa is the earliest known reference to Bhadrabāhu's southbound migration and connection with this site.[27] There is no reference to Chandragupta in this inscription, and, as Balcerowicz notes, the inscription is important as evidence of the 'social memory of religious historical account and how it reproduces the past' but not necessarily as a historical document for events that took place some 900 years previously.[28] In this context, he further suggests, Chandragupta's absence from the inscription is significant because it suggests that the story of Bhadrabāhu's conversion of Chandragupta and their ritual suicide at Śravaṇa Beḷgoḷa had either been forgotten by this time or had not yet been invented.[29]

A series of inscriptions at various locations at Śravaṇa Beḷgoḷa also mention figures named Bhadrabāhu and Chandragupta. However, not only are all the inscriptions late, dating from between the sixth or seventh and fifteenth centuries, but there is confusion between the characters mentioned in them. This is because different figures from a range of religious, literary and historical traditions have the names Bhadrabāhu

Figure 1.3 A detail from the carved screen inside Chandragupta Basadi which depicts events from the lives of Chandragupta and the Jain monk Bhadrabāhu. © Nicholas Barnard.

and Chandragupta, so it is not always possible to determine whether Chandragupta, the founder of the Mauryan dynasty, and his guru Bhadrabāhu are being referred to, or other individuals entirely.[30]

Overall, therefore, the evidence as it currently stands suggests that the story of Chandragupta's conversion to Jainism and abdication (if, indeed, he did abdicate), his migration southwards and his association (or otherwise) with Bhadrabāhu and the site of Śravaṇa Beḷgoḷa developed after *c*.600 AD.[31] And yet these stories remain popular and are invariably included in histories of the Mauryan period and also of Śravaṇa Beḷgoḷa. Their frequent repetition, without recourse to and integration of detailed analysis of the evidence for the events in question, has led to their widespread acceptance in scholarship, much as other aspects of Chandragupta's reign and dates have been.

Echoes of Hemacandra's story are found in a later Buddhist source, the *Mahāvaṃsa-ṭīkā*. This text provides some tantalising information about Chandragupta's early life and rise to power that is not found elsewhere. As in Hemacandra's work, Cāṇakya plays a vital role. Here, Cāṇakya is impressed with the young Chandragupta and teaches him for some six or seven years. Once he reaches adulthood, Cāṇakya retrieves his buried treasure and uses it to raise an army, and thenceforth begins to attack towns and villages. The population successfully rebels against this violent onslaught, causing Chandragupta and Cāṇakya to put down their arms, listen to people and decide upon their next move.

It was during this phase of their activities that they overheard a mother talking to her child. The child would only eat the middle of the pancakes she cooked for him, and she responded that his 'conduct is like Chandagutto's [Chandragupta's] in his attempt to take possession of the kingdom'. She went on, 'Chandagutto also in his ambition to be a monarch, without subduing the frontiers, before he attacked the towns, invaded the heart of the country and laid towns waste. On that account, both the inhabitants of the town and others, rising, closed in upon him, from the frontiers to the centre, and destroyed his army. *That* was *his* folly.'[32] As in Hemacandra's story, Cāṇakya and Chandragupta learned from her words and worked their way from the outskirts of the kingdom to the centre, eventually overthrowing it.

The *Mahāvaṃsa-ṭīkā* is a commentary on the *Mahāvaṃsa* ('Great chronicle'; see also Chapter 7). The *Mahāvaṃsa* was composed in Pāli by various monks of the Mahāvihāra ('Great monastery') in Anuradhapura, Sri Lanka. Over the fifth and sixth centuries, it was compiled into a single document by a Buddhist monk named Mahānāma about whom nothing more is known. This text relates the history of

Sri Lanka from a Buddhist perspective.[33] The *Mahāvaṃsa-ṭīkā* was written to comment on words that were unclear in the *Mahāvaṃsa*. It was composed before the twelfth century, but lack of evidence means that it is not possible to be more specific than that. However, as Hinüber notes, it frequently refers to the *Aṭṭhakathā*, the Pāli commentaries on Pāli canonical literature, which means it includes information from much older sources.[34] Notably, the stories about Chandragupta are not found in the earlier Sri Lankan chronicle, the *Dīpavaṃsa*.

Unfortunately, it is not always possible to locate the origins of the information contained within the *Mahāvaṃsa-ṭīkā*, and this is the case with the details of Chandragupta's early life and rise to power. However, it does seem that Hemacandra and the author of the *Mahāvaṃsa-ṭīkā* were drawing on the same, or very similar, tradition or sources concerning Chandragupta, his relationship with Cāṇakya and his rise to power. Thomas Trautmann's detailed investigation of these sources with a primary focus on Cāṇakya leads him to suggest that there may have existed a popular cycle of stories, a *Cāṇakya-Candragupta-Kathā*, that was anecdotal in character and from which the stories were ultimately drawn via intermediary sources.[35] Trautmann further argues that, of the two surviving accounts, the Jain version is not only superior, because of the additional details it includes, such as the rationale for certain actions, but also the older of the two. His reasoning as to the age of the Jain version is compelling. He highlights the way in which it preserves the integrity of the *Cāṇakya-Candragupta-Kathā* while conserving its original features.[36]

Two additional texts retell the *Cāṇakya-Candragupta-Kathā*. Somadeva's *Kathāsaritsāgara* ('Ocean of the streams of stories') and Kṣemendra's *Bṛhatkathāmañjari* ('Collection of great stories'), both of which are Kashmiri sources, draw on Guṇāḍhya's *Bṛhatkathā* ('Great narrative'). However, there is precious little information here about Chandragupta. For example, Kṣemendra writes merely, 'Candragupta, son of the previous Nanda, was established in sovereignty by the energetic Cāṇakya.'[37] They do not add detail to the Jain and Buddhist sources included above.[38]

Justin's *Epitome of Pompeius Trogus* adds some detail to the stories as related in the *Sthavirāvalīcaritra* and the *Mahāvaṃsa-ṭīkā*. In Justin's work, Chandragupta's outspokenness is said to have annoyed 'King Nandrus' (ruler of the Nanda dynasty) so much that he was sentenced to death and had to escape quickly. After his flight, Chandragupta fell into an exhausted sleep and a lion licked the sweat from his body.

This strange event apparently inspired Chandragupta to seek the throne and, to this end, he gathered a band of outlaws and incited 'the Indians' to revolt.[39] As with the information concerning Chandragupta in the *Sthavirāvalīcaritra* and the *Mahāvaṃsa-ṭīkā*, the source for this story is unclear.

Pompeius Trogus, a historian who flourished in the first century AD, wrote the *Book of Philippic Histories and the Origins of the World and Descriptions of the Earth* in Latin in 44 books.[40] The central theme of the narrative is the history of the Macedonian empire founded by Philip II and expanded by Alexander and Alexander's Successors, including the regions they travelled through or which came under their control, such as India. Unfortunately, this work does not survive complete: it was epitomised by Justin, about whom little is known, at some point during the second, or perhaps third, century AD.[41] Many of the details about Chandragupta contained in the *Epitome* are not found in any other source, meaning that it is not possible to reconstruct, with any degree of certainty, the origin of much of this information. This has not prevented some degree of speculation; Jain sources and Megasthenes' *Indica* have been suggested.[42] However, the historical accuracy of many of these details cannot be confirmed and each event and reference must be carefully evaluated in turn.

The *Milindapañha* ('Questions of Milinda') briefly refers to a battle between Chandragupta and Nanda: 'There was, revered Nāgasena, the general's son named Bhaddasāla of the Nanda (royal) family between whom and King Candragutta [Chandragupta] a battle was raging.'[43] This Pāli Buddhist text is a dialogue that took place over two days between the Indo-Greek King Menander ('Milinda' in the work; reigned *c.*155–130 BC) and a sage named Nāgasena. Menander is undoubtedly a historical character who ruled parts of Afghanistan, Pakistan and northern India. He is mentioned in Strabo's *Geography*, for example, and his coins survive in various museum collections and, according to tradition, he converted to Buddhism.[44] The *Milindapañha*, however, is not a historical text and it is not believed to record actual conversations between Menander and the otherwise unknown Nāgasena.[45]

The *Milindapañha* is a collection of different texts, the first of which dates roughly from between 100 BC and AD 200.[46] The section which mentions Chandragupta is from the second part, the *Meṇḍakapañha* ('Question about the ram').[47] The additional sections – parts two to five – had been added by the time the *Aṭṭhakathā* (Pāli commentaries) were composed in the fifth century.[48] This source reflects the enduring historical memory of Chandragupta's rise to power; it is a shame that such a small fragment of information, which cannot be corroborated elsewhere, has come down through it.

A Sanskrit source, Viśākhadatta's play *Rākṣasa's Ring*, also tells the story of how Chandragupta overthrew the previous Nanda dynasty (see Chapter 8). In this case, the drama revolves around the machinations employed by his minister Cāṇakya (also known as 'Kauṭilya') to win the Nanda minister Rākṣasa over to Chandragupta's side. Kauṭilya is mentioned in the *Sthavirāvalīcaritra* and the *Mahāvaṃsa-ṭīkā* as Chandragupta's advisor, suggesting that this traditional association between them has much older roots. However, as with other ancient Sanskrit plays, events in this drama cannot be taken as historically accurate; indeed, Michael Coulson, the modern translator of this play, described it as 'a fairy tale subjected to a further process of political sophistication'.[49]

A range of dates have been suggested for *Rākṣasa's Ring*. If the reference to Chandragupta in the final benedictory stanza is authentic, the play is likely to have been written during the reign of Chandragupta II (*r*. AD 376–415), ruler of the Gupta Empire. It is interesting to note that the titles of Viśākhadatta's father and grandfather suggest the author came from a princely family that was involved in some aspect of political administration, perhaps under Gupta rule.[50]

These, then, are the key sources for Chandragupta's rise to power, abdication and death, as well as his apparent conversion to Jainism at the end of his reign. All of the texts and inscriptions, as well as the temple and the associated narrative scenes rendered through sculpture, are much later in date than the events they claim to report. In addition, there is no way to verify the information contained in them, so while it is generally accepted that Chandragupta rose to power by harassing the outlying sections of the Nanda empire before moving to the centre and overthrowing the dynasty, there is no firm historical evidence for this story. It could just as easily be part of Mauryan-era (or later) myth-making around the figure of Chandragupta, and some of the myth-making at least could be religiously motivated. As shown in the next section, dates associated with Chandragupta's foundation of his empire are similarly problematic.

Reconstructing the date of Chandragupta's life and reign

South Asian sources from Buddhist, Jain and Brahmanic religious traditions help to broadly reconstruct the order of the Mauryan rulers and the number of years they ruled. These are complex texts and they cannot be used alone to establish specific historical dates. Any Mauryan regnal, or other, dates based on them must remain conjectural. It is only when particular events reported in these sources intersect with episodes in Graeco-Roman texts which are more securely dated that approximate dates can be assigned to them (see Chapter 3).

The *Purāṇic* ('ancient') king lists are of particular relevance here. The *Purāṇas* are a large and diverse collection of texts principally composed in Sanskrit and Tamil, from the Brahmanic, Jain and Buddhist religious traditions. The texts include genealogies and king lists, wide-ranging information about important political events such as wars, and geography and mythology. It has proved notoriously difficult to date the *Purāṇas*. Scholars generally accept that the earliest Sanskrit *Purāṇas* were written down during the Gupta period in approximately the fourth century, but it is clear that the texts may have been composed before this time and continued to evolve after it.[51] Additionally, the *Purāṇas* draw on information based in earlier written and oral traditions, most of which is now lost, meaning that it is very difficult to corroborate, and therefore confirm, the details contained in them.[52]

Mauryan king lists are contained in some of the Brahmanic *Purāṇas*, such as the Viṣṇu and Matsya *Mahāpurāṇas* ('Great *Purāṇas*'). Different *Purāṇas* often give different names and in different orders for the later Mauryan rulers, but the first three – Chandragupta, Bindusāra and Aśoka – are given in the same order.[53] Another point on which the *Purāṇas* agree is that the Mauryan dynasty lasted for 137 years,[54] the first three rulers accounting for 85 years between them, and Chandragupta's reign lasting 24 or 25 years. The nature and purpose of the *Purāṇas* mean, however, that it is difficult to date Mauryan (or other) reigns on the basis of these sources alone. It is also difficult to verify the details through comparison with other sources: often the information is either different or absent in other texts.

In contrast to the *Purāṇas*, Buddhist and Jain sources link the years of Mauryan rule to the lives of the Buddha and Mahāvīra, two religious figures believed to have been contemporaries. For example, the *Sthavirāvalīcaritra*, a Jain text, notes that Chandragupta became king 155 years after the *jina* Mahāvīra's *nirvana*.[55] Two Buddhist Sri Lankan chronicles, the *Dīpavaṃsa* and the *Mahāvaṃsa*, note that Aśoka became king 218 years after the Buddha's *nirvana*, and that Chandragupta reigned for 24 years, Bindusāra reigned for 28 years and, after a four-year interregnum, Aśoka reigned for 37 years.[56] These texts are historical chronicles about the arrival of Buddhism in Sri Lanka, a proselytising event that took place during Aśoka's reign. In works like this, created by and for the Sri Lankan Buddhist community, the way in which Buddhism first arrived in Sri Lanka was, obviously, a vital part of the narrative, and it was important to record it and pass it down.

As with the *Purāṇas*, it is difficult to extract and verify historical detail from the chronicles, because such information cannot always be confirmed elsewhere. Both chronicles are based on the commentary literature (the *Aṭṭhakathā*) of the Buddhist canonical writings that existed in different Sri Lankan Buddhist monasteries. Of these different versions, the recension at the Mahāvihāra ('great monastery') in Anuradhapura was used to write the *Dīpavaṃsa* and, later, the *Mahāvaṃsa*.[57] The events they describe begin in the sixth century BC and end in the fourth century AD. No author is named for the *Dīpavaṃsa*, but the author of the *Mahāvaṃsa* is known as Mahānāma ('great name') and he is thought to have been writing at the end of the fourth century AD.

While it is useful to have a link between Mauryan regnal dates and the lives of the Buddha and Mahāvīra, the historical dates of these religious figures remain uncertain, so they cannot be used as an absolute fixed point. For example, Buddhist sources agree that the Buddha was 80 years old at the time of his physical death. Pāli sources of Theravāda Buddhism note that this was 218 years before the start of Aśoka's reign and this approach to determining the Buddha's age is known as the 'long chronology'. In contrast, a 'short chronology', giving only 100 years between the Buddha's death and Aśoka's reign, is found in Sanskrit sources preserved in East Asia. Using the references to named Hellenistic kings in Aśoka's Major Rock Edicts – a series of 14 inscriptions carved into large rocks located around the boundaries of his empire during his reign – modern scholars traditionally place Aśoka's inauguration at *c.*268 BC. These Edicts were inscribed by Aśoka, the third Mauryan Emperor, However, according to the lineage of Buddhist teachers mentioned in the *Dīpavaṃsa*, Richard Gombrich argued that there were 136 years (not 218 or 100) between the Buddha's death and Aśoka's reign and that, with different margins of error, the Buddha died between 422 and 399 BC, most likely around 404 BC. However, these dates remain contested.[58] The importance of Mauryan dates, both in themselves and in relation to the dates of the Buddha, and conversely of the dates of the Buddha in relation to Mauryan dates, is clear.

So, for now, Graeco-Roman sources remain key to providing more accurate dates for Chandragupta and his successors, although considerable caution must be exercised here too. In his *Life of Alexander*, Plutarch tells us:

> Androcottus [Chandragupta], when he was a stripling, saw Alexander himself, and we are told that he often said in later times that Alexander narrowly missed making himself master of the country, since its king was hated and despised on account of his baseness and low birth.[59]

Scholars have combined this reference from Plutarch with information found in the *Mahāvaṃsa-ṭīkā* to suggest a possible date for Chandragupta's life. However, the link is tenuous at best. The *Mahāvaṃsa-ṭīkā* states that Cāṇakya lived in Taxila and travelled to Pataliputra, in whose environs he encountered Chandragupta.[60] It goes on to explain that Cāṇakya was impressed by Chandragupta and 'rendered him in the course of six or seven years highly accomplished and profoundly learned'.[61] It is not clear how old Chandragupta was at any point during his early association with Cāṇakya: the only information about his age in the text is that 'when he attained an age to be able to tend cattle' he was taken to the dwelling of a friend of his adoptive father in order to look after cattle.[62] And yet on this basis, R. K. Mookerji argues that Chandragupta was eight or nine years old when he met Cāṇakya and, moreover, that Cāṇakya took him to Taxila for his education.[63] There is no evidence for either of Mookerji's statements, nor, therefore, that Chandragupta was approximately sixteen when he met Alexander in this city.

So, we return to Justin's *Epitome*. According to Justin, it was around the time that Eudamus murdered Porus and travelled west, *c*.317 BC, that Chandragupta first entered the Punjab.[64] Justin fills in a little of the detail of what occurred in the Punjab and the Indus valley after Alexander quit the region, writing that Chandragupta 'gathered a band of outlaws and incited the Indians to revolution' against the Nanda dynasty, after which 'he was preparing for hostilities against Alexander's governors'.[65] Chandragupta does not appear to have fought against Alexander's governors because, once again according to Justin, they had already been put to death:

> [H]e [Seleucus] crossed into India, which, following Alexander's death [in 323 BC], had shaken from its shoulders the yoke of servitude and put to death his governors. The man responsible for this liberation was Sandrocottus [Chandragupta appeared in Greek sources as 'Sandrocottus']; however, after his victory he had turned the so-called liberty they had gained back into servitude; for on seizing power he began himself to enslave the people he had championed against foreign domination.[66]

Justin does not explain what Chandragupta's enslavement of the people involved. It may have been the imposition of his own political and military dominion. It is also not clear how long Chandragupta had been in power at this stage. While some scholars have argued that he was still in the process of challenging Nanda supremacy, the general consensus at present, with a few exceptions couched in tentative language, is that he had already established his own dynasty.[67] The language in Justin is ambiguous. For example, Chandragupta could equally have 'liberated' and 'enslaved' those people, formerly under the authority of Alexander and his governors, before or after his overthrow of the Nanda dynasty. There is no external, corroborating evidence to establish the order of events. Both positions remain possible, and this means that the date of Chandragupta's arrival in this region cannot be used to date the beginning or end of his reign. Instead, it is only possible to state that he held power, in some capacity, in *c.*317 BC.

Justin does, however, provide a useful temporal context for the date when 'Sandrocottus was ruler of India', specifically, 'at the time that Seleucus was laying the foundations for his future greatness'. This is a reference to the time when Seleucus was defending his satrapy of Babylonia against the Antigonids, which was between 311 and *c.*308 BC.[68] This statement is a key factor in Joe Cribb's argument about the date of the start of Chandragupta's reign.

Cribb re-evaluates the traditionally accepted Mauryan and Buddhist chronology through a reanalysis of South Asian and Graeco-Roman evidence. He begins by questioning the precision of the generally accepted starting point for this chronology: the start of Aśoka's reign in *c.*368 BC. As Cribb notes, the dating of Mauryan rulers was 'fixed' by a correlation with the comparatively well-established chronology of Greek rulers, particularly those mentioned in Aśoka's inscriptions.[69] The major flaw in the conventional presentation of the evidence, he suggests, is Justin's reference to Chandragupta's status as 'ruler of India' when Seleucus was 'laying the foundations' of his own empire.[70] As mentioned in the previous paragraph, this reference appears to refer to the period *c.*311– *c.*308 BC. If this date range is indeed accurate, then, according to Cribb's argument, it follows that Chandragupta acceded to the throne, and was therefore 'ruler of India', at some point between this period and when he met Seleucus in *c.*303 BC.[71] Cribb further refines the earlier date to *c.*309 BC because this was the year Seleucus secured his control over his Babylonian satrapy.

While it is tempting to accept this new date range as the start of Chandragupta's reign, not least because a neat solution to a tricky problem is always welcome, caution must be exercised. It is not clear, for example, what Trogus' sources were for this statement, or therefore what the basis of this information, which temporally links events connected with Seleucus and Chandragupta, actually was. Similarly, there is no statement in Justin relating to the start of Chandragupta's reign, simply that he was 'ruler of India' while Seleucus was securing and establishing the foundations of his own empire. Chandragupta's location in the Punjab at this time could suggest that he either was on his way to securing (from the geographical periphery to the centre in Magadha), or had already secured, his authority in the Magadhan heartlands and was moving from the centre to the periphery again. However, as we have seen, the story about his rise to power in the *Sthavirāvalīcaritra* is problematic and unverifiable, and cannot therefore be used to reconstruct his movements or, indeed, the start date of his reign due to his presence in the Punjab.

Instead, all that can be said with any confidence is that Chandragupta gained power, and was possibly already the first Mauryan king, between *c*.311 and *c*.305 BC. The widespread belief that Chandragupta established his dynasty in *c*.320/319 BC cannot yet be wholly rejected on the basis of Cribb's argument, nor can it continue to be uncritically repeated in scholarship as it has been hitherto. Similarly, the regnal dates for his successors, and therefore the Buddha and Mahāvīra, cannot be based on a Mauryan start date of *c*.320/319 BC.

A clash by the banks of the Indus

Chandragupta and Seleucus met for the first and only time by the banks of the River Indus. Aside from the information discussed in the previous section, little is known about Chandragupta's movements or actions leading up to this meeting. In contrast, considerably more is known about Seleucus' career before their encounter.

Seleucus was one of Alexander's Companions and accompanied him during his conquests across the Mediterranean world and the Persian Empire and in north-west India. At the mass wedding in Susa arranged by Alexander in 324 BC for marriages between himself and his officers, and women drawn from the Persian nobility, Seleucus was married to Apama.[72] Apama was the daughter of Spitamenes, the Sogdian chieftain whose power base lay in the eastern satrapies of Bactria and Sogdiana. Spitamenes had been killed some four years before his daughter's marriage took place. This wedding, which established family ties to a prominent family in this region, was to prove a useful strategic alliance in relation to Seleucus' claim to Persia and also his future aspirations in the East. Given Apama's usefulness in terms of legitimising her husband's claims, it is not surprising that Seleucus was one of the few men known not to have divorced the wife given to him at Susa after Alexander's death.[73] Their son, Antiochus I, later inherited the empire and maintained his eastern territorial interests.

Through a series of complex, ambition-charged manoeuvres, Seleucus' position changed profoundly in the years between Alexander's death in 323 BC and his return to India in *c.*305 BC. In the Babylonian Settlement which took place immediately after Alexander's death, Perdiccas, Alexander's regent, appointed Seleucus Commander of the Companions.[74] In 320 BC, after taking part in Perdiccas' murder while on campaign with him against Ptolemy in Egypt, Seleucus was granted the satrapy of Babylonia by Antipater, the new regent, at the conference in Triparadeisus.[75]

Considerable political and military manoeuvring between the Successors led to Antigonus driving Seleucus out of Babylonia in 316 BC. Seleucus only regained this satrapy with Ptolemy's help in 312 BC: this year is traditionally viewed as the foundation date of the Seleucid empire.[76] After securing his satrapy in 308 BC following further warfare against Antigonus and pro-Antigonid forces,[77] and when Antigonus shifted his attention westwards, Seleucus began to move eastwards towards the upper satrapies, Bactria, and India as far as the River Indus, where he met Chandragupta in *c.*305– *c.*303 BC.[78]

Over the years, scholars have been content to suggest a range of dates between *c.*305 and *c.*303 BC on the understanding that they are roughly accurate rather than specific. The date range is based on an estimation of how long it may have taken Seleucus to travel eastwards to Bactria and then on to the Indus after his final battle with Antigonus for control of the satrapy of Babylonia in 308 BC and his return west to Phrygia to fight the Battle of Ipsus against Antigonus in 301 BC.[79] A few examples illustrate the range of scholarly suggestions for the date-range: Susan Sherwin-White and Amélie Kuhrt suggest *c.*305 BC; both F. W. Walbank and John Grainger propose *c.*303 BC; Paul Kosmin mentions that it was at some point around 305–304 BC.[80] Upinder Singh provides one of the few outliers from this range when she suggests *c.*301 BC.[81] However, Singh's date is unlikely to be accurate because the Battle of Ipsus took place in the same year.

In terms of evidence, there are no references to Seleucus or the encounter between this ruler and Chandragupta in any South Asian literary or epigraphic texts. Instead, we are wholly reliant on

Graeco-Roman sources, namely Strabo, Appian, Plutarch and Justin, for any information relating to the meeting of these kings. The dependence on a small group of sources from only one literary tradition necessitates a cautious approach to these texts and the event they describe. For example, the propagandistic Seleucid ideology that underlies Megasthenes' *Indica*, which appears to form the basis of at least some of the information about the first Seleucid-Mauryan meeting and its outcome, must be taken into account. Megasthenes, his work and his travels are dealt with in more detail in Chapter 2.

Different authors provide different layers of information about this meeting and the resulting treaty. Justin, for example, provides a bird's-eye view of events: 'Seleucus made a truce with him [Chandragupta], settled matters in the East, and returned to the fight with Antigonus.'[82] It may be that Trogus originally included more information about this meeting and treaty that was subsequently lost during Justin's compression of his work. Unfortunately, little more can be said, for lack of evidence, including details about Trogus' original source(s).

Appian and Strabo add additional details about this meeting. Appian (*c*.95– *c*.165 AD) was a Greek author from Alexandria who wrote a *Roman History* in 24 books, of which only some sections remain. He mentions the encounter between the Seleucid and Mauryan rulers in Book 11, *Syrian Wars*. Appian notes that Seleucus 'crossed the Indus and waged war with Sandrocottus, king of the Indians, who dwelt on the banks of that stream, until they came to an understanding with each other and contracted a marriage relationship'.[83] While Appian is the only author to describe the eastern extent of Seleucus' territories before his encounter with Chandragupta, it is not surprising that the battle between Seleucus and Chandragupta receives only scant mention given the summary way in which he deals with Seleucus' life overall.[84]

Appian refers to the meeting and resulting treaty in the wider context of a Hellenistic and Roman history of Syria in which his emphasis is on military events. In this section, Appian digresses into a more personal history of Seleucus. Seleucus is depicted in an entirely positive light in Appian's work and even favourably compared to Alexander, which prompts Omar Coloru to write that Appian's testimony in relation to Seleucus' invasion of India is 'largely the fruit of [Seleucid] propaganda'.[85] However, there is not enough evidence to support or reject this suggestion, and Coloru himself notes that one must not 'rule out the possibility that some clashes of a certain magnitude took place [between Seleucus and Chandragupta]'.[86]

Strabo (*c*.62 BC–*c*.AD 24), the Roman geographer and historian, refers to two more parts of this treaty; he is, in fact, the only ancient author to mention all three sections of the treaty that have come down to us. Strabo writes, 'Seleucus Nicator gave them [territories previously held by Alexander, but it is not specified which these were] to Sandrocottus, upon terms of intermarriage and of receiving in exchange five hundred elephants.'[87]

One point of comparison can be made between Strabo's and Appian's references to the meeting and treaty: the authors used different words for the marriage alliance. Appian used 'kēdos' (κῆδος) and Strabo used 'epigamia' (ἐπιγαμία). While the meaning of both words is essentially a contract, alliance or connection by marriage, 'epigamia' can also mean the 'right of intermarriage between states'.[88] In contrast, 'kēdos' has more personal connotations attached to it, particularly in terms of contracting a marriage for one's own daughter.[89] Unfortunately, Appian rarely mentions his sources, and these sections are no exception.[90] The overall lack of information prevents a meaningful comparison between Appian's sources and those of Strabo for the purpose of determining how far their choice of word for 'marriage alliance' is a reflection of the sources they chose to follow.

Plutarch (born before AD 50; died after AD 120) was a Greek philosopher and prolific author. Among his many works, the *Life of Alexander* is most useful to us here. This is because Plutarch details Alexander's incursions into India and dealings with local rulers, and he also includes a reference to Seleucus' receipt of 500 elephants from Chandragupta.[91] This is precisely the same number of elephants mentioned by Strabo and in the same context, suggesting that both authors may have drawn on the same source. Unfortunately, neither Plutarch nor Strabo tells us what this source was. A further similarity between information provided by these authors may suggest that Megasthenes, who was probably Seleucus' ambassador to Chandragupta (see Chapter 2), was the ultimate source for the detail about the elephants, and conceivably even the encounter and treaty between Seleucus and Chandragupta. Strabo reports that Chandragupta had an army of 400,000 men in his camp – a piece of information known to have been derived from Megasthenes – while Plutarch notes that Chandragupta had an army of 600,000 men.[92] While Plutarch's figure is significantly larger than that reported by Strabo, it is the same order of magnitude, and this reference is not found elsewhere.[93]

Over the years, scholars have put forward a range of suggestions as to where Megasthenes may have derived the detail in relation to the number of elephants exchanged. W. W. Tarn, for example, believed a Buddhist informant may have been Megasthenes' source for the number.[94] More recently, Trautmann reiterated his suggestion that Megasthenes, in his capacity as an intermediary between Seleucus and Chandragupta, obtained the number from a memorandum of agreement negotiated between the rulers.[95] Given the limited evidence available, these suggestions must remain just that.

Overall, it is clear not only that little information survives about the encounter and treaty between Seleucus and Chandragupta, but that it is not even clear in which work(s) the details originated. It is particularly important to note at this stage that there are very limited details about the battle or skirmish they fought, and that none of the ancient authors depicted either Seleucus or Chandragupta as the clear victor of this battle. While three parts of the treaty have come down to us, the details and outcome of them are unclear. This lack of information and clarity about the encounter and the ensuing treaty means that it is impossible to reconstruct them. Similarly, it is not possible to determine whether Seleucus or Chandragupta, or neither, emerged more successful than the other in terms of the gains each made through their treaty. As we shall see in Part II, the uncertainty and complexity of this situation have not prevented some scholars from speculating about what may have taken place, particularly in terms of the land exchange and marriage alliance, or from making assertions as to which of the rulers emerged victorious.

Cāṇakya's role in Chandragupta's life and achievements is a curious one: he is not mentioned in any Graeco-Roman or early South Asian sources, only in two much later Jain and Buddhist texts. Despite this lack of early evidence associating the two figures, as time passes he is gradually made to play a greater and greater role in Chandragupta's success. This phenomenon as expressed through artwork, plays, films and popular literature from the late nineteenth century onwards is explored in Part III of this book.

Just as ancient authors selected their sources for and interpretations of this episode, so have modern historians. In Chapters 3 and 4, I show how differently British and Indian historians of the last two centuries have interpreted the same sources for the encounter and resulting treaty, and therefore the power relations, between Seleucus and Chandragupta. These often opposing interpretations can only be understood when set in the social and political context of the time, specifically, British colonial rule in India and eventual Indian independence. During this period, and within this context, the confrontation between Seleucus and

Chandragupta took on a special significance for some historians and politicians and the meeting was shaped to reflect the state of contemporary politics and British-Indian relations.

Before we explore the reception and transformation of the earliest Seleucid-Mauryan encounter, we must look at Megasthenes and his *Indica*. Megasthenes provides the only surviving contemporary eyewitness account of Mauryan India at the time of Chandragupta's rule. He may also have been involved in the establishment and continuation of diplomatic relations between these two rulers. For these reasons, Megasthenes is often invoked as a key source by scholars working on Seleucid-Mauryan contact as well as on early Mauryan rule. It is essential, therefore, to contextualise Megasthenes historically and geographically before embarking on any investigation of the fragments of his *Indica*. It is also necessary both to assess his involvement in any aspect of Seleucid-Mauryan relations and consider later interpretations and uses of his work.

Notes

1 Hdt. IV.44.
2 Arr. *Anab*. 5.13.4.
3 Curt. 8.13.2.
4 Arr. *Anab*. 5.8.2, 5.
5 Arr. *Anab*. 5.29.2, 6.2.1.
6 Arr. *Anab*. 5.8.3, 5.20.5–6, 5.29.5. Alexander continued the Achaemenid tradition of ruling through satraps and satrapies: a 'satrapy' is an Achaemenid administrative unit governed on behalf of the Achaemenid king by a satrap (Jacobs 2011).
7 Diod. 17.91.4, 7; Curt. 9.1.27–30; Oro. *Hist*. 3.19.4.
8 Arr. *Anab*. 5.8.3.
9 Arr. *Anab*. 5.25.1–26.8, 5.27.2–28.5.
10 Arr. *Anab*. 6.2.1.
11 Arr. *Anab*. 6.2.3, 6.14.3, 6.15.2.
12 Arr. *Anab*. 6.27.2.
13 Arr. *Anab*. 6.27.2; Curt. 10.1.20–1; Diod. 19.14.8.
14 Just. *Epit*. 15.4.12–13.
15 The commentary alongside this section of Justin in Yardley, Wheatley and Heckel (2011, 278–9) provides a good overview of the arguments, from those put forward by scholars writing in the early nineteenth century to those of recent decades, in relation to the timing of Chandragupta's arrival in the region before or after he took the Nanda throne.
16 The Sanskrit term '*jina*' means 'spiritual victor'. In Jainism, there are 24 *jina*; they are enlightened human beings who teach other people the path to liberation from *saṃsāra* ('cycle of rebirth'). The term *jina* is interchangeable with *tīrthaṅkara* ('ford-maker'), which means a person who builds a *tīrtha* ('ford') across the river of rebirth.
17 *Sth*. 8.242–55.
18 *Sth*. 8.291–7.
19 *Sth*. 8.435.
20 There are two main sects in Jainism: Digambara ('sky-clad') and Śvetāmbara ('white-clad').
21 Cort 1999, 1166.
22 Trautmann 1971, 29.
23 Balcerowicz 2018.

24 Sangave 1981, 29–36.
25 Narasimhachar 1923, 5.
26 TiP_1 4.1481 = TiP_2 4.1493 in Balcerowicz 2018, 35–6.
27 Narasimhachar 1923, 36–7 and Inscription 1.
28 Balcerowicz 2018, 36–7.
29 Balcerowicz 2018, 38.
30 Wiley 2009, 50–1.
31 Balcerowicz 2018, 53, 61.
32 Turnour 1837, xxxix–xlii.
33 Hinüber 1996, 88, 91.
34 Hinüber 1996, 92.
35 Trautmann 1971, 10, 19–21.
36 Trautmann 1971, 25–7, 30–1.
37 Trautmann 1971, 32.
38 For more information about the Kashmiri texts, see Trautmann 1971, 31–6.
39 Just. *Epit*. 15.4.16–18.
40 Yardley and Heckel 1997, 4, 6.
41 Yardley and Heckel 1997, 10–11.
42 Based on Bussagli's suggestion that Trogus may have drawn on a Jain source for information about Chandragupta, Stoneman (2019, 160) wonders if Megasthenes was the original source. This is because, he writes, Megasthenes was familiar with Chandragupta's court and, 'if Chandragupta ended his life as a Jain, there may well have been a number of them at his court.' However, as discussed above, the association between Chandragupta and Jainism is quite late and the tradition is not reliable, so, this becomes a circular argument.
43 Mil. 8.3 (292) = trans. Horner 1964, 120.
44 Strab. 11.11.1.
45 Hinüber 1996, 83; Fussman 1993.
46 Baums 2018, 33; Hinüber 1996, 83, 85. The text is preserved in Chinese and Pāli translations. The Pāli translation is the *Milindapañha*. The Chinese translation, the *Nàxiān bǐqiū jīng* ('Sūtra of the monk Nāgasena'), was prepared in the fourth century and based on an earlier translation dating from the third century, which is now lost. That, in turn, goes back to an Indian original text in a language other than Pāli, possibly Gāndhārī.
47 Hinüber 1996, 84, 84n298.
48 Baums 2018, 33; Hinüber 1996, 85–6. Hinüber notes that quotations from parts two to five of the *Milindapañha* are found in the *Aṭṭhakathā*.
49 Coulson 2005, 17.
50 Coulson 2005, 15.
51 Bailey 2003, 139.
52 Dimmitt and van Buitenen (1983, 4–13) give a good overview of the main problems with dating *Purāṇic* texts and the differences between them.
53 *Viṣṇu Purāna* 4.24: Chandragupta, Bindusāra, Aśoka, Suyaśas, Daśaratha, Saṃgata, Śāliśūka, Somavarman, Śatadhanvan, Bṛhadratha. After this list of Mauryan kings the text reads: 'These are the ten Mauryas, who will reign over the earth for a hundred and thirty-seven years' (trans. H. Wilson 1868, 90). *Matsya Purāna*: Chandragupta, Bindusāra, Aśoka, Daśaratha, Samprati, Śatadhanvan and Bṛhadratha (Thapar 1961, 182–3).
54 Thapar 1961, 184.
55 *Sth*. 8.339.
56 *Dip*. 5.97, 6.1; *Mah*. 5.61, 5.97. '*Dīpa*' means 'island', '*mahā*' means 'great' and '*vaṃsa*' means 'chronicle'. So the *Dīpavaṃsa* and the *Mahāvaṃsa* are the 'island chronicle' and the 'great chronicle'.
57 For more details, see Geiger 1908, Guruge 1989 and Malalasekera 1935.
58 Harvey 2013, 8; Cribb 2017.
59 Plut. *Alex*. 62.
60 Turnour 1837, xxxix, xli. In contrast, the *Sthavirāvalīcaritra* (8.194) gives Cāṇakya's home as Caṇaka in Golla District. This location remains unknown; sites as diverse as Gandhara, Punjab and southern India have been suggested.
61 Turnour 1837, xli.
62 Turnour 1837, xl.

63 Mookerji 1943, 16.
64 Just. *Epit*. 15.4.12–13.
65 Just. *Epit*. 15.4.18–19.
66 Just. *Epit*. 14.4.12–14. Trans. J. C. Yardley.
67 Yardley, Wheatley and Heckel (2011, 278–9) provide a good overview of the way the scholarship falls on both sides of the debate. Singh (2008, 330) suggests the possibility that Chandragupta was in the process of empire-building when he arrived in the Punjab at this time.
68 Just. *Epit*. 15.4.20. Yardley, Wheatley and Heckel 2011, 290; Wheatley 2002, 39–41.
69 Cribb 2017, 3–10. Interestingly, Cribb (2017, 4) writes that he was first prompted to rethink the conventional dating of Mauryan chronology when reading the pre-publication draft of Gombrich (1992), on the relevance of monastic succession for dating the life of the Buddha. Specifically, it was the sentence 'scholars now seem to agree in putting this [Aśoka's inauguration] between 269 and 267 BC'. This passive acceptance of dates and events, derived in many cases from repetitive assumptions published across multiple generations of scholarship, is precisely the situation I seek to challenge in this section.
70 Cribb 2017, 11.
71 Cribb 2017, 11. The date Seleucus and Chandragupta met is also approximate and variously given as, for example, *c.*303 BC or *c.*305 BC.
72 Arr. *Anab*. 7.4.6; Plut. *Dem*. 31.5.
73 Ogden 1999, 119.
74 Diod. 18.3.4; App. *Syr*. 11.9.57; Just. *Epit*. 13.4.17.
75 Diod. 18.36.1–5; 18.39.6.
76 Diod. 18.55.2-55.6; 19.86.5; 19.90.1-91.5.
77 Diod. 19.92.1–5; Polyaen. *Strat*. 4.9.1; App. *Syr*. 11.9.53–5; Babylonian *Diadochi Chronicle BCHP* 3 (=*ABC* 10; BM 34660) column 4.
78 Appian provides a list of those satrapies that Seleucus moved through (*Syr*. 11.9.55): Mesopotamia, Armenia, Seleucus Cappadocia, Persis, Parthia, Bactria, Arabia, Tapouria, Sogdia, Arachosia, Hyrcania 'and other adjacent peoples that had been subdued by Alexander, as far as the river Indus'.
79 Plut. *Dem*. 28–9; Diod. 21.1–4; App. *Syr*. 11.9.55.
80 Sherwin-White and Kuhrt 1993, 12; Walbank 1981, 54; Grainger 2014, 112; Kosmin 2014, 32.
81 Singh 2008, 330.
82 Just. *Epit*. 15.4.21.
83 App. *Syr*. 11.9.55 (trans. Horace White).
84 Even the Battle of Ipsus, in which Seleucus fought and defeated his old enemy Antigonus, receives only brief mention (App. *Syr*. 11.9.55).
85 Coloru 2009, 142. Translation kindly provided by Omar Coloru. Appian himself acknowledges his digression, writing at the end of this section (*Syr*. 11.9.55): 'So much, in the way of digression, concerning the Macedonian kings of Syria.' The positive comparison between Seleucus and Alexander is also included in this section: 'he [Seleucus] ruled over a wider empire in Asia than any of his predecessors except Alexander.' Notably, Appian writes nothing negative about Seleucus in his *Syrian Wars*.
86 Coloru 2009, 142. Translation kindly provided by Omar Coloru.
87 Strab. 15.2.9.
88 Liddell et al. 1953, ἐπιγαμ-ία, ἡ [I've added the word from the dictionary here].
89 Liddell et al. 1953, κῆδ-ος: 'contract the *marriage* for one's own daughter'. [I've added the word from the dictionary here.]
90 The closest that he comes is in the section dealing with Seleucus' history, in reference to the foundation of the city of Seleucia-on-the-Tigris (*Syr*. 11.9.59): 'This is what I have heard about Seleucia.' Sadly, this isn't particularly helpful information for our purposes here.
91 Plut. *Alex*. 62.2.
92 Strab. 15.1.53; Plut. *Alex*. 62.2.
93 Other arguments are inconclusive: Tarn (1940, 88), for example, tentatively suggests Duris as Plutarch's source for Seleucus' elephants. Bar-Kochva (1976, 77) emphatically rejects this link, writing, 'he [Tarn] credits Duris, Plutarch's main source, with a degree of elaborate arithmetical calculation and historical association which could hardly be expected of any Hellenistic historian, save perhaps Polybius, and certainly not of a Pathetic [a reference to Duris'

involvement in the development of 'tragic history'] writer like Duris'. Tarn (1940, 87) rejects Hieronymus of Cardia as Plutarch's source for the number of elephants because of the discrepancy in numbers: Diodorus (20.113), who is known to have used Hieronymus, gave 480 elephants, whereas Plutarch (*Alex*. 62.2) initially mentioned 500 and then 400 at Ipsus (*Dem*. 28.3). This discrepancy is not conclusive in itself: there is always the possibility that the sources Plutarch used contained errors. Bar-Kochva (1976, 77) counters this argument of Tarn's as well, stating that it would have been very curious if Diodorus, who used Hieronymus as his main source for Book 20 of his *Library of World History*, chose to disregard the numbers provided by Hieronymus, especially as the latter had first-hand information, having been present at Ipsus (Luc. *Macr*. 11).

94 Tarn 1940.

95 Trautmann 1982, 269; 2015, 233–4. Stoneman (2019, 261) agrees with Trautmann's suggestion.

2
Megasthenes: travelling between empires

As we saw in Chapter 1, during Alexander's conquest of north-west India in 329–326 BC, a number of embassies were sent between Alexander and Indian rulers in the north-western regions of the subcontinent. For example, Alexander sent Cleochares to Porus, and Abisares sent his brother and other leading men to Alexander.[1] These embassies constituted the very first instances of official Graeco-Macedonian and Indian ambassadorial contact and exchange. Surviving details about the embassies provide a unique insight into the complexity of the political situation in north-west India at this time. Furthermore, they form the foundation of the later relations that developed and matured among the Graeco-Macedonian and Indian satraps and rulers appointed by Alexander and his Successors.

Megasthenes was the first of only three Greek ambassadors of the Hellenistic period known to have been sent to Indian courts, and he was also the first to be sent to a Mauryan ruler.[2] There remains some uncertainty about who sent him to whom, but he has been linked with Sibyrtius, Porus, Seleucus and Chandragupta. Megasthenes' association with Sibyrtius, one of Alexander's satraps stationed in the East, and Porus ties him to the diplomatic framework established by Alexander in Punjab. His links with Sibyrtius and Porus also place him among the wave of Graeco-Macedonian envoys who originated with Alexander's satraps. Among these, he appears to be the first and the best known.

Megasthenes' connection with Seleucus and Chandragupta suggests that he is contemporary with the establishment of Seleucid-Mauryan relations and closely linked to the key actors in that event.[3] It may also associate him with the two rulers' meeting in *c.*305–*c.*303 BC. It is because of Megasthenes' possible involvement in these earliest, founding stages of Seleucid-Mauryan relations that he and his work are so important here.

Megasthenes wrote an *Indica* based on his travels and experiences in India, which survives in fragmentary form quoted in the work of later authors, sometimes at great length.[4] From these fragments, it is clear that he travelled into Mauryan India and had some level of personal and direct access to Chandragupta in his capacity as an ambassador to the Mauryan court. The *Indica* fragments provide the earliest surviving references to various aspects of contemporary early Mauryan India, including its history, mythology, ethnography and geography.[5] It was also the first work to provide a Greek audience with first-hand knowledge of the Indian interior and the Mauryan court. Megasthenes' work did not, of course arise in a vacuum: there were a few earlier works, including those arising from Alexander's expedition, that touched on aspects of India, and Megasthenes' work fitted into this context.

The earliest descriptions of India found in Greek literature comes from Scylax of Caryanda (sixth–fifth centuries BC). Scylax wrote about an expedition he took part in sponsored by Darius I (r.522–486 BC), that went along the Indus and the Indian lands bordering those of the Achaemenid empire, as well as the Indian Ocean.[6] While the name of the book is now lost, fragments of it (collected together in *FGrH* 709) are found in a range of works, including Herodotus' *Histories*, Aristotle's *Politics*, Athenaeus' *Deipnosophists*, and Philostratus' *Life of Apollonius*.[7] In Book 3 of his *Histories*, Herodotus (early fifth century BC) includes a section on India that is primarily ethnographic but also includes some geographic elements.[8] The first monograph on India was the *Indica* written by Ctesias of Cnidus (late fifth–early fourth century BC), the Greek physician to Artaxerxes II; it only survives in fragments.[9] Unlike Scylax, neither Herodotus nor Ctesias travelled to India; instead they drew their information from sources such as Scylax, and in Ctesias' case from first-hand accounts from those people he met at the Persian court.[10]

Unlike these earlier Greek authors, Megasthenes travelled to and wrote about India beyond the Indus, and his importance to later authors is due to the originality of his information. This ancient focus on Megasthenes' work, rather than his life, means that basic information about him is lacking: his life, travel and political dealings have to be pieced together from fragments of information that, more often than not, raise more questions than they answer. The situation becomes more complicated still because the type, quality and volume of information that secondary authors provide about Megasthenes vary greatly, as do, where given, their opinions of him. One important point quickly becomes apparent in any modern assessment of Megasthenes: the evidence is limited and open to interpretation, with the result that much of what is written about him is necessarily speculative.

Brunt's observation that fragments are rarely what the word 'fragment' implies – namely, word-for-word quotations from now lost historians – is an important consideration here. He urges caution when using fragments, writing that 'every collection of "fragments" abounds in mere allusions, paraphrases, and condensations, which are often very inadequate mirrors of what the lost historians actually wrote'.[11] While not ideal, the availability of multiple fragments of Megasthenes' work in a range of later authors allows their cross-comparison and thus a more nuanced appraisal of the information presented by the original author than that offered by later interpolations. However, there are a number of instances where only one author reports a particular piece of information, which means that this 'checking' process is not always possible. Other limitations are based on the simple fact that comparisons often reveal little about the original authors' agenda(s), literary or otherwise, or intentions. In addition, there is always a tension between our reaction to an author's reproduction of an original source, and how we think the original may have read.[12]

Megasthenes' importance is such that his association with the four rulers, Sibyrtius, Porus, Seleucus and Chandragupta, are investigated here in turn. After this examination, the full range of Megasthenes' geographical references are investigated with the aim of locating him geographically. The aim is to better understand which regions of India he most likely travelled to and therefore saw at first hand, compared with those he is less likely to have visited and for which he required second-hand information.

Reconstructing the *Indica*?

Some scholars have attempted to reconstruct the original structure of the *Indica*. Barbara Timmer, for example, suggested the following order for the work: firstly, the borders and extent of India, and nature; secondly, Indian history, customs, society and urban life; thirdly, Indian religion and philosophy.[13] More recently, Stoneman tentatively proposed a structure broadly similar to that of Timmer and slotted in both Jacoby's and Schwanbeck's fragments in the order 'which seems to provide the most logical disposition of the material within the ethnographic template'.[14] Notably, both Timmer and Stoneman accept Jacoby's emendation of Josephus' reference to Book 4 of Megasthenes *Indica*:

Jacoby did not believe there was a Book 4 of the *Indica*, so he thought Josephus' reference to Book 4 was wrong and it should have been Book 1. In this way, Timmer and Stoneman dispense with Book 4 in their proposed structure of the *Indica*. As discussed below, my approach to the fragments is different from that of Timmer and Stoneman, and I do not accept Jacoby's emendation. However, my work broadly supports their conclusions in relation to the *Indica*'s original structure and provides more detailed insight into the organisation of the content of this work.

From an initial consideration of the authors in whose work most of the Megasthenes-derived material is found,[15] it appeared that there was some thematic correlation between the ways in which these authors organised the information they took from Megasthenes. I refined my approach to look at only those writers who included fragments of the *Indica* in single, lengthy sections of their work rather than shorter, individual sections. This is because, in a short section, it is easy to slot in one or two particular points that fit with the topic under discussion. In a longer section that deals with various aspects of a single topic – in this case India – it is possible to get a clearer idea of how information is brought together and discussed. Here, therefore, I turn to Diodorus' lengthy passage on India, which I discuss alongside Book 15 of Strabo's *Geography* and Arrian's *Indica*.

When all of the references from Megasthenes' *Indica* are arranged in the order in which they are included by Diodorus, Strabo and Arrian, an interesting pattern emerges. There are eight points (marked in **bold** type in Table 2.1) at which the order of the material matches in either two or all three authors. There are also a number of points where similar material is found in a different order in the different authors (marked in *italics* in Table 2.1). If the pattern only held true at a handful of points, or in relation to a particular topic within an overall discussion on India, this could be put down to coincidence. However, the trend is in evidence all the way through the three passages on India. Given the limited number of Megasthenes-derived fragments included in these three works, this is a striking correlation. We find the same order of information in all three works, for example, in relation to the division of Indian society and elephant hunting. However, in other cases it is necessary for the details to remain in a particular order for the contents to make sense. Reorganising them would produce nonsensical text.

A number of factors can be put forward to try and explain this pattern. Firstly, and perhaps most tantalisingly, it is possible that it reflects the original structure of Megasthenes' *Indica*. There are hints that the three authors had first-hand access to the original work, which would

Table 2.1 The order in which Megasthenes' fragments are found in Diodorus, Book 15 of Strabo's *Geography* and in Arrian's *Indike*.

Diodorus, *Library of World History*	Strabo, *Geography*	Arrian, *Indike*
	15.1.6-7 Ancient rulers who did not conquer India	
2.35.1-2 Size and shape of India	**15.1.11-12 Size and shape of India**	**3.6-8 Size of India**
2.35.3 Brief overview of Indian landscape, including animals and birds		
2.35.4 Elephants		
2.36.1 Fruitfulness of India and benefit to health		
2.36.2 Minerals in India		
2.36.3-5 Indian crops, monsoon and harvest	**15.1.20 Indian harvests and fruits**	
2.26.6-7 Inviolability of farmers and farms		
2.37.1-6 Indian rivers	**15.1.35 Indian rivers**	**4.2 Indian rivers**
		5.4-5 Ancient rulers who did not conquer India
	15.1.36 Description of Pataliputra	
	15.1.37 Indian animals	
2.37.7 River Silla	**15.1.38 River Silas**	**6.1-3 River Silas**
2.38.1 Indian people autochthonous		
2.38.3-7; 2.39.1 Dionysus' arrival in India; Dionysus and his descendants		**7.1-8.3 Outline of early India and role played by Dionysus**
		8.4.9-8 Heracles' role in Indian history

Diodorus, *Library of World History*	Strabo, *Geography*	Arrian, *Indike*
		9.9-12 Indian kings; no one invaded India
2.39.5 No slaves in India		
2.40.1-2.41.5 Division of Indian society	**15.1.39-49 Division of Indian society**	
		10.1 Indians do not make memorials to the dead
2.42.1-2 Elephants	**15.1.42-43 Elephant hunting**	
	15.1.44 Gold-digging ants	
		10.2-4 Description of Indian buildings by riverbanks and coasts
		10.5-6 Description of Pataliputra
		10.8-9 No slavery in India
2.42.3 Magistrates for foreigners	**15.1.50-52 Mauryan administrative divisions**	**11-12 Division of Indian society**
	15.1.53-55 Megasthenes in Chandragupta's camp; description of king's daily life	
	15.1.56-57 Marvellous peoples of India	
	15.1.58-60 Indian philosophers	
	15.1.68 Calanus	
		13-14 Elephant hunting
		15.4-7 Gold-digging ants

have provided an obvious model for them to follow. However, not all of the different aspects of Megasthenes' work were relevant to the aims and scope of later authors, and they may also have found it necessary to move certain sections of pieces of information to better serve the purpose of their own writings. Therefore, references to information found in particular books of the *Indica* provide a way of cross-checking whether or not the order of the references in Diodorus, Strabo and Arrian mirrors the original structure of Megasthenes' work.

No author mentions the first book of the *Indica*, but Athenaeus, Clement and Josephus, respectively, do refer to books two to four.[16] According to Athenaeus, Book 2 of Megasthenes' work includes information about Indian dining customs that appears to apply to a court, because of the reference to a golden bowl. Clement of Alexandria includes a reference from Book 3 of the *Indica*, which states that Megasthenes mentions that philosophers from outside Greece, including those from India, discussed nature. Finally, Josephus notes that Megasthenes wrote in Book 4 that Nebuchadnezzar surpassed Heracles in bravery and deeds.

Interestingly, the references associated with Books 2 and 3 of the *Indica* do appear to fit the overall pattern found in the order of the Megasthenes-derived information in Diodorus, Strabo and Arrian. After descriptions of Indian geography, climate and crops, which might reasonably have come from a putative Book 1, there is a grouping of fragments that concern Indian society. In all three authors this includes the different sections of Indian society; in Strabo there are descriptions of the Mauryan king's daily life, while Arrian includes a description of Pataliputra in this section as well as a note that Indians do not make memorials to the dead. The reference from Athenaeus concerning Indian dining practice that is found in Book 2 of the *Indica* therefore correlates well with this group of fragments. Strabo's final passages from Megasthenes concern Indian philosophers, and come after the section on Indian society. Clement's reference to Indian philosophers in Book 3 of the *Indica* therefore fits within the overall sequence of relevant fragments found in Strabo.

There are more difficulties in relation to the information contained in Book 4: of all the authors who include fragments from Megasthenes, only Josephus, Eusebius and Strabo mention Nebuchadnezzar, while Arrian refers to some of the other ancient rulers that Strabo also includes as part of his discussion of Nebuchadnezzar. Diodorus does mention Heracles in his section on Indian society and after his section on Indian geography. Of the three authors who include the largest number of fragments from Megasthenes, not one of them places this information at the end of their fragments from the *Indica*: it comes halfway through Diodorus' section on India, while it is the first reference from Megasthenes that Strabo includes in Book 15 of his *Geography* and the third fragment that Arrian includes in his *Indike*. Clearly, there is no correlation between the position of this particular fragment in Diodorus, Strabo or Arrian, and its position in the *Indica*. Without Josephus' note that this particular material was contained in Book 4 of the *Indica* – a piece of information there is no reason to doubt – it would be impossible to attempt to locate it within Megasthenes' work.

The trends seen in the organisation of the fragments of Megasthenes that are found in the work of later authors suggests they do reflect to some extent the original structure of Megasthenes' work. However, there are of course other reasons why the pattern of the use of Megasthenes' *Indica* is similar across all three authors, one of which is the use of intermediary sources. Diodorus, Strabo and Arrian all used Eratosthenes' *Geography* for information on India and, of particular relevance here, as a source for at least some material from Megasthenes. It is possible, therefore, that the order in which the details are included reflects, at least in part, the order in which Eratosthenes included Megasthenes' references in his own work. However, it is difficult to reconstruct the order in which Eratosthenes discussed various aspects of India in his *Geography*. Most of the fragments of Eratosthenes' *Geography* are found in Strabo's own *Geography*, and it may be that Strabo echoes Eratosthenes' own organisation of material. This is a circular argument and without further evidence little more can be said.

Overall, therefore, when looking at writers who include fragments of Megasthenes' *Indica* in single, lengthy sections – namely Diodorus, Strabo and Arrian – we find patterns in which the order of the material matches. From these correlations at multiple points in their respective works, it is possible to suggest, albeit tentatively, a structure for the *Indica*. While no ancient author refers to Book 1 of the *Indica*, looking at the order of the Megasthenes-derived material in Diodorus, Strabo and Arrian one can surmise that this book may have contained information about Indian geography, climate and crops. Of the remaining three books, Book 2 appears to have focused on Indian society and cultural practices, Book 3 perhaps on philosophers and religion, and Book 4 on ancient rulers from across the known world, as well as gods, who did and did not conquer India. This structure appears to be echoed in ethnographies written by authors broadly contemporary with Megasthenes, which suggests he was following an established format and therefore provides additional support for the organisation of the *Indica* presented here.[17]

Megasthenes and Sibyrtius

Arrian explicitly links Megasthenes with Sibyrtius:

> The latter [Megasthenes], who was with Sibyrtius the satrap of Arachosia, says that he frequently travelled to Sandrocottus [Chandragupta] the king of the Indians.[18]

Alexander appointed Sibyrtius satrap of Gedrosia in 326 BC and of Arachosia in 325 BC.[19] Sibyrtius was confirmed in these satrapies both at the Babylonian conference held after Alexander's death in 323 BC and at Triparadeisus in 320 BC.[20] Sibyrtius is last mentioned in the sources when, just five years later, Antigonus Monophthalmus restored him to his satrapy, after Sibyrtius had been charged with treason and deposed by Eumenes.[21] No information survives about the end of Sibyrtius' rule. So, for at least ten years, Sibyrtius controlled a vast swathe of land in the upper satrapies that bordered Porus' realms on the eastern bank of the Indus.

The capacity in which Megasthenes was with Sibyrtius is not clear: Stoneman suggests that Megasthenes was a member of Sibyrtius' staff until he was appointed ambassador to Chandragupta, most likely after the Seleucid-Mauryan treaty in *c.*303/305 BC.[22] Megasthenes could have been with Sibyrtius at any point, and in any of Sibyrtius' satrapies, up to this time. On the basis of this association, it is tempting to suggest that Megasthenes had come east with Alexander. However, Arrian does not include Megasthenes alongside Nearchus as one who campaigned with Alexander, which suggests, but doesn't prove, that Megasthenes was not with Alexander.[23]

Arrian writes:

> However, I shall write a special monograph about India including the most reliable descriptions given by Alexander's fellow campaigners, especially Nearchus, who coasted along the entire Indian part of the Great Sea, and further all that Megasthenes and Eratosthenes, both men of repute, have written.[24]

Bosworth argues convincingly that this reference from the *Anabasis* suggests that Megasthenes did not travel with Alexander.[25]

When historians try to link Megasthenes and Sibyrtius more closely together, or to develop arguments as to their relationship, the limited available evidence inevitably leads to supposition and speculation. Bosworth stands out in his suggestion that Sibyrtius sent Megasthenes to both Porus and Chandragupta over the course of only one, long ambassadorial mission between 320 and 318 BC, and that one of the aims of this mission may have been to obtain war elephants.[26] While parts of this argument are compelling, overall it does not convince. Bosworth rejects Megasthenes as Seleucus' ambassador despite the close relationship indicated by Clement of Alexandria.[27] He also overlooks Pliny's statement that the territory between the Hyphasis and Palimbothra (Pataliputra) was explored for Seleucus.[28] As Kosmin points out, in an argument rejecting Bosworth's dating of Megasthenes' embassy, the only individual both associated with Seleucus and known to have done this is Megasthenes.[29]

Other suggestions, while tempting, are also problematic because of lack of evidence. Coloru and Stoneman, for example, suggest that Megasthenes did not reside continuously in Pataliputra, but used Sibyrtius' residence at Alexandria-in-Arachosia as his base.[30] Kosmin points to a series of possibilities, some based in earlier scholarship, in an attempt to reconcile Megasthenes' association with Sibyrtius and Clement's reference to Megasthenes' having lived with Seleucus (see below). Firstly, Megasthenes could have started his career with Sibyrtius and then transferred to Seleucus.[31] Secondly, if Sibyrtius retained his satrapy of Arachosia and became one of Seleucus' 'recognised subordinates' when Seleucus extended his authority over the upper satrapies, Megasthenes may have been Seleucus' agent while associating with Sibyrtius.[32] Lastly, given that Seleucus ceded Arachosia to Chandragupta, Kosmin refers to Habib and Jha's suggestion that Chandragupta might have retained Sibyrtius as a Mauryan governor.[33] Unfortunately, there is not enough surviving evidence to confirm or reject these suggestions.

Megasthenes and Porus

Arrian links Megasthenes with both Porus and Chandragupta:

> But even Megasthenes, so far as I can see, did not visit much of India, though he visited more than the followers of Alexander, son of Philip, did: he states that he was in the company of Sandrocottus, the greatest king of the Indians, and Porus, who was yet greater than him.[34]

Although there are no problems with the received Greek text, it has been suggested that Porus' name is a later interpolation, but the lack of evidence makes this point difficult to accept.[35]

An alternative editorial amendment, which has become the standard version,[36] renders the final part of this passage as follows:

> he states that he was in the company of Sandrocottus, the greatest of the Indian kings, with that one who was even greater than Porus.[37]

However, this emendation is based on unfounded modern assumptions about Megasthenes' assessment of the respective greatness of Porus and Chandragupta. Brunt, for instance, writes, 'The text is amended, as Megasthenes knew that Chandragupta was more powerful than Porus.'[38] And yet, nowhere else in Arrian's work is it stated that Megasthenes thought Chandragupta was the 'greater' or even the more 'powerful' king compared with Porus. The received Greek text is problem-free and straightforward. For this reason, the original, unemended text is preferred here.[39]

Kosmin rejected Bosworth's suggestion that dating Megasthenes' embassy to 320–318 BC allows Arrian's statement that Porus was a 'greater' king than Chandragupta on the grounds that the latter was not yet at the full height of his power.[40] And, in relation to the unemended sentence, Stoneman has remarked that 'on any reading this is nonsense'.[41] While he appears to be more – if not entirely – accepting of the revised sentence, Stoneman questions Bosworth's assessment that it refers to a time when Porus was a greater king than Chandragupta. This is because Bosworth's interpretation would, logically, mean the superlative was used at a time when Chandragupta was the supreme ruler in India and not Porus. Stoneman attempts to rationalise Bosworth's acceptance of the unemended text by suggesting that Megasthenes' reference to Porus was perhaps retrojected into the past, meaning that he had met Porus at a time when Porus was indeed greater than Chandragupta.[42]

However, Stoneman, Kosmin and Bosworth overlook a reason why Porus was depicted as 'greater' than Chandragupta, namely Porus' relationship with Alexander, as described in the next paragraph. Arrian's work reflects his positive opinion of Alexander: points of criticism directed at Alexander were occasional and generally muted in tone and Arrian wrote explicitly that Alexander's many achievements outweighed any faults.[43] Bosworth justly writes that the *Anabasis* was a narrative of achievement, 'with a favourable verdict built into the texture of the narrative'.[44] A ruler such as Porus, whom Alexander held in high regard and treated like a king as requested, would therefore be 'greater' than another.[45] The date is thus not relevant.

Before his defeat by Alexander at the Battle of the Hydaspes in 326 BC, Porus ruled the land between the rivers Hydaspes and Acesines.[46] After the battle, Alexander appointed Porus satrap and returned his original lands to him, and he also handed to Porus huge tracts of land to the north which Alexander had acquired during military operations.[47] Porus ruled until he was murdered by Eudamus in *c.*317 BC.[48] This provides a *circa* nine-year window of opportunity for Megasthenes to meet Porus, a period that is chronologically compatible with the hypothesis that it was Sibyrtius who sent Megasthenes on this mission.[49] Unfortunately, as ever in matters pertaining to Megasthenes, all of these suggestions must remain speculative.

Megasthenes and Seleucus

Clement of Alexandria (*c.* AD 150–*c.*215) was the head of the catechetical school in Alexandria and the author of numerous works of which the most important is the *Stromateis* ('Miscellanies'). While this a complex work whose aims and purpose are still debated, Clement himself states that his goal is to explain the meaning of scripture to Greeks and Jews.[50] The book also served as a resource for Christian teachers (like Clement) that could be used to convert others to Christianity.[51] Clement makes extensive use of Greek literature in his work and his frequent reference to Indian philosophers and philosophy suggests they were of particular interest to him.[52] Clement links Megasthenes to Seleucus in Book 15 of his *Stromateis*:

> The clearest evidence [for the antiquity of the Jews] comes from Megasthenes, the historian who lived with [or, 'was closely associated with'] Seleucus Nicator. He wrote in the third volume of his *History of India*: 'However, all that has been said by the ancients about nature is also said by philosophers outside Greece, the Brahmans in India, and the people called the Jews in Syria.'[53]

The key word here is 'συμβεβιωκὼς', which is indicative of a very close relationship.[54] A search for this word across Clement's writings in the *Thesaurus Linguae Graecae* reveals that Clement used this word in the context of personal relationships, as opposed to the more temporal equation which is suggested by Ferguson's translation of the word as 'contemporary'.[55]

Clement's close association of these two individuals is valuable because this information is likely to be accurate. A detailed analysis of Clement's use of Megasthenes in his *Stromateis* reveals that he may have had direct access to a copy of the *Indica*. He was therefore well placed to know with whom Megasthenes associated himself.[56] It is also important to note that Clement's scholarship was highly regarded by his contemporaries: Cyril, for example, called Clement 'exceptionally excellent in Greek history', while Jerome noted Clement's knowledge of secular literature.[57]

As discussed in Chapter 1, Seleucus first travelled to India alongside Alexander in 326 BC, returning as a king in his own right in *c.*305 BC, having gained control of the lands between Babylon and the Indus.[58] He met Chandragupta on the banks of the Indus in *c.*305–*c.*303 BC, and after a military engagement they concluded a treaty which comprised at least three parts. Seleucus then returned west to face Antigonus at Ipsus in 301 BC and did not travel to the upper satrapies or India again. Kosmin's work on the politically driven, ideological basis of Megasthenes' *Indica* argues for a stronger link between Megasthenes and Seleucus than has hitherto been acknowledged.[59] Kosmin suggests that Megasthenes' *Indica* served a 'legitimizing purpose' for Seleucus by justifying Seleucus' retreat from India and emphasising the martial qualities of Chandragupta's elephants (which Seleucus received from Chandragupta as part of their treaty).[60] Overall, it is not clear when or where Megasthenes' association with Seleucus began or ended. While it is doubtful that Seleucus sent Megasthenes to Porus,[61] Seleucus' meeting with Chandragupta and his conclusion of a treaty with him gave him the perfect opportunity for dispatching an ambassador to Chandragupta.[62]

Megasthenes and Chandragupta

Two references from Arrian and three from Strabo link Megasthenes with Chandragupta. The first relevant passage from Strabo is included in the context of his writing that both Daimachus and Megasthenes provide bizarre and unreliable information about India: 'they [Megasthenes and Daimachus] were sent on an ambassadorial mission to Palimbothra (Megasthenes to Sandrocottus, Daimachus to Amitrochades the son of Sandrocottus)'.[63] The second reference is found in the context of a description of Palibothra [Pataliputra] at the end of which Strabo notes that the ruling king must be named after the city in addition to his personal name, giving Chandragupta as an example: 'King Sandrocottus to whom Megasthenes was sent on an embassy'.[64] The third reference is found in a section concerning theft among Indians (found in a longer ethnographic description of Indians) where Strabo includes Megasthenes' example of how few thefts occurred in Chandragupta's army camp: 'Megasthenes says that when he was in the camp of Sandrocottus …'.[65]

As discussed in Chapter 1, little is known about Chandragupta's rise to power or his movements during his reign. Justin provides some information when he writes that Chandragupta invaded the regions of Punjab and the Indus valley when Seleucus was defending his satrapy of Babylonia against the Antigonids; this was between 311 and *c.*308 BC.[66] Chandragupta re-emerges in the available sources in *c.*305–*c.*303 BC, when he met Seleucus by the Indus and concluded a tripartite treaty with him.[67] These dates give a period of some three to eight years during which Megasthenes could have met Chandragupta in north-western India. The surviving fragments of Megasthenes' *Indica* describe a prosperous and successful realm with an already implemented administration running the empire centred on the capital at Pataliputra. Although one must concede the influence of utopian literature on his work, the suggestion remains that Megasthenes travelled in India sometime after Chandragupta's conquest and his consolidation of his rule.

Overall, and given the limited evidence available, the traditional hypotheses linking Megasthenes with Sibyrtius for the embassy to Porus, and Megasthenes with Seleucus for the embassy to Chandragupta, remain the most plausible. The dates available for the individuals with whom Megasthenes was associated help to constrain the dates of his own travels broadly to 325–317 BC for his first embassy and 320–297 BC for his second. While it is tempting to suggest that he travelled to India in *c.*326 BC with Alexander, information from Arrian makes this unlikely.[68] Instead, the evidence suggests that Megasthenes may have had over 20 years' experience of living, working and travelling in the upper satrapies and northern India.

Megasthenes' geographical horizons

In this section, the full range of Megasthenes' geographical references are investigated with the aim of locating him geographically and thereby understanding the basis of his authority as a source for the Indian interior during the early Mauryan period. Such an analysis is important because, since antiquity, authors have mined his work for information pertaining to various aspects of ancient India. This type of scholarly excavation of the *Indica* for snippets of information pertinent to specific studies, including the attempt to reconstruct knowledge of the Mauryan empire or Seleucid-Mauryan relations ever more minutely, continues to the present day.

Details about the areas in which Megasthenes lived and travelled are derived from his links with the individuals discussed above and information extracted from the surviving fragments of his *Indica*. Given that more of these fragments concern geography than in the *testimonia* relating to his personal associations, it might be assumed that it is straight-forward to determine the routes and places he visited over the course of his travels. But, as we will see, this is not the case. So many of the geographical details have been summarised by later authors that few details survive specifically linking Megasthenes with particular locations and regions. Much, therefore, remains uncertain.

Given his Greek name and the language in which the *Indica* was written, it would be easy to assume that Megasthenes was of Greek ethnicity, but this is not necessarily the case: non-Greek people sometimes adopted Greek names.[69] Indeed, very little is known about Megasthenes. No information survives about where he was born, raised or died, or about the regions through which he travelled before he arrived in the upper satrapies and went to India.[70] It is interesting to note that Megasthenes' reference to the River Maeander in Asia Minor has been taken to suggest that this may have been his place of origin, but there is no clear evidence for this.[71]

Megasthenes' association with Sibyrtius locates him in the upper satrapies, and he may have resided in any or all of this governor's satrapies of Carmania, Gedrosia and Arachosia.[72] The available evidence does not permit this list to be narrowed down any further. As argued above, Megasthenes' embassy to Porus came after the former king had been installed as satrap by Alexander and his territories had been considerably extended. It is not known where Megasthenes met Porus, or how extensively he travelled within Porus' territories. Appian only mentions that Seleucus 'crossed the Indus and waged war with Sandrocottus, king of the Indians, who dwelt on the banks of that stream', a meeting at which Megasthenes may have been present.[73] Neither the location of this crossing, nor the meeting itself, is known.

More details survive about Megasthenes' meetings with Chandragupta, but it is difficult to determine their location. For example, as mentioned above, Strabo tells us that 'Megasthenes says that ... he was in the camp of Sandrocottus',[74] but this camp could be anywhere Chandragupta campaigned across northern India, including on the banks of the Indus where he met Seleucus.[75] Similarly, it seems that Megasthenes accompanied Chandragupta to the law courts, 'sacrifices', and a 'Bacchic' hunt,[76] but it is nowhere stated where these events took place. Where there is more detail about royal advisors and administration, it is not known where Megasthenes encountered them.[77] For example, Strabo mentions 'city inspectors', 'camp inspectors' and 'advisers and councillors of the king', as do Diodorus and Arrian. While Diodorus and Arrian note that overseers are located in various Indian cities, it is not known where the camps are situated, nor which city is referred to. It is tempting to suggest that the city is Pataliputra, Chandragupta's capital, but it is important to remember that there were numerous other important cities dotted across northern India during the early Mauryan period.

From the surviving fragments of his work, it is clear that Megasthenes did not travel the length and breadth of India, nor did he meet all of the people he described, something that ancient authors were aware of. Pataliputra, however, looms large in Megasthenes' surviving fragments, and his detailed descriptions strongly suggest that he travelled at least this far east from north-west India, possibly along the royal road.[78] Strabo notes that the length of this 'royal road' to Pataliputra has been measured, and extends for 20,000 stadia.[79] This detail may derive from Megasthenes because of the reference to Pataliputra. The starting point of the royal road and the measurement to this city is difficult to gauge from this context.[80]

Megasthenes recorded various details about Pataliputra, including its location at the confluence of the River Ganges and the River Erannoboas (ancient River Śoṇa, modern River Son), and the presence of a defensive ditch and 570 towers with 64 gates.[81] Later excavations at this site, albeit limited in their scope, reveal structures that correspond with Megasthenes' descriptions and thereby add credibility to them.

The European search for Mauryan cities and sites, particularly Pataliputra, began in the mid-eighteenth century and was closely based on information contained in Megasthenes' fragments.[82] By the end of the eighteenth century, Sir William Jones (see Chapter 3) had identified the modern city of Patna as the location of ancient Pataliputra.[83] Almost a hundred years later, after initial surveys by Sir Alexander Cunningham, first Director General of the Archaeological Survey of India, Laurence Waddell started excavations in the Bulandibagh area of the site in 1895. Waddell's work confirmed that Patna was indeed constructed on top of the ancient city of Pataliputra.[84] Further excavations by David Brainerd

Figure 2.1 Wooden palisade revealed during excavations by J. A. Page and M. Ghosh at Bulandi Bagh, Patna in 1926–27. Source: Archaeological Survey of India 1926–1927, Wikimedia Commons, bit.ly/3BMVWei.

Spooner in 1915 and by J. A. Page and M. Ghosh in 1926–7 revealed a wooden structure thought to be Pataliputra's outer palisade as described by Megasthenes (Figure 2.1). These fortifications comprise two parallel walls of *śāl* wood posts, and there was another wooden structure, believed to be a drain bringing wastewater out of the city.[85] Notably, the wooden palisade is assumed to be Mauryan because of the similarity to Megasthenes' description, but it may be pre-Mauryan. Radiocarbon dating of the wooden rampart provides a broad timespan: results suggest it was constructed in the second century BC ± 250 years.[86]

All of these excavations took place at and beyond the boundaries of ancient Pataliputra. While modern building works have revealed some objects and structures such as Mauryan terracottas and ring wells, it is unlikely that the heart of this city will be excavated in the foreseeable future because the modern city of Patna has been constructed directly on top of it. For this reason, virtually nothing is known through archaeology about the city itself and little about the environs or material culture represented at the site. Despite some re-excavation by A. S. Altekar and Vijayakanta Mishra in 1959, overall the reports and data are not as reliable and accurate as could be hoped for. One of the results of this situation is that further links between Megasthenes' text and the city remain tantalisingly out of reach.

How widely Megasthenes travelled in northern India beyond Pataliputra in the Ganges valley, and what he did and did not personally see, are difficult to determine because of the limited available evidence. An interesting series of references in Arrian's *Indike* point to the possibility that Megasthenes visited – or at least had some familiarity with – the region in which Mathurā was located. There is a reference to the 'Surasenians' (probably the Surasena people), their cities 'Methora' (probably modern-day Mathurā) and 'Cleisobora', and the river 'Iomanes' (probably modern-day Yamunā, formerly called the Jumna) which flowed through their land.[87] Pliny also mentions the 'Suari' people who live 'up country' (in the interior) of India, as well as the city 'Chrysobora'.[88] Megasthenes associates an indigenous Heracles with the Surasenians, and the context in which Arrian and Diodorus include this information suggests that his original account went into some detail about the stories associated with this Heracles.[89]

Śūrasena was one of the 16 *Mahājanapada* (*'maha'* means 'great'; *'janapada'* means, literally, 'the place where the tribe places its foot'), and Mathurā was indeed its ancient capital. This city is located by the River Yamunā, a tributary of the Ganges which is on the way to Pataliputra.[90] The Hindu deity Kṛṣṇa is believed to have been born in Mathurā and this city remains sacred to him. It is possible that Megasthenes equated Kṛṣṇa with the 'indigenous Heracles' although, of course, as Stoneman notes, this is not an argument for linking every reference to Heracles in an Indian context to Kṛṣṇa.[91] In addition, Stoneman makes the important point that, for Megasthenes, Heracles had to be identified in India because Alexander had insisted he was there.[92] The city of Cleisobora is otherwise unknown, but if it did refer to a place named Kṛṣṇapura ('city of Kṛṣṇa'), as Schwanbeck suggests, its association with Mathurā would, of course, be important and relevant here.[93] More recently, Stoneman returned to Cunningham's suggestion that Cleisobora might be identified with Keśavapura, a district of Mathurā located on the Yamunā.[94] 'Keśava' is one of Viṣṇu's names and Kṛṣṇa is his eighth avatar, which makes the possible link more tantalising.

Extant information about Indian rivers and peoples reinforces the impression that Megasthenes only travelled as far as Pataliputra and possibly its close environs. Arrian, who provides the most detail, and Diodorus, include information derived from Megasthenes about rivers in India, focusing on the Indus and Ganges and listing their tributaries.[95] According to Arrian, Megasthenes noted that the Ganges is 'much greater than the Indus', but in fact the Indus is the longer river.[96] This detail may point to Megasthenes' greater experience and familiarity with the Ganges than with the Indus. Where the tributaries of the Ganges have been identified, these are on the upper Ganges. The extant fragments of the *Indica* do not show an awareness of the lower Ganges. In relation to the Indus, there is no information about this river below the Acesines (modern Chenab).[97] Taken together, these points suggest that Megasthenes travelled south along the Indus as far as the Acesines and east along the Ganges perhaps little or no further than Pataliputra.

While not perfect, a general rule may be that the more outlandish the description, the less likely it is that Megasthenes had personal experience of what he describes.[98] For example, a considerable amount of information comes from Megasthenes about the 'Brachmanes' and the 'Garmanes', who spend time 'in a grove in front of the city', suggesting that he personally encountered these holy men, perhaps outside Pataliputra.[99] It is also possible that he met sages living in or near Taxila.[100] In contrast, it seems highly unlikely that he travelled to the eastern limit of India, because his description of the *Astomoi* ('mouthless ones'), whom he locates around the source of the Ganges, is so peculiar.[101] It is worth noting that it is the mouth of the Ganges, which empties into the Bay of Bengal, that is in eastern India, rather than the source, which is in the western Himalayas.[102] As with the information about the Indian rivers, this error coupled with the bizarre description of the *Astomoi*, further strengthens the suggestion that Megasthenes' travels were limited to northern India and that he did not visit the limits of eastern India.

Ancient descriptions of the size and shape of India, with the Ocean bounding east and south, Mount Emodus (Himalayas) the north, and the River Indus to the west, are derived from Megasthenes, as are a number of statements relating to India more generally.[103] Some information is specific to certain types of location, for example riverbanks or coastal areas. Given the type of surviving details, such as the material from which structures located near rivers or coasts are made, it is not possible to narrow down the identity of these places any further.[104] Megasthenes also provides information about places far from northern India, including Taprobanê (Sri Lanka), an island that was also known to contemporaries of Alexander such as Onesicritus.[105] There is no indication that Megasthenes personally travelled there; it is more likely that such information was based on knowledge about such regions obtained during his travels in northern India. Few of the surviving fragments of Megasthenes' work make explicit reference to others' testimony and

Pliny's reference to Megasthenes' information about Sri Lanka is no exception.[106]

The earliest known Mauryan embassy to Sri Lanka came during the reign of Chandragupta's grandson, the third Mauryan emperor Aśoka. Aśoka sent a proselytising embassy to the Sri Lankan king Devānaṃpiyatissa.[107] This mission presupposes knowledge of the island, and archaeological evidence reveals extensive lines of commerce and communication extending to the Gangetic plain from regions such as coastal and western India, Afghanistan and Sri Lanka.[108] Given the long-standing trading relationship between the two regions, and the transfer of knowledge that accrued over time, Megasthenes may well have obtained his information about Sri Lanka during his travels in northern India, including during his residence in Pataliputra.

The details that Megasthenes provides about the island appear to be accurate. Sri Lanka does have a river – the Mahaweli Ganga – running centrally through it for over 200 miles.[109] The ethonym 'Palaeogonoi' that Megasthenes associates with the people of Sri Lanka sounds like the old name for the island 'Palaisimundu' ['Palaesimundu']. Interestingly, this name for the island is found in Pliny and the *Periplus Maris Erythraei*, a trading document written in *c.* AD 70 and which includes information about aspects of trade across the Indian Ocean.[110] According to the *Periplus*, Sri Lanka did export gold and pearls, as previously reported by Megasthenes.[111]

Megasthenes locates the gold-digging ants among the Derdae, 'a large tribe of Indians living towards the east and in the mountains, [where] there is a plateau about three thousand stadia in circumference', but he does not add much more to Herodotus' description.[112] In addition, Arrian was in no doubt that Megasthenes had not seen these ants at first hand, writing, 'Megasthenes, however, merely recounts hearsay, and as I have no more accurate information to record on the subject I readily pass over the tale about the ants.'[113] Just before this section, Arrian notes that 'Nearchus says that he himself saw none of the sort [gold-digging ants] which some writers have described as native to India but that he did see many of their skins brought into the Macedonian camp.'[114] Megasthenes most likely borrowed the framework of the story from Herodotus, later adding extra geographical detail, perhaps from authors such as Nearchus, to give verisimilitude to his own account. It is highly unlikely that Megasthenes visited this area, wherever it may have been.[115]

In his *Indica*, Megasthenes includes an accurate dynastic list of the Babylonian kings of the sixth century BC, although Jacoby did not include this fragment in his *FGrH* 715, nor is it in *BNJ* 715. This information was preserved by Abydenus and survives in Eusebius' *Chronicle*.[116] Eusebius (*c.* AD 260–339) is a Christian historian, author and Bishop of Caesarea, while Abydenus is a Greek historian about whom little is known aside from the fact that he wrote a *History of the Chaldaeans* and may have lived during the Second Sophistic.[117] Abydenus may have derived part of his work from Alexander Polyhistor, a Greek author of the first century BC who wrote numerous works on diverse topics, including the Chaldaeans, and it is possible that Eusebius did too.[118] In his work *Against Apion*, the Jewish author Josephus (AD *c.*37– *c.*100) notes that Megasthenes included a discussion of the Babylonian kings in the fourth book of his *Indica*, but Josephus does not include this information in either of his own passages about Nebuchadnezzar.[119]

The way in which Megasthenes appears to have presented the information in his own work suggests that it was transmitted orally: 'the Chaldaeans say'. However, Sack notes that the prophetic literature upon which Megasthenes drew for his information had a long written tradition and was associated with the Chaldean dynasty that Megasthenes discussed.[120] More specifically, the *Dynastic Prophecy*, an Akkadian text which outlines the reigns of the Chaldean and Persian rulers of Babylon before wishfully predicting the downfall of Alexander at the hands of Darius III, very closely parallels the information provided by Megasthenes.[121] This suggests written rather than oral transmission.[122]

Whether or not Megasthenes consulted these written sources in Babylon is more difficult to ascertain. Kosmin, for example, suggests that Megasthenes' reference to this information locates him in the Seleucid court at Babylon.[123] While this may be the case, it overlooks the possibility that such writings circulated around the Greek world at this time, something about which little is known before Berossus in the mid-third century BC.[124] There are also the questions of language and transmission: how was Megasthenes able to consult a source written in Akkadian? Did he read a Greek translation? Seymour tackles such questions with respect to Ctesias, but conclusions are impossible given the lack of evidence.[125]

Conclusion

Ancient authors made use of Megasthenes' *Indica* but did not provide much detail about him, his unusual career or his links with other known historical figures.[126] Their foci remained elsewhere, and included Alexander the Great, power struggles among the Diadochi, geography and ethnography. Megasthenes the ambassador was not, apparently, a significant enough character to warrant detailed mention in either the Alexander or Diadochic narratives. Megasthenes' importance may have been recognised and explored more fully in works that dealt with the upper and Indian satrapies, and Seleucid or Mauryan histories.[127] Instead, his importance rested on the originality of his descriptions of and perspective on India. For this reason, little is known about Megasthenes himself.

Notes

1 Curt. 8.13.2; Arr. *Anab*. 5.8.3.

2 The other two ambassadors are Daimachus and Dionysius. Strabo (2.1.9) writes that Daimachus was sent on an ambassadorial mission to 'Allitrochades the son of Sandrocottus', surely a reference to Bindusāra, the son and successor of Chandragupta. Pliny (*NH* 6.21.58), the only author to mention Dionysius, notes that he is an ambassador dispatched by Ptolemy II Philadelphus to an Indian ruler, but does not specify which ruler this was.

3 Sibyrtius: Arr. *Anab*. 5.6.2. Seleucus: Clem. Al. *Strom*. 1.15.72.5. Porus: Arr. *Ind*. 5.3. Chandragupta: Arr. *Anab*. 5.6.2; Arr. *Ind*. 5.3; Strab. 2.1.9, 15.1.36, 53. Stoneman (2022, 1, 2–3) suggests his dates are *c*.350–*c*.290 BC.

4 *FGrH* 715; Stoneman 2022, 2.

5 Stoneman (2019, 137–8) provides a useful overview of the many ways in which Megasthenes' *Indica* has been understood and presented.

6 Hdt. 4.44.

7 Hdt. 4.44; Arist. *Pol*. 7.13.2; Ath. *Deip*. 2.82; Philost. *Ap*. 3.47.

8 Hdt. 3.97–106.

9 Nichols (2011) is the most recent scholar to collect together and translate the fragments of Ctesias' *Indica*.

10 Ct. Fragments 45–51 = Phot. *Bibl*. 72, 50a 4.

11 Brunt 1980, 477. Brunt notes that he prefers the term 'reliquiae' to 'fragments'. However, the term 'fragments' is too well established in scholarship to be dispensed with and is used here.

12 The ideas that he developed when he made his new translation of Megasthenes' fragments (Stoneman 2022, 16–17).

13 Timmer 1930 in Stoneman 2019, 182.

14 Stoneman 2019, 183.

15 This study was included in my PhD thesis and subsequently reworked, significantly expanded and published in Jansari 2020.

16 Ath. *Deip*. 4.153d–e; Clem. Al. *Strom*. 1.15.72.5; Joseph. *AJ* 10.227.

17 Stoneman 2019, 140–6, 178.

18 Arr. *Anab*. 5.6.2. Translation by Stoneman 2022, 33–4. Mehl (1986, 187–8) agrees with this translation, which says that Megasthenes often visited Chandragupta (rather than often saying he visited Chandragupta). He suggests that it is logical that Megasthenes had a single, prolonged stay with Sibyrtius, and several short stays with Chandragupta at Pataliputra.

19 Curt. 9.10.20; Arr. *Anab*. 6.27.1. See also Billows 1990, 432–3; Bosworth 1996, 118.

20 Arr., *Ta Met'Alexandron* 1.36 in Billows 1990, 433; Schober 1981, 4–5, 40.

21 Diod. 19.48.3; Plut. *Eum*. 19.3; Polyaen. *Strat*. 4.15. Antigonus also provided Sibyrtius with one thousand Argyraspids. These were Alexander's elite 'Silver Shield' soldiers. For more details about the Argyraspids' role in the battle between Eumenes and Antigonus, see Just. *Epit*. 14.1–4. Schober (1981, 82–3, 86, 93) discusses this in more detail.

22 Stoneman 2022, 88.

23 Arr. *Anab*. 5.5.1; Bosworth 1995, 235–6.

24 Arr. *Anab*. 5.5.1, translation Brunt 1983.

25 Bosworth 1995, 235–6. Also, Arr. *Ind*. 5.3: 'But it seems to me that Megasthenes did not visit much of the Indian land, although it was more than those with Alexander son of Philip visited.'

26 Bosworth 1996, 120.
27 Bosworth 1996, 114; Clem. Al. *Strom*. 1.15.72.5.
28 Kosmin 2014, 267–8; Plin. *NH* 6.63: 'The remaining distances after the [River] Beas were ascertained by the exploration of Seleucus Nicator.'
29 Kosmin (2014, 261–72) outlines his arguments *contra* Bosworth.
30 Coloru 2009, 144; Stoneman 2022, 4.
31 Kosmin 2014, 267, drawing on Bosworth 1996, 123.
32 Kosmin 2014, 267–8, drawing on Primo 2009, 54–5; Capdetrey 2007, 42; Heckel 2006, 259; Billows 1990, 432–3; T. S. Brown 1957, 15.
33 Kosmin 2014, 268 drawing on Habib and Jha 2004, 18.
34 Arr. *Ind*. 5.3. My translation based on Brunt 1983. Stoneman's translation (2022, 34, 38) is as follows: 'But even Megasthenes does not seem to me to have visited very much of India, though he did see more of it than those who accompanied Alexander the son of Philip. He says that he associated with Sandrocottus, the greatest king of the Indians, and still greater than the aforementioned Porus.'
35 See, for example: Lassen 1827; *FHG* 2.398; Timmer 1930 – mentioned in T. S. Brown 1957, 12–13 – and Kosmin 2014, 265.
36 For example, Schwanbeck 1846; *FHG* 2.398, followed by Roos and Wirth 1967.
37 Arr. *Ind*. 5.3: 'ἀλλ ' οὐδὲ Μεγασθένης πολλὴν δοκέει μοι ἐπελθεῖν τῆς 'Ινδῶν χώρης, πλήν γε ὅτι πλεῦνα ἢ οἱ ξὺν 'Αλεξάνδρῳ τῷ Φιλίππου ἐπελθόντες· **συγγενέσθαι γὰρ Σανδροκόττῳ λέγει, τῷ μεγίστῳ βασιλεῖιλΙνδῶν, καὶ Πώρου ἔτι τούτῳ μείζονι**', according to the standard edition by Roos and Wirth (1967, 9).
38 Brunt 1983, 319.
39 *Contra* Kosmin 2014, 263–5. Unamended text of Arr. *Ind*. 5.3: 'ἀλλὰ οὐδὲ Μεγασθένης τὴν πολλὴν δοκέει μοι ἐπελθεῖν τῆς Ἰνδῶν χώρης, πλήν γε δὴ ὅτι πλεῦνα ἢ οἱ σὺν Ἀλεξάνδρῳ [τῷ Φιλίππου] ἐπῆλθεν: **συγγενέσθαι γὰρ Σανδρακόττῳ λέγει, τῷ μεγίστῳ βασιλέι τῶν Ἰνδῶν, καὶ Πώρῳ, ἔτι τούτου μέζονι**' (Hercher and Eberhard 1885: http://www.perseus.tufts.edu/hopper/text?doc=Perseus%3Atext%3A2008.01.0531%3Achapter%3D5%3Asection%3D3, accessed 10 November 2022).
40 Kosmin 2014, 263–4; Arr. *Ind*. 5.3.
41 Stoneman 2019, 131–2.
42 Stoneman 2019, 132.
43 Arr. *Anab*. 7.30.1.
44 Bosworth 1995, 15.
45 Arr. *Anab*. 5.19.
46 Arr. *Anab*. 5.9–19.
47 Arr. *Anab*. 5.19.3, 5.20.2–4, 5.29.2, 6.2.1; Plut. *Alex*. 60.8.
48 Diod. 19.14.8, 19.15.5, 19.19.30.
49 Our knowledge about any problems Sibyrtius faced while satrap is so limited that we cannot be certain when or why he may have sent Megasthenes to Porus. Bosworth (1996, 120), for example, suggests that Megasthenes was sent to Porus (and then to Chandragupta) to obtain war elephants when Peithon staged a coup in Parthia in 318 BC, killing its satrap Philotas and installing his brother Eudamus in his place (Diod. 19.14.1). The upper satraps united and mustered a force of over 20,000 men under Peucestas' command, driving Peithon and Eudamus out of Parthia (Diod. 19.14.1–2).
50 Clem. Al. *Strom*. 4.1.1.3. For an overview of the ongoing debate about the *Stromateis*, see Osborn 2005, 5–18.
51 Osborn 2005, 14–15.
52 Osborn 2005, 2. Clement quotes over three hundred different literary sources for over one thousand references to other writers. Clement's interest in India may have originated with his teacher Pantaenus, who, according to Eusebius (*Hist. Ec*. 5.10) travelled to India as a missionary (Ferguson 1991, 10).
53 Clem. Al. *Strom*. 1.15.72.5. Translation by Ferguson (1991) with the exception of the words 'the historian who was contemporary with Seleucus Nicator', which is my translation.
54 From 'συμβιόω': 'living together', 'companion', 'partner', 'live with' (Liddell et al. 1953, 1675). Notably, this word is used by Antiochus III of his wife: 'she lived with me' (Welles 1934, no. 36, 1.6).
55 For example Clem. Al. *Strom*. 1.14.62. Kosmin (2014, 265–6) also notes the personal, rather than purely temporal, connotations of the verb 'συμβιόω', including in Clement's work.

56 Jansari 2020, 38. Ferguson (1991, 18) points out that the mention of an author by Clement does not necessarily imply that he read him at first hand. There were numerous compendia and anthologies in circulation and it is likely that Clement drew on these. However, in this case, Clement specifically refers to the 'third volume of his [Megasthenes'] *Indica*. It is unlikely that he would have done so if he had not personally had access to the *Indica*, a work that may have piqued his interest because of his particular attraction to and expertise in Greek and religious history. His references to Indian philosophy and the Buddha demonstrate his interest in, and knowledge of, Indians and their religions (Clem. Al. *Strom.* 1.15.71.6; 1.15.71.4–6). This interest has struck some scholars as unusual: some reason that Clement's teacher Pantaenus may have travelled to India (Ferguson 1991, 35n338 - in relation to Clem. Al. *Strom.* 1.15.71.6). Dihle (1984, 78) also notes Clement's familiarity with Megasthenes.

57 Cyril, *Contra Julianum* 6.215; Jerome, *De viris illustribus* 38 (both quoted in Ferguson 1991, 4). Clement spent over 20 years learning and teaching in Alexandria (Ferguson 1991, 3), the leading centre of Greek literary culture in this period, and the numerous and diverse references in his *Stromateis* are testimony to the rich literary milieu there. He aimed to preserve his teaching notes and compile them into a single body of work so that others might learn from them and be converted to Christianity. This latter point emphasises the importance accorded to the information he included in his work. Clement explicitly set out his goals in the introduction to his *Stromateis*. See especially: Clem. Al. *Strom.* 1.11.1, 1.11.2, 1.14.2, 1.16.1, 1.18.1, 1.71.3–5; Osborn 2005, 6–7; Rankin 2006, 125.

58 Seleucus also took part in the operations against Porus at the Battle of the Hydaspes (Arr. *Anab.* 5.13.1). For details about his return to India see: Diod. 20.53.4; Plut. *Dem.* 18.3; App. *Syr.* 11.9.57.

59 Kosmin 2013a, *passim*; Kosmin 2013b, *passim*. This goes beyond Sherwin-White and Kuhrt's suggestion (1993, 95–7) that Seleucus decided to abandon any thoughts of attempting to conquer the Indus area on the basis of the information Megasthenes (and local satrapal knowledge) provided about the might of the Mauryan empire.

60 Kosmin 2013a, 204; Kosmin 2013b, 97–9, 204.

61 When he first travelled to India alongside Alexander, Alexander sent Cleochares to Porus (Curt. 8.13.2); no other ambassadors are named, and Seleucus is most unlikely to have sent an ambassador to Porus, certainly not on his own account. Porus died in *c.*317 BC and Seleucus only regained control of the satrapy of Babylonia in 312 BC, extending his control over lands to the east until *c.*305 BC, when he met Chandragupta. Seleucus is unlikely, therefore, to have had either reason or opportunity to send an ambassador to Porus.

62 See, for example: Stein 1931, 232; Gruen 2006, 304; Errington 2008, 67; Walbank 1981, 199 (although Walbank also wrote that Megasthenes went to Pataliputra as Antiochus I's ambassador: Walbank 1981, 19); Shipley 2000, 285; Grainger 1997, 103. Billows (1990, 433) suggested that Sibyrtius hosted Megasthenes, and that the latter was Seleucus' ambassador to India.

63 Strab. 2.1.9.

64 Strab. 15.1.36.

65 Strab. 15.1.53.

66 Just. *Epit.* 15.4.20; Yardley, Wheatley and Heckel 2011, 290; Wheatley 2002, 39–41.

67 Strab. 15.2.1; Arr. *Syr.* 11.9.55.

68 Arrian (Arr. *Anab.* 5.5.1) does not include Megasthenes among those authors whose work Arrian used *and* who campaigned with Alexander: 'However, I shall write a special monograph about India including the most reliable descriptions given by Alexander's fellow campaigners, especially Nearchus, who coasted along the entire Indian part of the Great Sea, and further all that Megasthenes and Eratosthenes, both men of repute, have written.' Bosworth (1995, 235–6) argues convincingly that this reference from the *Anabasis* suggests that Megasthenes did not travel with Alexander. Also, Arr. *Ind.* 5.3: 'But it seems to me that Megasthenes did not visit much of the Indian land, although it was more than those with Alexander son of Philip visited.'

69 The name 'Megasthenes' appears once in the *LGPN* volumes published thus far, and this example is from the eighth century BC in Chalcis, Euboea (*LGPN* 1, 301). There is a 'Megasthenes' on Paros (*IG* XII,5 212) that is dated to the fourth century, and one at Pergamum (*MDAI* (A) 24, 1899, 188, 51) that is undated. These do not help to locate the ambassador Megasthenes, but they do suggest that the name is properly Greek. It is also notable that names ending in '-sthenes' are very common on the Greek mainland and in the Aegean. *Pace* Stoneman (2022, 2) who refers only to the Megasthenes in Chalcis.

Stein (1931, 230), for example, noted that Megasthenes' name pointed to his Greek descent. However, Greek names were adopted by non-Greek people for different reasons and in different contexts. There is good evidence for this practice in Hellenistic Babylonia (see Van der Spek 2009), and Mairs (2006) has also studied this phenomenon in the upper satrapies.

70 Kosmin (2013a, 205) notes Megasthenes' familiarity with Babylonia through the reference to Nebuchadnezzar and setting Megasthenes within a Chaldaean historical tradition (Strab. 15.1.6). Whether this link suggests that Megasthenes himself spent time in Babylonia is unclear.

71 Arr. *Ind.* 4.6. Duane W. Roller (commentary on *BNJ* 715 F9a), for example, suggests the reference to the Maeander may point to Megasthenes' place of origin. Notably, inscriptions found at Miletus (located near the mouth of the Maeander) mention that a number of Milesians campaigned with Seleucus I, including Demodamas of Miletus (Robert 1984, 470). So it is not impossible that Megasthenes was from the Maeander region, but it is impossible to prove. Stoneman (2019, 130) makes the point that Nearchus, who was from Crete, also used the Maeander, alongside other large rivers, for comparative purposes, and that 'no conclusion can be drawn from any of these pieces of evidence'.

72 The capital of Arachosia was Alexandria-in-Arachosia (Fraser 1996, 139) and it is possible that Megasthenes spent time in this city founded by Alexander.

73 App. *Syr.* 11.9.55.

74 Strab. 15.1.53. Further details are found in Strab. 15.1.52, which strongly suggest personal experience of the Indian army camp.

75 Just. *Epit.* 15.4.13-14; App. *Syr.* 11.9.55.

76 Strab. 15.1.55.

77 Strab. 15.1.48–9; Diod. 2.41.3–4; Arr. *Ind.* 12.5–7.

78 This city is called variously 'Palimbothra' (Arr. *Ind.* 10.5) and 'Palibothra' (Strab. 15.1.36; Plin. *NH* 6.63) in the Greek sources.

79 Strab. 15.1.27.

80 Roller (commentary for *BNJ* 715 F6c) suggests that the starting point may have been the River Indus, but this cannot be confirmed. Roller also notes that Strabo's figure is 'absurdly high' and 10,000 stadia is more likely.

81 Arr. *Ind.* 10.5, 10.6; Strab. 15.1.36; Diod. 2.39.3.

82 Chakrabarti 2009, 5.

83 Jones 1799, xxvi.

84 Waddell 1903; Ray 2014, 127.

85 Waddell 1903, 21–3; Spooner 1916; Page 1930; Lahiri 2015, 57.

86 S. D. Chatterjee et al. 1955.

87 Arr. *Ind.* 8.5.

88 Plin. *NH* 6.69.

89 Arr. *Ind.* 8.4–9.8; Diod. 2.39.1–4.

90 Thapar 2004, 138; Singh 2008, 262.

91 Stoneman 2019, 88, and further discussion about Kṛṣṇa/Heracles in an Indian context, including from Megasthenes' *Indica*: 87–8, 192–7; Karttunen 1989, 211.

92 Stoneman 2019, 88.

93 Schwanbeck 1846, 37–8; Karttunen 1997, 120n143.

94 Stoneman 2019, 28.

95 Diod. 2.37.1–6; Arr. *Ind.* 4.2–5.2. Also, Arr. *Ind.* 5.2: 'Megasthenes has in fact recorded the names of many other rivers beyond the Ganges and the Indus which run into the eastern and southern outer sea, so that he states the total number of Indian rivers to be fifty-eight, all navigable.' There is no known location for the River Silas, a river on which nothing floated, but everything sank to its depths (Arr. *Ind.* 6.2; Strab. 15.1.38; River 'Silla' in Diod. 2.37.7).

96 Arr. *Ind.* 4.2.

97 See Roller, commentary for *BNJ* F9a.

98 This criterion, which is certainly not without its problems, has been used as a methodological tool to assess the likelihood that ancient authors had first-hand experience or knowledge of peoples, events, places, etc. See, for example, Munson 2013, 130–1.

99 Strab. 15.1.59–60. For more information about these holy men, see: Karttunen 1997, 55–64.

100 In relation to the sage Calanus whom Alexander met in Taxila, Arrian (*Anab.* 7.2.4) writes, 'by Megasthenes' account, he was a man they themselves regarded as specially lacking self-control'.

101 Plin. *NH* 7.25; Strab. 15.1.57, 2.1.9. The same is true of the eight-toed people who Megasthenes located on the otherwise unknown 'Mount Nulus' (Plin. *NH* 7.22), and the Pygmies who lived in the 'furthest region of the mountains' (Plin. *NH* 7.26; also mentioned in Strab. 2.1.9 and 15.1.57, but without details of their location).

102 Although Diod. 2.37.2 writes: '[the Ganges] flows from north to south, emptying out into the Ocean, marking the boundary of the tribe of the Gandaridae toward the east'.

103 Diod. 2.35.1–2; Strab. 2.1.4, 2.1.7, 15.1.11–12; Arr. *Ind.* 3.7–8. In relation to general statements about India see Diod. 2.35.3–2.36.5. Also, Megasthenes noted that there were 118 tribes in India (Arr. *Ind.* 7.1; Plin. *NH* 6.60) but, as Arrian writes, 'I cannot conjecture how he learned and recorded the exact number, since he [Megasthenes] visited only a small proportion of India'.

104 Arr. *Ind.* 10.3–4.

105 Plin. *NH* 6.81.

106 Occasionally, secondary authors note, for example, ''Ινδοὶ λέγουσιν' ('Indians say') (Arr. *Ind.* 9.9). Even more rarely particular groups of people are mentioned as providing information: for example 1) Arrian (*Anab.* 7.2.4) mentions the sages giving their reaction to Calanus' actions; 2) Diodorus (2.38.3) notes 'the most learned Indians' who tell a legend; 3) there are also multiple references in Arrian (*Ind.* 8.4, 8.6, 8.8) to Indians themselves talking about Heracles.

107 *Dip.* 11.32–4, 12.1–4; *Mah.* 11.28–32.

108 Lahiri 2015, 265–7; Coningham and Young 2015, 392.

109 Ptolemy (*Geography* 7.4.6, 7.4.8) refers to this river as the Ganges; Weerakkody 1997, 34.

110 Plin. *NH* 6.85–6; *Periplus* 61; Weerakkody 1997, 34–5.

111 *Periplus* 61; Weerakkody 1997, 36.

112 Strab. 15.1.44; Arr. *Ind.* 15.4–7; Hdt. 3.102–5. Pliny (*NH* 11.111) also mentions these gold-digging ants in the 'region of the North Indians called the Dardae'.

113 Arr. *Ind.* 15.7.

114 Arr. *Ind.* 15.4.

115 Stoneman 2019, 271–4.

116 Euseb. *Praep. Evang.* 9.41.

117 *BNJ* 685 = Abydenus *FGrH* 685 F 6.

118 Geert De Breucker commentary for *BNJ* 685 F1a. Eusebius notes the similarity between Abydenus and Polyhistor in the section on Chaldaean history (Euseb. *Chron.* section 9 in R. Bedrosian trans.): 'Abydenus' Chaldean history confirms this. In agreement with Polyhistor, he relates it as follows.' And (Euseb. *Chron.* section 14 in R. Bedrosian trans.): 'Abydenus, after providing this account of the Chaldean kings, which is similar to Polyhistor's [account], then separately describes the Assyrian kings.'

119 Joseph. *Ap.* 1.144.

120 Sack 1991, 23.

121 Sack 1991, 33, 116n7, 116n8; Grayson 1975, 31–3. See also Neujahr 2005.

122 Sack 1991, 34.

123 Kosmin 2014, 52, 287n160. Kosmin does not refer to Sack.

124 For more information on Berossus, see: Verbrugghe and Wickersham 2001; Haubold et al. 2013.

125 Seymour 2014, 67–8.

126 The same is true of Daimachus and Dionysius, the other Greek ambassadors to the Mauryan court.

127 It would also be interesting to find out whether or not Hieronymus of Cardia used Megasthenes. Hornblower (1981, 85) wrote that Hieronymus would have known the works of Megasthenes and Daimachus, but was unable to provide evidence for this claim. She was mildly optimistic that some of Hieronymus' work might 'emerge from the sands of Egypt' (1981, 2).

Part II
Establishing the narrative

Part II of this book comprises three chapters which look at histories of ancient India, including multi-authored volumes, written by British and Indian historians between the late eighteenth and mid-twentieth centuries. Three distinct periods in the relationship between Britain and India are covered: the East India Company hegemony in India, the British Raj, and Indian independence from colonial rule.

Sir William Jones's identification in 1793 of the 'Sandrocottus' of Graeco-Roman literature with the 'Chandragupta' of the South Asian literary tradition opens the first chapter. The association that he made was vital. Without this link, Chandragupta might well have remained a little-known, obscure figure in the history of India, overshadowed by his grandson Aśoka, in much the same way that his son Bindusāra still is. The economist and historian James Mill took up this connection in his *History of British India* (1817). He recognised the inherent value in the encounter between Seleucus and Chandragupta, interpreting it in accordance with his own views of British compared with Indian people, history and civilisation.

Mill had patently different ideas about Indian history and culture from Jones, and he was writing for very different reasons. From his work, it is immediately apparent that Mill, who, unlike Jones, had no personal experience of India, was deeply prejudiced against the country and its people. Indeed, his book is unabashedly racist in its language and underlying assumptions. It was also influential and remained the most popular – in fact the only – general history of India for almost a century. Mill's division of India's history, for the first time, into Hindu, Muslim and British periods, for example, remains pervasive. It has taken a long time for this approach to be challenged. Similarly, his interpretation of the Seleucid-Mauryan encounter has long been influential, and the first time it was seriously challenged was in the early twentieth century, by the historian and former Indian Civil Service official, V. A. Smith.

Smith is much maligned as an arch-orientalist who reinforced stereotypes about the subcontinent, but in many ways this seems an unfair criticism. The way he dealt with the clash between Seleucus and Chandragupta and interpreted its outcome, for example, shows that there is considerably more careful analysis and nuance in his approach than is usually granted him. His interpretation stands in contrast to that of his contemporary, the historian E. J. Rapson, who maintains a paternalistic attitude towards India.

The most significant change in the presentation of the Seleucid-Mauryan encounter came in the work of Indian historians of ancient India. While Smith handed victory to Chandragupta, R. C. Dutt was the first to make the conceptual link between Chandragupta's defeat of Seleucus and the unification of northern India. It is this interpretation that won out in India through the work of the second generation of Indian historians, such as R. C. Majumdar and R. K. Mookerji. This latter group of scholars transformed Chandragupta from a minor ruler into the consummate Indian and Hindu hero who pushed the European Seleucus out of the subcontinent. Their strong nationalist allegiance and commitment to independence led them to reject the earlier British interpretations of the Seleucid-Mauryan encounter. Instead, like Mill, they imposed their own ideas and prejudices onto the meeting and its outcome. Their reading of this event was to leave a lasting legacy not only in historical scholarship but in Indian popular culture, as explored in Part III.

3
Sir William Jones and James Mill: synchronising histories and creating a divide

Making the link between 'Sandrocottus' and Chandragupta

In 1783, Sir William Jones (1746–94), barrister, radical political thinker and linguist, set sail for India to take up his appointment as Judge to the Supreme Court of Judicature at Fort William in Calcutta.[1] He worked with men such as Sir Warren Hastings (1732–1818), Governor-General of India, who had practical administrative as well as scholarly reasons for encouraging the pursuit of knowledge about ancient India. Hastings believed that to govern India the British needed to understand the history, laws and customs of the people. This approach laid the lasting foundations for British claims to rule India and for the methods by which rule was implemented.[2] It also informed the scholarly activity of organisations such as the Asiatic Society, founded in 1784 by Jones, who was also its first president, with the help of Charles Wilkins (1749–1836), a fellow Indologist under the patronage of Hastings.

While members were reliant on local teachers and experts for their information, until 1829 only Europeans were elected to this society. The Society was the focal point for scholarly activities pertaining to India; its influential journal, *Asiatick Researches*, was a vital means of recording and disseminating the new knowledge it generated. Jones's linguistic ability and interests, as well as the wider imperial, philosophical, judicial and social context in which he was working, meant that he soon began to learn Sanskrit under the tutelage of the pandit Rāmalocana. Under the Marquess Cornwallis (1738–1805), Governor-General of India between 1786 and 1793, Jones went on to work with a team of Indian scholars to compile and translate a digest of Hindu and Muslim law for use in the administration of India.[3]

Alongside his extensive judicial and administrative work, Jones used his leisure time to study other aspects of India, including botany. He also translated literary texts, most famously Kālidāsa's celebrated play *Abhijñānaśākuntalam* ('The recognition of Śakuntalā'). Jones's Sanskrit studies, allied with his knowledge of Greek and Latin, led to one of his most important scholarly breakthroughs: at a meeting of the Asiatic Society in 1786, and in the Society's journal in 1798, Jones presented his observation that Sanskrit, Greek and Latin had a common root.[4] It was at another meeting of the Society that he presented another momentous discovery that has particular relevance here.

On 28 February 1793, in his capacity as President of the Bengal Asiatic Society, Sir William Jones delivered his tenth, and final, anniversary discourse, 'On Asiatic history, civil and natural'.[5] It was here that he made public his research that equated, for the first time, the ancient Mauryan king 'Chandragupta' of the Sanskrit literature with the 'Sandracottus' of the Graeco-Roman sources. The basis of this association was his identification of Megasthenes' toponym 'Palibothra' as the modern city of Patna:[6]

> This discovery led to another of greater moment; for CHANDRAGUPTA, who, from a military adventurer, became, like SANDRACOTTUS, the sovereign of *Upper Hindustàn*, actually fixed the seat of his empire at *Pataliputra*, where he received ambassadors from foreign princes; and was no other than that very SANDRACOTTUS who concluded a treaty with SELEUCUS NICATOR.[7]

This link was of vital importance: it meant, for the first time, that Indian and Graeco-Roman history could be synchronised and dates assigned to this period of ancient Indian history and therefore others. The significance of this discovery was later emphasised by F. M. Müller (1823–1900), the Sanskrit scholar and Indologist, who referred to the start of Chandragupta's reign as the 'sheet-anchor' of Indian chronology, a term still used in reference to this date.[8] However, this synchronicity was not quite the panacea for the problem of dating events in the history of ancient India that scholars had hoped for. As seen in Chapter 1, for example, the date when Chandragupta's reign began remains elusive, and so therefore do the dates of his successors, as well as those of key religious figures such as the Buddha and Mahāvīra who preceded him.

Meanwhile, scholars sought immediately to build upon Jones's important work. For example, in the very next volume of *Asiatick Researches*, Captain F. Wilford wrote an article on 'The chronology of the Hindus' in which he noted that events recorded in the Sanskrit play *Mudrārākṣasa* (*Rākṣasa's Ring*) agreed 'remarkably well' with the account of Chandragupta/Sandrocottus transmitted in the Graeco-Roman authors.[9] Jones's link was (and still is) regularly cited in modern histories of ancient India.

Mill's *History of British India*

Unexpectedly, perhaps, one of the most prominent early adopters of Jones's equation of the two figures was James Mill (1773–1836), the economist and political philosopher and associate of Jeremy Bentham. Mill spent 12 years researching and writing a three-volume *History of British India* (1817), a publication that established his reputation as an expert on India and led directly to his employment by the East India Company (EIC).[10] In addition to Graeco-Roman sources, Mill drew upon the work of two broadly contemporary scholars when writing about the Seleucid-Mauryan encounter in his book: the Rev. W. Robertson (1721–93) and John Gillies (1747–1836). All three were figures of the Scottish Enlightenment, and they wrote within a few decades of one another, but had different aims and approaches to studying and understanding the past and its connection with the present. As we shall see below, Mill rejects Robertson's interpretation and follows that of Gillies. It is also important to note that, of these three authors, only Robertson wrote in ignorance of Jones's recognition of the equation of Sandracottus with Chandragupta.

Mill's aim was to produce 'a work, of considerably utility, on the subject of India'.[11] At the time of its publication, there was no comparable work available to an English-reading audience. For this reason, it was especially popular and influential, going through numerous editions and becoming the standard nineteenth-century reference work on the subject until the publication of V. A. Smith's *Early History of India* in 1904.[12] The book's immediate utility to the EIC can be seen from its inclusion as a standard textbook at Haileybury College, where the Company's civil servants underwent their training, as part of a wide curriculum of study.[13] Mill was well aware of the gap in the market that he sought to fill through his *History of British India*, noting in his Preface: 'Hitherto the knowledge of India, enjoyed by the British community, has been singularly defective. ... [N]othing is so rare as to meet with a man who can with propriety be said to know anything of India, and its affairs.'[14] And this was at a time when British influence in India was on the rise following the first conquest, in Bengal in 1757, and the rapid succession of campaigns and victories resulting in its becoming the paramount power on the subcontinent in 1818, after the Company's defeat of the Marathas.

Mill's approach to his work is, to a modern audience, astonishing in its undisguised contempt for the subject at hand from the very start. Early on in his Preface, Mill explains that he has not been to India and has 'a very slight, and elementary acquaintance' with any Eastern languages.[15] His expertise therefore comes at second hand. Mill proceeds to explain, at length, why this is unimportant, and one can soon conclude that it is because he does not think very highly of Indian history or culture. He writes, for example, 'Whatever is worth seeing or hearing in India, can be expressed in writing. As soon as every thing of importance is expressed in writing, a man who is duly qualified may attain more knowledge of India, in one year, in his closet in England, than he could obtain during the course of the longest life, by the use of his eyes and his ears in India.'[16] Through statements such as these, Mill's attempt to justify his own lack of personal experience of India in writing his book comes across strongly in his Preface.

In addition, while relying on the flood of new knowledge being generated and published in India, Mill fails to note that it is also there that the biggest breakthroughs and scholarly developments in the broad sphere of Indological studies are taking place. Indeed, he owed a debt to men such as Warren Hastings with whose approach to India he disagreed ideologically. Hastings believed that if the British were to govern India successfully, they needed to understand, respect and apply the laws and customs of the Indian people. In order to pursue this Enlightenment ideal, which aimed to understand all cultures, Hastings and his administrators, including William Jones, committed themselves to the study of ancient India for both practical administrative reasons and out of scholarly curiosity.[17] One of the outcomes of such scholarly pursuits was the establishment of the Asiatic Society of Bengal. As discussed above, it was in this context that Jones made and presented his discovery that the 'Sandrocottus' of Greek literature and the 'Chandragupta' of Sanskrit literature were one and the same.

Mill's approach has its philosophical origins in Montesquieu's (1689–1755) meteorological climate theory, which asserted that climate influenced man and the society in which he lived.[18] Its political origins, meanwhile, can be traced to Edmund Burke (1729–97), who believed that the English qualities of freedom and virtue were corrupted when they came into contact with despotic Indian traditions and institutions, exemplified in the person of Hastings, against whom Burke led the impeachment, supported by Mill, which was to prove unsuccessful.[19] Mill's writing (like that of Burke before him) therefore represented a particular strain in Georgian thought which emphasised English liberty contrasted with Oriental despotism. One of the ways in which this particular idea found expression in Mill's writing was through the argument that Indians were 'morally depraved as a race by long eras of despotism'.[20] With this pejorative and racist stereotype about Indians at their core, Mill's ideas about a 'primitive' ancient India in comparison with ancient Greece and Rome took shape and proved to be enduringly influential. Moreover, while Mill declares himself to be in the 'sincere and determined pursuit of truth',[21] his partiality is evident throughout his work, including in reference to ancient Indian history. The way in which he presents the meeting between Seleucus and Chandragupta and its outcome is no exception.

Establishing a narrative: Mill's interpretation of the meeting between Seleucus and Chandragupta

In Book II, titled 'Of the Hindus', of the first volume of his work, Mill includes a section on the 'Chronology and ancient history of the Hindus'. Mill finds that the lack of available evidence makes it impossible to 'describe the lives of their [India's] Kings, or the circumstances and results of a train of battles'.[22] However, he is unconcerned at the poor state of the available source material, writing, 'we have perhaps but little to regret in the total absence of Hindu records'.[23] The implication is clear: while little is known about India's ancient rulers, little would be gained through any greater knowledge because the details are so gory and horrible. India's ancient rulers are, for Mill, peripheral figures in India's overall history. However, he goes one step further by denigrating the whole people of India both in antiquity and modernity in a short, pithy statement:

> From the scattered hints contained in the writings of the Greeks, the conclusion has been drawn that the Hindus, at the time of Alexander's invasion, were in a state of manners, society, and knowledge, exactly the same with that in which they were discovered by the nations of modern Europe; nor is there any reason for contradicting this opinion.[24]

This type of deeply prejudiced opinion of and judgement on the people of India echoes with unremitting regularity through Mill's work. It is worth quoting the following section in full because his opinion of Indians clearly has a significant impact on how he chooses to interpret the meeting between Chandragupta and Seleucus. According to Mill:

> It is certain that the few features of which we have any description from the Greeks bear no inaccurate resemblance to those which are witnessed at present. From this, from the state of improvement in which the Indians remain, and from the stationary condition in which their institutions first, and then their manners and character, have a tendency to fix them, it is no unreasonable supposition that they have presented a very uniform appearance from the visit of the Greeks to that of the English.[25]

In Mill's view, therefore, India's contemporary rulers could be equated with her unimportant and marginal ancient rulers, and her people who were defeated by the Greeks as well as those in more recent battles by the English, similarly so. Against this background, Mill's portrayal of the ancient Indian ruler Chandragupta in comparison with the Macedonian Seleucus is all too predictable.

Mill was aware of the link Jones had made between 'Sandracottus' and Chandragupta Maurya, writing that the new king was 'a man of the Maurya race, named Chandragupta. This prince is reckoned, by our Oriental antiquarians, the same with Sandracottos or Sandracuptos, the contemporary of Alexander the Great.'[26] So he knew that Seleucus encountered Chandragupta, the founder of the important Mauryan dynasty, and not an otherwise unknown and insignificant ruler in India.

According to Mill, Seleucus 'gained victories' over Chandragupta, but before Seleucus could consolidate these victories he had to make peace with Chandragupta.[27] However, this peace agreement was not due to any military advantage the local ruler had gained. Rather, it was because Seleucus had to return and defend the western portion of his realm against Antigonus Monophthalmus, a more powerful opponent in a more important (western) part of his empire. The suggestion in Mill's work is that if Seleucus had not had to abandon the East in such a hurry, his victories over Chandragupta would have continued: 'He [Seleucus] gained victories over Sandracottus, the sovereign of a people living on the Ganges. But, as he was recalled to the defence of another part of his dominions against Antigonus, he made peace with the Indian.'[28] Given the lack of importance Mill accords Indian rulers, it is highly unlikely that he would countenance one of them equalling in military prowess, let alone defeating, one of Alexander the Great's generals.

In a footnote, Mill provides his sources for the information about the meeting between Seleucus and Chandragupta. Alongside Strabo and Appian, Mill refers to two works: firstly, the Rev. W. Robertson, *An Historical Disquisition Concerning the Knowledge Which the Ancients Had of India: And the progress of trade with that country prior to the discovery of the passage to it by the Cape of Good Hope* (henceforth '*Historical Disquisition*'); secondly, John Gillies, *The History of the World, from the Reign of Alexander to that of Augustus* (henceforth '*History of the World*').[29] Mill's presentation of the Seleucid-Mauryan encounter is strikingly different from that of Robertson, and echoes that of Gillies. This is despite all of the modern authors being reliant on the same group of ancient sources. As seen in Chapter 1, these sources do not permit the encounter, including the military skirmish and treaty, to be reconstructed with any degree of accuracy, especially in relation to which ruler emerged victorious. Each author's interpretation of events is, therefore, of particular interest.

Robertson's *Historical Disquisition*

Robertson was a leading figure of the Scottish Enlightenment and, like Edward Gibbon, David Hume and Voltaire, one of the most notable and influential historians and thinkers of his day.[30] For 30 years he held the office of Historiographer Royal for Scotland, a position to which he was succeeded by Gillies. As a historian, Robertson was best known for his histories of Scotland, America and Charles V, but it is his final work, on India, that is of particular interest here. His *Historical Disquisition* focuses closely on the history of European trading relations with India in three chronological sections: the earliest times up to the Roman conquest of Egypt; the period up to and including the Arab conquest of Egypt; and the discovery of the route to India via the Cape of Good Hope.

While the *Historical Disquisition* explored European-Indian trading relations in antiquity, Robertson was not an ancient historian and his primary interests did not lie in this period. Like Mill and Gillies, however, he had excellent Greek and Latin, which permitted him to read ancient Graeco-Roman sources.[31] Robertson was preoccupied with contemporary problems posed by the burgeoning commercial trade with India and the expansion of British power in India, which included both military domination and the creation and institution of a legal framework with which to establish British rule there. It is in this wider political and philosophical context that Robertson contributed, through his *Historical Disquisition*, to the maelstrom of ideas concerning the nature and future of British rule in India. The work quickly gained popularity and became influential not only in Britain, but also in Germany and France, as attested by the rapid translation of his book into both German and French.[32]

Robertson's ideas about the nature and future of British relations with India combined with those of other Enlightenment figures, including Adam Smith and Montesquieu, in his *Historical Disquisition*.[33] However, Robertson was also clear in his own beliefs and used his book as a vehicle for a political and moral message: while he thought that a strong military presence in India was necessary to protect and expand Britain's commercial interests in India, he also urged British respect for India's enduring, never-changing culture and traditions.[34] This broadly tolerant outlook, probably inspired by Montesquieu, contrasted strongly with that of Mill and others who were debating British policy with respect to India at the time.[35] Indeed, Mill found Robertson's opinions on Indian society so abhorrent that Briant refers to Book II of his *History of British India* as an 'orderly demolition of Robertson's theses' and it is difficult to disagree with this assessment.[36] While Robertson does not overtly set out the practical policies his position entailed, he did intend his book to inform legislative opinion.[37] In this context, and bearing in mind his history of America, the way in which he ended his *Historical Disquisition* is particularly apposite with its 'moving appeal to the European imperial powers then present in India to avoid the abuses of power that so darkened European expansion in the Americas and to show respect for the rich and ancient cultural heritage of India'.[38]

Robertson's views about contemporary British relations with, and intentions towards, India influenced the way in which he presented earlier European encounters with India, including during the Hellenistic period.[39] Robertson argued, for example, that Alexander the Great was a benevolent ruler, moved by reason rather than passion, and with commercial intentions. Furthermore, he contended that if the British modelled their rule after this ideal of Alexander, which in turn was based on Montesquieu's image of Alexander, they would help uplift the Indian people.[40] Robertson's view of Alexander, including Alexander's beneficent intentions towards Indians and in relation to trade with India, also influenced his interpretation of the reasons behind Seleucus' march towards India and even of Seleucus' relations with Chandragupta. Robertson was writing nearly a decade before Jones made the link between 'Sandracottus' and Chandragupta. Given the reasons that underlay the way in which Robertson chose to present the Seleucid-Mauryan encounter, it is unlikely that knowledge of the link Jones had made would have had any real impact on his interpretation.

Robertson asserted, for example, that Seleucus travelled to India at least in part for commercial purposes, writing: 'Seleucus, like all the officers formed under Alexander, entertained such high ideas of the advantages which might be derived from a commercial intercourse with India, as induced him to march into that country, partly with a view of establishing his own authority there, and partly in order to curb Sandracottus.'[41] Robertson presents Sandracottus as a rising and substantial power who had already 'acquired the sovereignty of the Prasii, a powerful nation on the banks of the Ganges, [and] threatened to attack the Macedonians, whose Indian territories bordered on his dominions'. However, there is no doubt that Seleucus is the dominant, active figure in the relationship: *he* concluded a treaty with Sandracottus by which the latter 'quietly retained the kingdom he had acquired',[42] because Seleucus was 'constrained to stop short in his career [in India] in order to oppose Antigonus, who was preparing to invade his dominions at the head of a formidable army'.[43] Similarly, it was Seleucus' decision to cultivate 'friendly intercourse' with Sandracottus, choosing Megasthenes as his ambassador.[44]

Gillies's *History of the World*

Given the significant Scottish intellectual contribution to the Scottish, British and European Enlightenments, it is not entirely surprising that the other historian cited by Mill with respect to the encounter between Seleucus and Chandragupta is another Scot, the classical scholar and ancient historian John Gillies. As well as numerous translations of ancient Greek texts into English, Gillies wrote two lengthy tomes on Graeco-Roman history. His *History of the World from the Reign of Alexander to that of Augustus* (1807) is of particular interest here. Gillies spent some 20 years working on the subject, and he used and cited many more ancient and modern sources than Robertson. He embraced the work of Enlightenment thinkers such as Montesquieu and Voltaire even more wholeheartedly than Robertson did, as demonstrated by his very sympathetic portrayal of Alexander.[45] As shown below, this impression of Alexander influences the way Gillies presents Seleucus.

Notably, Scots were disproportionately represented in imperial endeavours, both in the Atlantic world and in the East India Company.

Gillies, Robertson, and of course Mill had links with British expansion abroad. In Robertson's case, this association was personal: both of his sons saw active service in India in the late eighteenth century.[46] It is not surprising to find, therefore, that ancient and contemporary commercial interests were of considerable interest to Gillies, as to Robertson before him, and found expression in his work. While his *History of the World* was not especially well received by his peers,[47] one aspect has proved enduringly influential: his interpretation and presentation of the Seleucid-Mauryan encounter. This interpretation was markedly different from that presented by Robertson and much more closely aligned to the version later accepted and propagated by Mill.

Robertson wrote his *Historical Disquisition* before Sir William Jones had made his now famous breakthrough, whereas Gillies was aware of it. In his *History of the World from Alexander to Augustus*, Gillies referred to the link made by Jones, albeit without attribution, between the ancient Mauryan capital 'Palibothra' and modern-day 'Patna', and he also noted that this was Sandracottus' capital city. However, interestingly, he chose to omit the other important connection that Jones had made, namely the recognition that 'Chandragupta', the important and powerful ruler from Sanskrit literature, was the Indian king 'Sandracottus' found in Graeco-Roman texts. Gillies did not explain the reasons behind this omission, but his interpretation of the ancient sources and the way he described Sandracottus in comparison to Seleucus are suggestive.

Seleucus is introduced as the active and dominant character in the section dealing with his approach to India. Not only did Seleucus' 'will' have the 'force of law over the vast regions between the Euphrates and Indus', but he 'spurned the latter boundary, and claimed for his own the valuable territory between the Indus and Ganges'.[48] It is not clear whence Gillies derived the evidence for Seleucus' claim to this territory; it is not found in the ancient sources. However, Seleucus was 'defeated [in] his purpose' because of Sandracottus.[49] While Sandracottus was 'endowed with abilities equal to his ambition', his military knowledge, and therefore his agency, were derived from Alexander. This is because, according to Gillies, Sandracottus 'learned the art of war in the camp of Alexander'.[50] Notably, there is no evidence for this statement: Plutarch writes that Sandracottus saw Alexander, but this statement does not, of course, equate to his having learned the art of war in Alexander's camp.[51] However, this link with the idealised Alexander who featured so prominently in his work conveniently enabled Gillies to account for Sandracottus' power.

The Sandracottus of Gillies's work was not, however, imbued with the honour and enlightened values of Alexander, or indeed Seleucus. Instead of using the knowledge Sandracottus had gained from Alexander to support and further the Greek aims and value system, 'he deceived and deserted his instructors', before becoming the head of 'a great army' in India. Despite his military might, Sandracottus is not allowed a 'victory' over the Macedonians: Gillies only permits him to reduce the 'feeble' Macedonian garrisons in the Punjab, receiving the submission of their 'reluctant' tributaries. Gillies's view that an Indian ruler could raise an army that posed a military challenge, albeit a minor one, to the Macedonians only with the benefit of a European education in warfare may have been influenced by events in India in the years leading up to the publication of his book in 1807. The late eighteenth century saw a spate of difficult British East India Company victories against powerful Indian adversaries, including Tipu Sultan at the end of the Anglo-Mysore wars in 1799. Other campaigns, such as the Anglo-Maratha wars, were ongoing. These Indian armies had received European training and in many cases included European soldiers among their forces. For Gillies, therefore, there is a clear parallel to be drawn between the real challenge posed by the European-trained Indian armies to their British adversaries. This link between India's ancient and contemporary rulers was highlighted by Mill in his *History of British India*.

In the event, according to Gillies, Seleucus asserted his power through a treaty with Sandracottus: 'Instead of persevering in an unprofitable war with this illustrious usurper, Seleucus gained his friendship, accepted his daughter in marriage, and, amidst other nuptial gifts [there is no evidence for any 'other' gifts], was strengthened for his western warfare [against Antigonus], by a present of five hundred elephants.'[52] In contrast, and despite his previous and impressive display of military might, Sandracottus' role in these events is a passive one according to Gillies. Gillies further asserted that both Seleucus and Sandracottus maintained this treaty with 'great fidelity' and that it led to commercial benefits. The close link between attempting to curtail or sidestep warfare through treaties and attempting to increase revenues and further commercial interests finds parallels with East India Company activities in India during the late eighteenth and early nineteenth centuries, when Gillies was writing. One of the most famous of these treaties is the Treaty of Allahabad signed in 1765 between the Mughal Emperor Shah Alam II and Major-General Robert Clive of the East India Company.[53]

The Treaty of Allahabad was agreed in the aftermath of the Company victory at the Battle of Buxar in 1764, against an alliance formed of Shah Alam II, Mir Qasim the former Nawab of Bengal and Shuja-ud-Daulah the Nawab of Oudh ('Awadh'). According to the Treaty, the Mughal Emperor surrendered the sovereignty of Bengal to the East India Company, which was granted *diwani* (the right to collect the provincial land tax revenue on behalf of the Emperor in return for a fixed payment) in Bengal, Bihar and Orissa.[54] British contemporaries presented the process of conquest – by war and by post-war treaty – as legitimate and moral because, according to them, it saved India from further degradation as a result of its 'Muslim interregnum' and the despotism of Oriental potentates.[55]

A closer look at the way in which Gillies discusses the commercial benefits of the Seleucid-Mauryan treaty is revealing. It quickly becomes apparent that the commercial aspect was as important to Gillies as it was to Robertson. Gillies embellishes his account with information that overinterprets the sources or is not found in the ancient sources at all. For example, he writes that 'the rich staples on the Ganges, particularly Callinypaza, the modern Canoge [present-day Kannauj in Uttar Pradesh], were opened to the commercial enterprize of the Greeks'. This comment is entirely speculative. He goes on to explain: 'In this place, the natives of Taprobana [Taprobanê], or Ceylon [present-day Sri Lanka], might be seen trading with the European subjects of Seleucus.' There is no specific evidence for this sentence either. It is possible that Gillies has taken Megasthenes' reference to Taprobanê and reshaped it to better fit his own ideas about the past. Similarly, he notes: 'For the convenience of caravans, a secure and spacious route, called the Royal road, was traced between the Indus and the Ganges.'[56] Megasthenes also mentions this royal road, but there was no suggestion that it was newly 'traced' to support this trade; rather, it pre-existed the formation of Seleucid-Mauryan ties.[57]

As mentioned previously, the Enlightenment figure of Alexander as a benevolent ruler with commercial intentions found in Robertson's work is also found in that of Gillies. This particular vision of Alexander clearly influenced the way in which Gillies presents his Successor, Seleucus. Gillies makes this link at the very end of his discussion of the encounter between Seleucus and Sandracottus. He writes, 'through the wise policy of Alexander's immediate successor in the East [Seleucus], a part of his great plan was carried into execution, and Assyria again enriched through the commerce of India'.[58] In this way, Alexander's, and therefore Seleucus', aims are neatly aligned with an inevitable, commercially beneficial outcome for all. Gillies's underlying sentiment here is not very subtle: if only the India of the early nineteenth century would set aside arms, abide by the treaties agreed and embrace Britain's benevolent intentions towards the country, then all would enjoy the fruits of commerce.

Conclusion

Overall, there are some inevitable similarities between the way in which Robertson, Gillies and Mill write about the Seleucid-Mauryan encounter because of their reliance on the same sources. In addition, all three give Seleucus the upper hand in various ways. However, there are also fundamental differences between Robertson's approach to India, and therefore to Indian history, and those of Gillies and Mill. Robertson's broadly tolerant vision and sympathetic attitude towards India more closely echoes those of his late eighteenth-century compatriots and contemporaries such as William Jones and Warren Hastings.

In contrast, Gillies and Mill, writing in the following decades, as Britain's relationship with and attitude towards India was changing irrevocably, rejected this approach towards the subcontinent. Instead, they contributed to the creation of what Thomas Metcalf describes as 'an array of polarities' between the British and Indians that went on to shape much of the ideology of the British Raj.[59] These moralistic approaches towards India found expression in the way each of these authors wrote about the character and behaviour of the Indian king in contrast with that of the Greeks. Gillies, for example, writes that he was 'endowed with abilities equal to his ambition' and, after he learned the 'art of war in the camp of Alexander', 'he deceived and deserted his instructors'.[60]

Other examples can be found. Firstly, Gillies and Mill were aware of Jones's association of Sandracottus with Chandragupta Maurya, the founder of the important Mauryan dynasty. Despite this knowledge, Gillies rejected the use of the Indian name, preferring to retain the Greek version in his *History of the World*. Mill, meanwhile, used the name Chandragupta a number of times in his book but only in specific contexts: to explain the link between Sandracottus and Chandragupta, in Indian king lists, and in quotations from Wilford, who had built on Jones's work. The only time Mill did not use the Indian name was in the section dealing with his encounter with Seleucus. The way Gillies and Mill either used or rejected the names 'Sandracottus' and 'Chandragupta' is telling. It suggests that they preferred to retain authority, as well as military victory, over this Indian ruler when he was confronted by a Western king who was closely connected with the idealised Alexander. Secondly, Gillies and Mill deny Chandragupta any of the agency that Robertson had granted Sandracottus. They transform the encounter into a conquest, stating explicitly that Seleucus 'gained victories' over Chandragupta.[61] The first Indian dynast to begin the process of uniting much of the northern part of the Indian subcontinent under his authority is no longer allowed to retain, albeit 'quietly',[62] the land he acquires by military force, but must be conquered.

This change in emphasis originates in Gillies's work: as we saw in Chapter 1, there is no evidence whatever that either ruler conquered the other or emerged more successful from the treaty. The recognition that 'Sandracottus' is Chandragupta is of the utmost significance here: while Sandracottus is an inconsequential ancient Indian king, he is permitted to retain agency and power. However, when the link is made between Sandracottus and Chandragupta, the powerful unifier of India, this king's ability to respond militarily to Seleucus' threat and deny Seleucus victory is downplayed. Mill readily adopts Gillies's position and it is from this point that it becomes more generally accepted.

A century later, in his *Oxford History of India*, Vincent Smith notes the continuing importance of Mill's work, writing that it 'will always be valuable for reference', despite the need for a new history of the British period 'planned on somewhat different lines'.[63] Rapson only mentions Mill once in his *Cambridge History of India*, in a section relating to the division of criminal and civil law in ancient Hindu law, and not at all in his earlier volume *Ancient India*.[64] Interestingly, neither Smith nor Rapson refers specifically to Mill's inclusion or handling of ancient Indian history, suggesting that this section was not, for them, especially worthy of consideration. However, as Chapter 4 shows, both Smith and Rapson had views on the Seleucus–Chandragupta encounter, which proved to be abidingly influential.

Notes

1 Numerous books and articles have been written about Sir William Jones's life and work, as well as the wider social and political context in which he operated. These include Franklin's (2011) biography of Jones.
2 Metcalf 2008, 9–10.
3 Franklin 2011, 4, 34.
4 Jones 1798, 422–3.
5 This lecture was later published in *Asiatick Researches* 4 (1799; rpt. 1801), xiii–xxxv.
6 Jones 1801, xxv–xxvi.
7 Jones 1799, xxvi. All words in italics and small capitals are as in the reprinted article.
8 Müller 1859, 298, 300.

9 Wilford 1799, 284.
10 Trautmann 1997, 117.
11 Mill 1817, xiii.
12 Trautmann 1997, 117.
13 Inden 1990, 45.
14 Mill 1817, xii.
15 Mill 1817, xii.
16 Mill 1817, xv.
17 Metcalf 2008, 10.
18 Montesquieu outlined his theory in *The Spirit of the Laws*, first published as *De l'esprit des lois* (1748).
19 Langford 1989, 619.
20 Bayly 2012, 63. For a longer discussion about race in India from *c.*1770–1880, see Kapila 2007.
21 Mill 1817, xxiv.
22 Mill 1817, 101.
23 Mill 1817, 101.
24 Mill 1817, 100–1.
25 Mill 1817, 101.
26 Mill 1817, 95.
27 Mill 1817, 482.
28 Mill 1817, 482.
29 Mill 1817, 482†.
30 S. Brown 1997, 7.
31 Briant 2005, 4.
32 As Briant (2005, 2) notes, Robertson's book was translated into these languages within two years of publication.
33 Smitten 2016, 232; Briant 2005, 2.
34 Smitten 2016, 231.
35 Smitten 2016, 231.
36 Briant 2005, 7.
37 Smitten 2016, 231.
38 S. Brown 1997, 34. Sebastiani (2013, 19) notes that as British imperial interests turned from America to India, so too did the attention of figures of the Scottish Enlightenment, including Robertson. His *Historical Disquisition*, written a decade after his retirement from political and institutional life, bears some witness to this shift.
39 Briant (2005, 6; 2017, 72) notes that Robertson also referred to Alexander in his monumental *History of America* (1777). In this work, Robertson presented a very positive view of Alexander that came directly from his reading of Montesquieu's *The Spirit of the Laws*. While Robertson's narrative mentioned that 'The expedition of Alexander the Great to the east, considerably enlarged the sphere of navigation and of geographical knowledge among the Greeks', he also wrote, 'The revolution in commerce, brought about by the force of his genius, is hardly inferior to that revolution in empire, occasioned by the success of his arms.' (Robertson 1777, 14). It is this vision of Alexander that Robertson expands upon in his *Historical Disquisition*.
40 Briant 2005, 1, 7–8; Vasunia 2013, 41.
41 Robertson 1791, 29.
42 Robertson 1791, 30.
43 Robertson 1791, 29–30.
44 Robertson 1791, 30.
45 Briant 2017, 74–5, 292; Vasunia 2013, 40–1.
46 Smitten 2016, 226.
47 Briant 2017, 77.
48 Gillies 1807, 442, 443.
49 Gillies 1807, 443.
50 Gillies 1807, 443.
51 Plut. *Alex.* 62.8.
52 Gillies 1807, 443.
53 The Treaty of Allahabad is held at the British Library (Mss Eur G49), along with Clive's draft copy (GB 59 Mss Eur G37/5/4 ff.7–10).

54 Harris 2006, 359.
55 Alam and Subrahmanyam 2011, 3.
56 Gillies 1807, 443.
57 Strab. 15.1.11.
58 Gillies 1807, 443.
59 Metcalf 2008, 6.
60 Gillies 1807, 443.
61 Mill 1817, 482.
62 Robertson 1791, 30.
63 Smith 1919, xxiii.
64 Rapson 1922, 281. Rapson's reference to Mill in the section devoted to law in ancient India is important because it was one of the ways in which Mill attempted to show that India was a primitive society in comparison with ancient Greece and Rome. Mill argued, *contra* Sir William Jones and other British orientalists, that classical Indian justice was not a rational system but, rather, one that emerged from religion and superstition (Bayly 2012, 66; Majeed 1992, 182).

4
Embedding the divide: competing accounts during the British Raj

From the East India Company to the Raj

The British relationship with India changed dramatically between the time Mill was writing and almost a century later, when scholars such as V. A. Smith and E. J. Rapson were working. A pivotal moment in this relationship came with the Indian Rebellion in 1857.[1] This was a major, albeit ultimately unsuccessful, uprising against East India Company (EIC) rule in India by some of their sepoys (locally recruited soldiers) and a small number of local rulers, including the Rani of Jhansi (1828–58). Company forces put down the rebellion in 1858, and the Government of India Act followed later in the same year. The passing of this Act brought Company rule in India to an end and established in its place the British Raj, whereby the Crown assumed direct control of India. From this point onwards, the India Office in Whitehall oversaw the administration of India.

These profound changes in the British relationship with India deeply influenced British scholarship pertaining to ancient India. The study of ancient Indian history and languages became increasingly popular and gradually more professionalised over the nineteenth century, with formal inclusion in the curricula of some British universities. Chairs of Sanskrit were established at, for example, University College London in 1828, the University of Oxford in 1832 (Boden Professor of Sanskrit), the University of Edinburgh in 1862 (Regius Chair of Sanskrit), and the University of Cambridge in 1867.[2] In 1884, the Indian Institute was opened in Oxford. Proposed by Sir Monier Monier-Williams (1819–99), Boden Professor of Sanskrit and previously a language teacher at the East India College, it was to be a centre of study for Indian Civil Service (ICS) probationers and Indian students. This institution brought together teaching, an extensive library and newspapers, and a museum, all of which related to India.[3]

The Asiatic Society, established by Sir William Jones during Company rule in 1784 as a focus for studies pertaining to India, continued to flourish, as did its journal. Like the Indian Institute in Oxford, which appears to have been modelled on it, the Society had an extensive library and museum. Over the years, numerous other Asiatic societies, some with their own journals and collections, were formed as focal points for sharing and publishing research; they included ones in Bombay, Ceylon and London. In 1879, collections of Indian objects that had originally been held at the EIC's Indian Museum were divided between various London-based institutions including the British Museum and the South Kensington Museum (now the Victoria and Albert Museum).[4]

Gradually, through these institutions and wider networks, and the considerable knowledge gained in India by colonial officials and their local assistants, expertise in the study of Indian objects developed in Britain alongside India's history and languages. This combined knowledge and experience is reflected in the careers of the two British scholars on whom this chapter focuses: Vincent Arthur Smith (1848–1920) of the Indian Civil Service and a scholar of ancient India, and the professional Indologist Edward James Rapson (1861–1937).

Smith and Rapson were two of the most prominent and influential British historians of ancient India since Mill and their work superseded his *History of British India*. The two had very different personal and professional experiences of India and diverging ideas about this land, its people and history. So while their respective histories echoed some of Mill's ideas, significant differences between them were inevitable, including their interpretations of the meeting and treaty between Seleucus and Chandragupta.

The ICS and knowledge of ancient India

Alongside a number of other changes and appointments, the 1858 India Act saw the creation of two senior positions: Secretary of State for India, based in London, and Viceroy of India, who resided in India. India was administered through the offices of the Secretary of State for India, the Governor-General (or Viceroy) of India, and a professional, highly trained Indian Civil Service. Lord Stanley (1826–93), the first Secretary of State for India, had no direct experience of India, and nor did most of the new

ICS recruits before their despatch to that country. And yet, members of the ICS such as Smith made considerable contributions to the study and understanding of ancient India, including the Mauryans. To further a better understanding of how this came to be, an overview of the selection process and training ICS recruits underwent, and their underlying rationale, is provided here.

In 1858, when power was transferred from the EIC to the Crown, the Company already had a system of administration, which included the framework of a civil service, in place. The administrators were taught at the Company's training college, Haileybury, from 1806 until it was closed in 1858.[5] Each of the three presidencies – Madras, Bombay and Bengal – had its own administration, employing hundreds of civil servants.[6] As Kirk-Greene notes, this system was 'inherited and adapted rather than abolished by the new ICS'. For example, the nomenclature used by the Company, such as commissioners and district officers, remained largely the same, as did the route for entry into the Civil Service.[7]

Entrance into the ICS involved passing rigorous and highly competitive examinations, and the subsequent training was no less arduous: the subjects studied included Indian history and modern and classical Indian languages. The result was a small and highly educated elite of British and, eventually, some Indian men who were responsible for administering all aspects of British rule in India. From 1855, entrance into the Civil Service was by open, competitive examination that took place in London. This reform was originally suggested in 1813 by Lord Grenville (1759–1834), previously Prime Minister, and supported by Thomas Babington Macaulay (1800–59), whose 1854 Report on the matter was largely accepted and implemented by the government.[8]

Macaulay, a Whig politician and historian, Secretary of the EIC's Board of Control and member of the Supreme Council of India, went on to draft the now infamous 'Minute on education' (see Chapter 5). He wanted a highly educated cadre of men drawn from universities, particularly Oxford and Cambridge, for the ICS. This sentiment was shared by others on the committee set up to discuss the Civil Service in India.[9] The reason 'the best, the most liberal, the most finished education' was required of these administrators was that their duties 'are of so high a nature that in [the civil servant's] case it is peculiarly desirable that an excellent general education, such as may enlarge and strengthen his understanding, should precede the special education which must qualify him to despatch the business of his cutcherry [an administration office in India].'[10]

The first examinations set included a range of subjects, from Greek, Latin and mathematics, to natural and moral sciences, English literature and language, and modern European languages, as well as Sanskrit and Arabic. However, while no subjects were compulsory, the weight given to Greek, Latin and mathematics was significantly greater than that given to any other subject. Notably, and despite the inclusion of French, German and Italian alongside English, no vernacular Indian languages were included in the tests; they were taught only to those who passed the examinations.[11]

Macaulay mentioned in his Report that the probationers (those who had passed the open examination) who aspired to be 'eminent Orientalists' should be encouraged in their study of ancient and contemporary Indian languages.[12] Probationers would also receive instruction in Indian history, including through Mill's *History of British India* and the work of Sir William Jones, and in religion and other aspects of the subcontinent, such as geography.[13] This knowledge would give Smith and his fellow members of the ICS a basis from which to conduct further research in India, if they so wished, and many of them did.

Ever-increasing numbers of ICS administrators and army personnel arrived in India from the mid-nineteenth century onwards, providing a larger pool of people interested in the history and culture of the country. The result was an explosion of knowledge about ancient India and the acquisition of objects from the subcontinent and their transfer to countries abroad. Britain's global reach combined with international scholarly links with India led to worldwide dissemination of this information and these collections. It also meant that both curatorial and academic expertise pertaining to India was developed and honed beyond the subcontinent, including in Britain.

Hearing the Mauryans speak: setting the scene in the nineteenth century

The nineteenth and early twentieth centuries saw a number of key discoveries that radically changed how the Mauryans were perceived. These breakthroughs had an impact on how this dynasty was seen and presented in all later scholarship, including in the work of the British and Indian historians discussed in this chapter and the next.[14]

While eighteenth-century Indological scholarship focused primarily on literary sources, the nineteenth century saw the burgeoning of many different lines of scholarly enquiry that used a wide range of source material. The numerous fields of research, some of which were new, served to open up fresh ways in which to study and understand the ancient past. These subjects included, but were not limited to, archaeology, numismatics, epigraphy, art history and the ancient indigenous religious traditions of South Asia, particularly Hinduism, Buddhism and Jainism.

With some important exceptions during the 1840s and 1850s, this range of work did not have a central focus, funding or publication outlet for reports until the establishment of the Archaeological Survey of India (ASI).[15] An archaeological survey was initially founded in 1861 by Sir Alexander Cunningham (1814–93), formerly of the Bengal Engineers, whose deep-seated interest in the archaeology of ancient India was partly inspired by his friend James Prinsep. After a temporary suspension due to lack of funds, the ASI was refounded in 1871 and allocated governmental funds by Lord Mayo (1822–72), Viceroy of India, who also appointed Cunningham as its first Director General.[16] There was genuine interest in learning more about India's ancient past and conserving its monuments among those on the ground and in the upper echelons of the Government of India.[17] However, the establishment of the ASI was not a purely altruistic act on Mayo's part.

The Archaeological Survey was one of numerous surveys launched by the colonial government in the decades following the establishment in India of direct rule, and thereby of greater control of the land and its people. Many built on pre-existing surveys, formalising and centralising them. The state harnessed its administrative and military resources in order to better understand the topography, climate, tides, people, languages and numerous other aspects of the subcontinent and its inhabitants. Alongside other aims and ambitions, this knowledge was used to implement, extend and justify British colonial rule in India.[18] With respect to archaeology and associated fields of study, imperial operations also served to shape knowledge about the Indian past. The government's involvement in the field of archaeology through the ASI was limited and short-lived until Curzon's reforms as Viceroy in 1899.[19]

The cumulative effect of Cunningham's archaeological investigations and collecting activity, through the auspices of the ASI and independently, must be seen in conjunction with the manifold, often haphazard, discoveries of others during this period. On the one hand, Cunningham conducted extensive field surveys and limited archaeological excavations in the subcontinent with his small ASI team. This work was done with an official, governmental mandate and the results of its work were regularly published in *Archaeological Survey Reports*.[20] This work was influential and remains essential reading for anyone interested in Indian archaeology, not least because, as Dilip Chakrabarti notes, it gave Indian archaeology its features and bearings.[21]

These archaeological excavations coupled with breakthroughs in the decipherment of ancient scripts brought forth startling new discoveries about the ancient past that were to radically transform knowledge and understanding of the Mauryans. The crucial breakthrough pertaining to Mauryan history in the eighteenth century was Jones's recognition that the Sandrakottus of Graeco-Roman literature was the Chandragupta of Sanskrit literature (see Chapter 3). Building on this initial work, the nineteenth century saw multiple, significant developments across a variety of disciplines, from epigraphy to archaeology and more. One, however, stands out among them, and it concerns not Chandragupta, but one of his successors.

Numerous inscribed pillars, rocks and caves had long dotted the landscape of what are now India, Pakistan, Afghanistan, Bangladesh and Nepal. Some of these pillars and sites remained important to later rulers as well as to both lay and religious communities. Their original purpose had long been forgotten, as had knowledge of the Brāhmī script in which most of the inscriptions had been written.[22] Similarly, the names and dates of the people under whose impetus these works had been undertaken were lost.

The decipherment of Brāhmī in 1836–8 by James Prinsep (1799–1840), assay master, philologist, numismatist and founding editor of the *Journal of the Asiatic Society of Bengal*, marked a seminal moment in the history of ancient South Asia.[23] Once it was discovered how to read the script, it became clear that these pillar, rock and cave inscriptions were the subcontinent's earliest monumental inscriptions. They are traditionally divided into minor rock edicts, major rock edicts, minor pillar edicts and major pillar edicts. Further work by Prinsep and George Turnour (1799–1843), philologist and member of the Ceylon Civil Service, revealed that these inscriptions were all disseminated and inscribed under Aśoka Maurya's authority.

Aśoka was Chandragupta's grandson and the third Mauryan emperor, who ruled the empire at the peak of its power, extent and influence.[24] His inscriptions revealed his conversion to and patronage and propagation of Buddhism, his definition and practice of *dharma* ('right way of living'), and information about numerous practical affairs including the roles of his officials. Intriguingly, Major Rock Edicts II and XIII revealed that Aśoka, like his father and grandfather before him, had ties with his Seleucid counterpart. In Aśoka's case, this was Antiochus II Theos (*r*.261–246 BC). Antiochus II was Seleucus I's grandson and he had succeeded his father, Antiochus I Soter (*r*.281–261 BC), to the Seleucid throne. Not only this, but Major Rock Edict XIII reveals that Aśoka sent *dharma* missions to five Hellenic kings: Antiochus II Theos of the Seleucid empire, Ptolemy III Philadelphus of Egypt, Antigonus Gonatus of Macedonia, Magas of Cyrene and Alexander of Epirus. Evidently, the relations Chandragupta and Seleucus had established in *c*.305–303 BC lasted for some three generations.

At this point, it became clear that Chandragupta was not merely a minor Indian ruler but the founder of a major, powerful dynasty and an empire that spread over large swathes of the subcontinent. Mauryan political authority and military dominion were primarily concentrated in the heartlands of the empire, and Mauryan power and influence varied the further one got from the Mauryan polity. As Aśoka's inscriptions showed, there was a desire to reach out beyond their centre of power in India, to kingdoms in South East Asia and Sri Lanka as well as the Mediterranean world.

Further archaeological evidence supported this vision of Mauryan strength and authority. One example concerns the Mauryan capital Pataliputra. Sir William Jones identified Patna as the location of ancient Pataliputra (see Chapter 3), and almost a century later a series of surveys and excavations took place at and beyond the boundaries of the city. Cunningham undertook initial surveys at Bulandibagh and these were followed by excavations by Laurence Waddell in 1895, David Brainerd Spooner in 1912–13, and J. A. Page and M. Ghosh in 1926–7. P. C. Mukharji (also known as 'Mukherjee' and 'Mukherji') also excavated at Lohanipur in 1897–8.

Among other things, the digs revealed the Pataliputra stone capital (Figure 4.1), a wooden structure believed to be the city's outer palisade described by Megasthenes, punch-marked coins terracotta figurines, and inscribed glass seals. Separately from the digs, important stone sculptures linked with the Mauryan period were found: the Parkham *yakṣa* Māṇibhadra in 1882 and the Didarganj *yakṣī* in 1917. The association between some of these structures and objects and the Mauryans has been challenged in more recent years. However, and importantly here, at the time they were discovered, it was believed that they were dateable to the Mauryan period.

The combined result of all of these discoveries was that the Mauryans were no longer relegated to a minor historical footnote but recognised as a major dynasty that left an enduring impact on the landscape and imagination of South Asia. Numerous books and articles were – and still are – written about the dynasty and its empire. The legacy

Figure 4.1 The Pataliputra stone capital found during L. A. Waddell's excavations at Bulandi Bagh, Patna in 1895. It is on display at Patna Museum, Bihar. Source: Nalanda001 and Gary Todd. Shared under a Creative Commons Attribution-ShareAlike 4.0 International licence (CC BY-SA 4.0), Wikimedia Commons, bit.ly/3DV7BL4.

of these findings still resonates today, not only in scholarship but also in the realms of culture and politics in India (see Part III).

Smith and Rapson: different experiences of Empire

In 1871, Vincent Smith passed top in the final examination for the Indian Civil Service and, along with many other Irishmen, made his career in India. Smith took up his posting in the North-West Provinces and Oudh ('Awadh'),[25] where he lived and worked for almost 30 years. During this time, he rose rapidly up the ranks until, in 1898, he was appointed Chief Secretary to the Government of the North-West and Oudh and, in the same year, became a Commissioner.[26] Like many of his contemporaries, and indeed earlier colonial officials such as Sir William

Jones, Smith took every opportunity to indulge and develop his interests in the history and antiquities, particularly coins, of India alongside his administrative duties.

Smith's colleagues and senior colonial officials, including his fellow Irishman Sir Antony MacDonnell (1844–1925), Lieutenant-Governor of the United Provinces of Agra and Oudh (1895–1901), recognised and made use of his interest in Indian history, ancient sites and collections. For example, in 1896, MacDonnell sent Smith to visit the historic monuments near Kasia in Gorakhpur District, Oudh (now in Uttar Pradesh), in order to submit proposals for the conservation of the ruins there.[27]

In 1900, Smith took early retirement to concentrate on his research. It is during this period that he published extensively on his scholarly pursuits in India. In 1910, he was elected to a fellowship at St John's College, Oxford, and was also appointed Curator of the Indian Institute, Oxford. In 1919, he was awarded the Companion Order of the Indian Empire by the Government of India in recognition of his historical works.[28] Among his books were three in which Smith mentioned the meeting between Seleucus and Chandragupta: *Asoka, the Buddhist Emperor of India* (1901b; 3rd edn 1920); *The Early History of India: From 600 B.C. to the Muhammadan Conquest, including the invasion of Alexander the Great* (1904; 2nd edn 1908); *The Oxford History of India: From the earliest times to the end of 1911* (1919).

The career of numismatist and Sanskrit scholar E. J. Rapson took a different trajectory from that of Smith. Rapson remained within the professional sphere of academia for the whole of his career and, unlike Smith, he did not spend any time in India. After reading Indian languages at Cambridge, Rapson was appointed Assistant Librarian at the Indian Institute, Oxford. Soon afterwards, he held, jointly, the positions of Assistant Keeper in the British Museum's Department of Coins and Medals, and Professor of Sanskrit at UCL. In 1906, he left both institutions to take on the role of Professor of Sanskrit at Cambridge, retiring in 1936.[29] His book *Ancient India: From the earliest times to the first century A.D.* (1914) was written for a general audience, providing a summary of current knowledge about ancient Indian history. Shortly afterwards, he was appointed editor of the *Cambridge History of India* (1922), most of which was completed before the outbreak of the First World War, but the publication of which was delayed until long after peace had been declared.

Despite the advances in knowledge about Indian history that had been made in the hundred years since Mill's book, Rapson echoes Mill when he advises his readers to 'study Ancient India always in the light of our knowledge of Modern India'.[30] Smith has less sympathy with this type of back projection of contemporary India onto the ancient past, writing for example: 'Much sentimental nonsense with little relation to the actual facts has been written about the supposed indestructible constitution of the Indo-Aryan village in the north.'[31] This comment among others suggests that his experience of living and working in northern India shaped his thoughts in this area.

Rapson is at pains to emphasise the glories and achievements of the British Empire, especially in comparison to the earlier Mauryan and Mughal empires. For example, he notes that neither of these empires encompassed the whole of the subcontinent, and that they were 'won by conquest and maintained by power', so that when this 'power failed, the various countries which constituted these empires reasserted their independence'. In contrast, British dominion in India 'finds no parallel in history', because it was 'founded less on conquest than on mutual advantage', with all participants sharing a common interest in 'peace and security'.[32]

In this way, Rapson justifies what he sees as benevolent, paternalistic British rule in India, neatly overlooking the reality of how the colonial enterprise came to be and what its ramifications were for millions of Indians. Rapson's emphasis on political rather than military interaction is also found in his interpretation of the meeting between Seleucus and Chandragupta. He writes that Seleucus invaded India with the aim of reclaiming from Chandragupta Alexander's earlier conquests, but that no information about his engagement with Chandragupta survives, apart from their concluding 'a treaty of peace'. About this treaty, Rapson only notes that the 'Indian provinces' previously held by Darius and then Alexander were 'definitely' acknowledged as belonging to Chandragupta. Instead, for him, the most important consequence of this treaty was the 'establishment of political relations between the kingdom of Syria, which was now the predominant power in Western Asia, and the Maurya empire of Northern India'.[33] Rapson presents the two rulers and their empires as broadly equal.

Smith's interpretations are more detailed and his language more emotionally charged than Rapson's. In *Asoka, the Buddhist Emperor of India* (1901b), Smith deals only briefly with the encounter between Seleucus and Chandragupta, but the difference in the way in which he presents the two rulers is nevertheless visible. He writes, for example, that Seleucus 'directed his victorious army against India', whereas Chandragupta is said to lead 'the vast hosts of teeming India'. The language employed suggests that while Seleucus' men were an organised and disciplined military body, Chandragupta's forces comprised an undisciplined mass of men who kept Seleucus out of India by the sheer weight of their numbers, rather than by any skill. In terms of the outcome of this military engagement, Smith suggests that Seleucus was 'compelled to ... withdraw from the country', and that the 'terms of peace ... comprised a matrimonial alliance between the two royal houses, and the cession to Chandragupta of all the Indian provinces of Alexander's empire .... On his part, Chandragupta gave five hundred elephants to Seleucus.'[34] These details are neutrally stated and there is little to dispute here.

By contrast, in Smith's *The Early History of India* (1904), Seleucus is said to have concluded a 'humiliating' peace with Chandragupta. Concerning the marriage alliance, Smith suggests that this 'probably means that Seleucus gave a daughter to his Indian rival'. Overall, 'The facts that Seleukos retired from India, giving up valuable provinces in exchange for only 500 elephants out of the 9,000 possessed by Chandragupta, that he entered into a matrimonial alliance, and sent an ambassador, clearly indicate the real nature of the relations between the sovereigns.' Chandragupta is recognised as 'among the greatest and most successful kings known to history', the ruler who 'repulsed and humbled Seleukos the Conqueror'.[35]

In the third edition of *Asoka, the Buddhist Emperor of India*, published in 1920, Smith presents yet another power relationship between Seleucus and Chandragupta, although the overall encounter is still presented as a defeat for Seleucus. In relation to the terms of peace, for example, Smith writes that 'the plain facts are that the Syrian monarch failed [in his attempt to regain Alexander's Indian provinces] and was obliged to surrender four valuable provinces for very inadequate consideration [five hundred elephants]'.[36] His characterisation of Seleucus here as 'Syrian' rather than Greek or Macedonian, before he acquired territory in Syria (this is after the battle at Ipsus in 301 BC), is interesting: perhaps, in Smith's eyes, Seleucus' failures in the East led him to become a fallible 'Oriental'.[37] In respect of the marriage alliance, Smith rejects the idea that Seleucus gave his daughter to Chandragupta in marriage, suggesting instead that the evidence 'testifies merely to a "matrimonial alliance"'. It is notable that despite Seleucus' failure to defeat Chandragupta, Smith writes that '*Seleukos* never attempted to assert any superiority over his successful Indian rival, but, on the contrary, having failed in attack, made friends with the power which had proved to be too strong for him, and treated Chandragupta as an equal' (my emphasis).[38] Seleucus, according to Smith's interpretation, was the active force in all the dealings between him and Chandragupta and was even magnanimous in defeat.

It is interesting to observe the changes in emphasis that occur in Smith's work over the years. The most marked difference relates to his interpretation of the marriage alliance. Where he gave more detail about this in his earlier publications, he maintained that there was most likely a marriage between Seleucus' daughter and Chandragupta; it is only in the last publication that he rejects this interpretation, though without providing any reasons for this change of opinion. In this final work, he also emphasises Seleucus' graciousness in defeat, presenting a united, friendly outcome to this battle.

Rival Oxbridge histories of India

The *Oxford History of India* (1919; henceforth *OHI*) written by Smith, and the *Cambridge History of India* (1922; henceforth *CHI*) edited by Rapson, were published within a few years of one another. As mentioned above, the *CHI* was due to be published in 1914, but publication was delayed by the onset of the First World War. Consequently, the composition of the *CHI* pre-dates the publication, and perhaps the composition, of the *OHI*.[39]

Despite their very similar titles, these were very different types of book. The *OHI* was a single-volume monograph, comprising some 800 pages, which provided an overview of Indian history from ancient to modern times for a general audience: 'The purpose of this book is to provide in one volume of moderate bulk and price a compendious up-to-date History of India as a whole, based on the results of modern research and extending from the earliest times to the end of 1911.'[40] At this point, the *Oxford History of …* was not yet a well-established formula: the multi-volume *Oxford History of Music* began in 1901, followed by Smith's own *Oxford Student's History of India* (1st edn 1908) and the *Oxford History of England for Indian Students* (1912).

By contrast, the Cambridge project was not only different, but also more ambitious: six volumes written by experts in their field were planned to cover the full span of Indian history, with the first dealing with ancient Indian history up to the first century AD.[41] Rapson, like Smith, notes in the Preface to the first volume that the aim is to present the most up-to-date research available about the history of India. Rapson is aware that he is involved with a different type of work than has gone before, with this history marking 'a new departure'.[42] The reason for producing a multi-authored work was that 'the literature of the subject has become so vast, and is still growing with such rapidity, that the best hope of securing a real advance in the study now lies in a division of labour among scholars who have explored at first hand the main sources of information'.[43]

The *CHI* was modelled on the modern and mediaeval histories published by the Cambridge University Press.[44] These latter two histories were heavily European in focus. For example, the *Cambridge Modern History* in 14 volumes (1902–12) included only one volume (vol. VII) on the United States of America, and the European colonies abroad formed only small sections in volumes XI and XII, while the rest focused entirely on Europe. The *Cambridge Medieval History* in eight volumes (1911–36) only goes as far east as the Byzantine empire, meaning that its overall vision is Christian. Using these prestigious European-focused histories as a template for the *CHI* not only raised the profile of the *CHI*, but officially raised the standing of Indian history to a much higher level than it had held before.

Prominent scholars of Indian history and language were commissioned to write individual chapters, which meant that their knowledge of particular fields of expertise was harnessed under Rapson's editorship. These scholars included Rapson himself, A. Berriedale Keith (1879–1944), Regius Professor of Sanskrit and Comparative Philology at the University of Edinburgh, and T. W. Rhys Davids (1843–1922), formerly of the Ceylon Civil Service and later Professor of Pāli and Buddhist Literature at University College London and then Professor of Comparative Religion at the University of Manchester.[45] Smith was conspicuous by his absence as a contributor to the Cambridge volume, as were historians from South Asia (see Chapter 5). Instead, Indian involvement was limited to financial assistance given by Sir Dorabji Tata (1859–1932), the industrialist and philanthropist, to illustrate the volume 'more lavishly' than would otherwise have been possible.[46]

Despite the broadly similar aims of these rival histories, neither Smith nor Rapson reviewed the other's work. Rapson mentioned some summaries of Indian history, including Smith's *Early History of India* (2nd edn 1908), but not Smith's *OHI*.[47] In the Preface to his Oxford history, Smith when he writes, damningly, 'Composite histories, built up of chapters by specialists, suffer from the lack of literary unity and from the absence of one controlling mind so severely that their gain in erudition is apt to be outweighed by their dullness.'[48] From these words it is not clear whether Smith had sight of the *CHI* before publication, or if he was aware of it and generalising about works of its kind. Rapson is well aware of the problems associated with such 'cooperative enterprises' and justifies his approach in the Preface.[49]

While both the Oxford and Cambridge histories maintain Mill's division of Indian history into Hindu, Muslim and British phases, the works present very different interpretations of the meeting between Seleucus and Chandragupta, and its outcome.

In the *CHI*, the encounter between Seleucus and Chandragupta is presented in two different ways, in two separate chapters and by two different scholars: Frederick William Thomas (1867–1956) and Sir George Macdonald (1862–1940). Thomas was an India Office librarian and, simultaneously, held academic posts at UCL and London University and was Boden Professor of Sanskrit at Oxford. Like Rapson, he had studied under Professor E. B. Cowell at Cambridge.[50] Macdonald was both an academic and a civil servant, eventually becoming the Permanent Secretary to the Scottish Education Department. He had numerous archaeological and numismatic publications to his name, including a *Catalogue of Greek Coins in the Hunterian Collection* (1899).[51]

In Chapter XVIII, 'Chandragupta, the founder of the Maurya Empire', Thomas provides a cursory overview of the meeting. He writes that there was 'either no battle ..., or an indecisive one' between the rulers, after which Seleucus was 'content to secure a safe retirement and a gift of 500 elephants' upon 'the surrender of all the Greek dominions as far as the Kābul valley', and that 'a matrimonial alliance was arranged'.[52] In Chapter XVII, 'The Hellenistic kingdoms of Syria, Bactria, and Parthia', Macdonald goes into considerably more detail to arrive at broadly similar conclusions. In terms of their military engagement, Macdonald writes, 'the written record contains nothing to show that Seleucus suffered defeat, nothing even to suggest that the rival armies ever came to blows at all'. Instead, it is suggested, while Seleucus was assessing the situation before him, an 'urgent call for help' came from some of the other Successors against the threat posed by Antigonus. So Seleucus' 'instinct of self-preservation' meant that it was 'politic' for him to 'make the best terms he could with Chandragupta'. In this context, Chandragupta's 'gift' of 500 elephants is interpreted as an expedient one for Seleucus to accept for his forthcoming battle with Antigonus.[53]

However, it is still difficult to equate the receipt of these elephants with the handing over to Chandragupta of vast tracts of land that were formerly under Greek authority, something Macdonald freely acknowledges. But, with a little inventive speculation to save Seleucus' reputation against Chandragupta, this equation can be balanced: Macdonald writes, 'We may take it that there were further stipulations as to freedom of trade and the like.' Also, in relation to the transfer of land, there 'may even have been a nominal and unmeaning acknowledgment of suzerainty'. Any personal aspect to the marriage alliance part of the treaty is removed altogether: what little is known of Seleucus' family tree does not allow for any intermarriage with the Mauryans, and the presence of the caste system in India meant that 'a *jus connubii* between the two peoples is unthinkable'.[54] In this way, Macdonald takes to its logical conclusion Rapson's focus on political expediency rather than military engagement.

Thomas's and Macdonald's interpretations thereby echo Rapson's own understanding of this meeting and its outcome. This is materially different in emphasis from that of Smith, who maintains that Seleucus was the defeated party. The reasons behind these conflicting interpretations are difficult to explain, and it may be that Thomas and Macdonald were persuaded to follow Rapson's interpretation. Or perhaps Rapson chose to engage for this project scholars with views more closely aligned to his own.

Conclusion

The profound changes that took place in terms of the British relationship with India had an impact on how British academics presented the meeting between Seleucus and Chandragupta in histories of India written between the early nineteenth and the mid-twentieth centuries. In the first history of India, which was written at the start of the nineteenth century by Mill, Seleucus is presented as victorious over Chandragupta, an interpretation of the encounter that runs counter to the ancient evidence available. In contrast, Rapson and Smith, both of whom were writing in the first quarter of the twentieth century, present interpretations of the meeting that differ not only from Mill's reading, but from one another's.

Rapson, for example, prefers to focus on and emphasise political rather than military interaction and presents the Seleucid and Mauryan empires more or less as equals who concluded a 'treaty of peace'.[55] This point of view is reflected in the chapters of Vol. I of the *CHI* – a work edited by Rapson – that were written by Thomas and Macdonald. Smith, on the other hand, presented two wholly contrasting opinions on the meeting between Seleucus and Chandragupta in his works. He begins with a broadly neutral interpretation and later, in the *OHI*, presents Seleucus as concluding a humiliating treaty with Chandragupta.[56] It is possible that their different experiences of India – Smith's long association with the colony and Rapson's lack of personal knowledge of it – influenced their approaches and perspectives.

A notable and glaring omission in relation to the Oxbridge projects of writing histories of India is that not a single Indian historian contributed so much as a chapter to these volumes. This is despite the fact that there were, by this point, a number of professional Indian historians of ancient India. Their absence is especially pertinent to the discussion in Chapter 5 about the series of Indian histories written by Indian academics in India.

Notes

1 There are numerous books devoted to the Indian Rebellion, including Saul David, *The Indian Mutiny: 1857* (London: Viking, 2002) and James Frey, *The Indian Rebellion, 1857–1859: A short history with documents* (Indianapolis: Hackett, 2020). Alongside these volumes, Kim Wagner's book *The Skull of Alum Bheg: The life and death of a rebel of 1857* (2017) provides an insight into the Rebellion through the story of one of the sepoys involved in it and the rediscovery of his skull in an English pub in 1963.

2 Trautmann 2005, 188. One of the first academic appointments made by the Council of the University of London (later UCL) was that of Friedrich August Rosen (1805–37). He was appointed Professor of Sanskrit in 1828. (See https://www.ucl.ac.uk/bloomsbury-project/articles/individuals/rosen_frederick.htm, accessed 26 October 2022.) There is also a link with the British Museum: in 1834, he worked for the museum 'to assist in revising and correcting the Catalogue of the Syriac MSS' (Committee Minutes, 10 May 1834, vol. XIII, British Museum Central Archive). Rosen clearly made an impression at the British Museum: on his premature death in 1837, the Trustees commissioned a portrait bust of him 'in memory of the worth, services and learning' of the sitter (Minutes of Standing Committee, 20 April 1839, British Museum Central Archive). The bust, which is still held by the museum (Reg. No. 1839,0420.1) was carved by Richard Westmacott the Younger (1799–1872), son of Sir Richard Westmacott (1775–1856), who was responsible for the 'Progress of Civilisation' pediment sculpture which stands above the entrance to the British Museum.

3 Harrison 1994, 609. See also The Open University, 'Making Britain: Indian Institute', https://www.open.ac.uk/researchprojects/makingbritain/content/indian-institute (accessed 12 November 2022).

4 For an overview of the EIC's Indian Museum's collections and their dispersal, see Arthur MacGregor, *Company Curiosities: Nature, culture and the East India Company, 1600–1874* (London: Reaktion Books, 2018).

5 Vasunia 2013, 194–6.

6 The civil servants of the Bengal Presidency served most widely because any new territory acquired by the Company was placed under this Presidency (Kirk-Greene 2000, 89).

7 Kirk-Greene 2000, 89.

8 Moore 1964, 246; Vasunia 2013, 204.

9 One of the supportive Committee members was Benjamin Jowett (1817–93), classical scholar, Master of Balliol College, Oxford, and Anglican cleric (Vasunia 2013, 203–216). It is not surprising to find that Jowett, given his professional affiliation and position, was keen to see more Oxford graduates gaining roles in this prestigious work. For more information about the others on the Committee, and the reasons for their selection, see Moore 1964, 254–5.

10 This information is contained in *The Government Regulations for the Examination of Candidates for Appointments to the Civil Service of the East India Company* (London: Edward Stanford, 1855), 9, 13.

11 Macaulay et al. 1855, 10. Vasunia (2013, 205fn.52) notes that 'the place given to mathematics reflects the prominence it had at Cambridge'. He also notes that the terms 'Natural sciences' and 'Moral sciences' used in the Report are specific to Cambridge.

12 Macaulay et al. 1855, 19.

13 Macaulay et al. 1855, 15.

14 For an overview of Mauryan archaeological discoveries, see Jansari 2021.

15 The EIC's Court of Directors instigated and paid for a series of appointments and projects with an archaeological focus. In 1848, for example, the Bombay Presidency established the Bombay Cave Commission, under which the Ajanta, Aurangabad and Elephanta caves were cleared of debris. In 1851 the Bombay Presidency appointed the photographer and artist William Armstrong Fallon to make accurate copies of the Elephanta cave sculptures, while also drawing and measuring the caves themselves (Singh 2004, 56).
16 Singh 2004, 25. Singh (2004, xvii–xviii, 55–85) gives a good introduction to, and overview of, the ASI as well as the wider colonial context in which it was established. The ASI remains India's primary organisation dedicated to archaeological research as well as the conservation and protection of the nation's cultural heritage.
17 Singh 2004, 81–2.
18 Singh 2004, 2.
19 Chakrabarti 2009, 14–15.
20 Singh 2004, 85.
21 Chakrabarti 2009, 9.
22 Aśokan inscriptions were written in Prakrit (with local variations) written in Brāhmī and Kharoṣṭhī scripts, and in Greek and Aramaic. Kharoṣṭhī script had also been forgotten and, along with Brāhmī, was deciphered by Prinsep in 1835.

The majority of the inscriptions were in Prakrit written in Brāhmī; these were found across the northern part of the subcontinent in modern-day India, Bangladesh and Nepal. Prakrit inscriptions written in Kharoṣṭhī, and the Greek and Aramaic inscriptions, were all found in the north-western parts of the subcontinent in modern-day Pakistan and Afghanistan. There is a considerable literature on the Aśokan inscriptions, spanning more than 150 years. A useful introduction is Falk 2006. The https://gandhari.org/ database includes all of the Aśokan inscriptions with images and transcriptions, along with a dictionary and an extensive bibliography (accessed 12 November 2022).
23 Prinsep was assisted in this endeavour by his friend Sir Alexander Cunningham (1814–93), of the Bengal Engineers and, later, first Director General of the Archaeological Survey of India. They built on initial work by Christian Lassen (1800–76), the Norwegian linguist (E. Errington and Sarkhosh Curtis 2007, 21–2).
24 Salomon (1998, 208–15) provides a good overview of Turnour's discovery that the ruler named in the inscriptions was Aśoka of the Mauryan dynasty.
25 This administrative region was later called 'United Provinces'; it roughly corresponds to the modern Indian states of Uttar Pradesh and Uttarakhand in the north of India.
26 Pargiter 1920, 391.
27 Smith 1896, Preparatory note.
28 Pargiter 1920, 391–3.
29 Turner and Burn 1938, 639, 642.
30 Rapson 1914, 33; Mill 1817, 100–1.
31 Smith 1919, xii.
32 Rapson 1914, 34.
33 Rapson 1914, 101.
34 Smith 1901b, 12–13.
35 Smith 1904, 112n2, 113.
36 Smith 1920, 15.
37 Notably, for a brief period between 1918 and 1920, Syria became an independent kingdom at the collapse of the Ottoman empire in the aftermath of the First World War (Commins and Lesch 2013, xxiii, 94). Syria was then taken over by France, which ruled under a League of Nations mandate from 1920 until 1936 (Commins and Lesch 2013, xxiii–xxiv).
38 Smith 1920, 15n1, 16.
39 Pargiter 1922, 634.
40 Smith 1919, Preface.
41 Pargiter 1922, 633.
42 Rapson 1922, vi.
43 Rapson 1922, vi.
44 Rapson 1922, vi.
45 Rapson 1922, xii, xiii.
46 Rapson 1922, x.
47 For example Rapson 1914, 103, 176, 179, 197.

48 Smith 1919, Preface.
49 Rapson 1922, vi.
50 Turner and Burn 1938, 639; Barnett 1957, 142; A. J. Arberry, revised by J. B. Katz, 'Thomas, Frederick William', *ODNB*, 2004.
51 A. O. Curle, revised by L. J. F. Keppie, 'Macdonald, Sir George', *ODNB*, 2004.
52 Thomas 1922, 472.
53 Macdonald 1922, 431, 432.
54 Macdonald 1922, 431.
55 Rapson 1914, 101.
56 Smith 1901b, 1904.

5

Reaction and transformation: reshaping history for a new era

Introducing changes

There are significant differences between the ways British and Indian historians wrote about the meeting between Seleucus and Chandragupta and its outcome. However, the views of these two groups of historians defy easy categorisation along 'national' lines: after all, Smith's interpretation differed markedly from that of Rapson. In the case of Indian historians, differences in approach and interpretation are found between and within the first and second generations writing about the Seleucid-Mauryan encounter. The reasons for the dissimilarities are connected to India's changing relationship with the colonial power ruling India, and historians' involvement with the Indian nationalist cause. In this context, it is notable that it is in the work of one of the historians of the first generation that the link between Chandragupta's battle with Seleucus and his unification of India is first made.

The Indian nationalist movement emerged in the late nineteenth century.[1] During this time, numerous groups sprang up that were tentatively discussing ideas about better government, including national (rather than metropolitan colonial) government and, gradually, about independence from British rule. The assemblies were initially concentrated in the economic and administrative hubs of Bombay and Calcutta. With the establishment of the Indian National Congress (INC) in 1885, there emerged a national, mainstream organisation that was eventually to lead the struggle for independence. Representatives at the INC annual meetings were from a range of social and religious communities, although Hindus and the educated professional and commercial elites predominated. Alongside these political groupings, there were, increasingly, associations organised along religious and caste lines to protect their own interests.[2]

The study of the history of India by Indians fed into, and was influenced by, this complex and interwoven social, religious and political landscape. Significantly, that effect was less noticeable in the first generation of professional historians of India. Among these men, two of the most influential are discussed in this chapter: Romesh Chunder Dutt (1848–1909) and Sir Ramakrishna Gopal Bhandarkar (1837–1925). There are more overt statements of political and religious affiliation among some of the second generation of Indian historians. Of these, the focus here is on Radha Kumud Mookerji (1884–1963), Ramesh Chandra Majumdar (1888–1980) and Hem Chandra Raychaudhuri (1892–1957).

From Pataliputra to Patna and back again: translating into English Graeco-Roman texts pertaining to India

The only ancient references to the contact between Seleucus and Chandragupta are found in Graeco-Roman sources. While Greek and Latin were integral parts of the curriculum in British schools and universities, they were not typically included in the curricula of schools and institutions of higher education across India. The now infamous 'Minute on Indian education' (1835) by Thomas Babington Macaulay (1800–59), historian and politician, had a profound influence on British educational policy in India. It meant that the English language became the primary medium of communication in government schools and colleges (as well as administration), and that history would be a key component of the curriculum.[3] By 1857, universities had been established in Bombay, Calcutta and Madras. All of these universities offered Latin and Greek, and Latin was taught more frequently than Greek, but neither language was taken up by many Indian students. There were also pre-existing educational institutions founded by the British in Indian cities, such as Elphinstone College, established in Bombay some 30 years previously.[4]

The result of this was that Indian scholars were well versed in English. However, only a minority of Indian students would have knowledge of Latin, even fewer of Greek, and not all of these students would study history. For most Indian scholars, if they were to engage with the historical evidence for Seleucus and Chandragupta's meeting – most of which is written in Greek – translations of the classical sources into

English were essential. J. W. McCrindle (1825–1913), the Principal of the Government College in Patna, is central to this part of the story.

In 1877, McCrindle published an English translation of a collection of Megasthenes' fragments and Arrian's *Indike*.[5] By a neat circle of history, this translation was made in Patna, the modern site associated with the ancient Mauryan capital Pataliputra. It was this city that Megasthenes visited and wrote about millennia ago, and McCrindle was aware of this connection.[6] He was also mindful of the usefulness of his translation, noting that 'the identification of Greek proper names with their Sanskrit originals ... will, I hope, recommend [the work] to the attention of native scholars who may be pursuing, or at least be interested in, inquiries which relate to the history and antiquities of their own country'.[7] In this way, McCrindle was explicitly directing his work towards educated Indians, including his own students in Patna. The popularity and usefulness of this work can be seen in the continued reliance on it by Indian historians and authors of historical fiction (see Chapter 9) over a hundred years later. This is despite the availability of more up-to-date translations in print and online, including an anthology of updated translations produced by R. C. Majumdar in 1960 that is itself modelled on McCrindle's work.[8]

As helpful as McCrindle and Majumdar's collections have been, they imposed constraints on scholarship by making available translations of only those sections of Graeco-Roman literature that related in some way to India. In addition, they provide only meagre information about the classical authors themselves. For these reasons, attempts to contextualise information derived from the ancient authors, as found in the anthologies, are subject to inherent limitations. One of the results has been the mistaken impression that McCrindle's (and therefore Majumdar's) selection of texts represents the full complement of classical references to India.[9] Another result of this narrow and incomplete selection of sources has been to restrict the scope of some aspects of historical research undertaken in India which has, in turn, contributed to distortions in the outcomes of this scholarship, as shown below.

The first generation of Indian academic historians and the encounter between Seleucus and Chandragupta

R. C. Dutt was one of the first professional Indian historians of India. He studied and later lectured in ancient Indian history and civilisation at University College London after a long career in the ICS. One of his contemporaries was Sir Ramakrishna Gopal Bhandarkar who studied at the Elphinstone Institute of Bombay and later taught at Elphinstone College in the same city. Dutt and Bhandarkar chose to focus much of their research and teaching on the history and languages of ancient India, the period of Indian history that was increasingly seen as the pinnacle of Indian, particularly Hindu, civilisation.[10]

This belief emerged from early colonial scholarship that periodised Indian history into a classical Hindu age followed by a mediaeval decline during a Muslim interregnum that stunted Indian development, and a modern renaissance under European hegemony. As Vasunia notes, not only was this division of India's history based on 'European patterns of history' but its acceptance and propagation 'contributed both to British colonial and Indian nationalist agendas in the nineteenth century'.[11] Some British scholars, for example, used this neat division of India's history to argue that Mughal misgovernment was one of the reasons why British rule in India had become necessary, thereby attempting to justify the British presence there. And the idea of an 'authentic' Hindu antiquity filled with potential gained traction with emerging Hindu nationalist politics in India, feeding an ideology of Hindu revivalism and the need for a Hindu homeland, the legacy of which can still be seen in India today.[12]

Both Bhandarkar and Dutt were active during the early stages of discussions about nationalist politics and ideas about Indian independence. For example, alongside his academic work, Bhandarkar was elected to the Imperial Legislative Council in 1903 as a non-official member, and was also known as a social reformer.[13] Dutt was an early nationalist, which meant that he was pushing not for independence, but for a reform of the imperial relationship in directions that supported India's development. To this end, he evaluated colonial economic policy on its own terms, identifying ways in which it needed to be adjusted to better India's place in the world. He also contrasted the colonial and pre-colonial periods for the same reason. He collaborated with other prominent figures of the day on this subject, including Dadabhai Naoroji (1825–1917), political leader, merchant, scholar and the second South Asian to be elected to Parliament in Britain.[14] And, in recognition of his wide-ranging work, achievements and interests, Dutt was invited to preside over the 1899 meeting of the INC.

There had been significant breakthroughs in the study and understanding of Mauryan history from the mid-nineteenth century onwards, and this work had been published in journals and books to which both Dutt and Bhandarkar had access (see Chapter 4). Despite these advances and the availability of literature on the subject, along with the increasing importance accorded to ancient Indian history in scholarship, only Dutt discussed Chandragupta and the Mauryan dynasty at any length and in any detail.

Dutt refers to Chandragupta a number of times in the second volume of his *History of Civilization in Ancient India, Based on Sanscrit Literature* (1889), but at no point does he mention Seleucus. There are no references to Seleucus in Sanskrit literature, so this omission is not wholly surprising. In contrast, in *The Civilization of India* (1900), Dutt writes that Chandragupta 'drove out the Greeks from the Punjab, and thus formed the whole of Northern India into one united empire. Seleucus concluded a treaty of peace with the Indian Emperor, and gave his daughter in marriage with him.'[15] This is a significant moment in the interpretation and presentation of the Seleucid-Mauryan relationship: Dutt links Chandragupta's repulsion of the Greeks from India with the unification of northern India. Later Indian historians would take this idea further and link the action with Chandragupta's unification of India itself, and not only the northern part. In relation to the treaty, it is Seleucus who is said to make a treaty with Chandragupta, which indicates Dutt's belief that Chandragupta held the higher status in the relationship.

In the same year, Bhandarkar published his book *A Peep into the Early History of India: From the foundation of the Maurya dynasty to the downfall of the imperial Gupta dynasty (B.C. 322–circa 500 A.D.)* (1900). Bhandarkar mentions neither the military engagement nor the treaty concluded between Seleucus and Chandragupta in this work. Instead, he states that Seleucus 'kept up a regular intercourse' with Chandragupta, at whose court Megasthenes, Seleucus' ambassador, resided.[16] Overall, Bhandarkar writes very little about Chandragupta, which is odd given that the book explores the early history of India, beginning with the foundation of the Mauryan dynasty. In 1920, a second edition of this book was published. More information about Chandragupta and the Mauryans was available to Bhandarkar by this date. However, he did not make use of this new knowledge, nor did he make substantial revisions of his book.

Hugh George Rawlinson (1880–1957), a British historian of India and Christian theologian, commented on the lack of information about Chandragupta in his Preface to the second edition of Bhandarkar's work, but he had no answer for it.[17] One of Bhandarkar's stated aims in writing his book is to reconstruct the history of India through a range of sources, including by foreign authors. Graeco-Roman authors are indispensable for their references to Chandragupta, and McCrindle's translation was available, making Bhandarkar's omission even more curious.

The careers of both scholars peaked during the initial stages of the Indian nationalist movement. They were both aware of and involved in the developing ideas about national unity. However, these ideas appear to have influenced only Dutt's interpretation and presentation of the meeting and interaction between Seleucus and Chandragupta. For Bhandarkar, Chandragupta was not an especially important historical figure. In contrast, Dutt held Chandragupta in esteem as the individual who drove out the Greeks and, by this action, united northern India into one empire. For the first time, he linked these two ideas together and they took root in the work of the second generation of Indian scholars of ancient India. It is less clear whether this reading was influenced by Dutt's own burgeoning nationalist leanings. Given that the language he used – 'drove out' and 'one united empire' – echoes the words used by those involved in the movement, the inclination is to say that he was.

A change in emphasis takes hold: the second generation of Indian academic historians

In the first half of the twentieth century, three of the most prominent Indian historians of ancient India discussed the encounter between Seleucus and Chandragupta. Radha Kumud Mookerji (also Mukherjee) was Professor of Indian History and Head of the Department of History at the University of Lucknow. Hem Chandra Raychaudhuri was Carmichael Professor of Ancient Indian History and Culture, and Head of the Department of Ancient Indian History and Culture, at the University of Calcutta. R. C. Majumdar was both Professor of History and Vice Chancellor of the University of Dacca, before joining the Benares Hindu University (BHU) as Principal of the College of Indology. Raychaudhuri addressed the topic in his *Political History of Ancient India: From the accession of Parikshit to the extinction of the Gupta dynasty* (1923), Majumdar in *Outline of Ancient Indian History and Civilisation* (1927), and Mookerji in *Chandragupta Maurya and his Times* (1943).

This period was one of considerable change and increasing upheaval and violence in India relating to nationalist (and communalist) activism. Figures such as Lala Lajpat Rai (1865–1928), Bal Gangadhar Tilak (1856–1920) and Bipin Chandra Pal (1858–1932), collectively referred to as 'Lal Bal Pal', began to agitate for *swaraj* ('self-rule') in the early twentieth century. Tilak famously stated, '*Swaraj* is my birthright and I will have it'. They particularly advocated the boycott of British goods and promoted *swadeshi* (the use of goods 'of one's own country') in their place. After his return to India from South Africa in 1915, Mahatma Gandhi (1869–1948) engaged in and spread a radically new form of non-violent political action: *satyagraha* ('truth force').[18] By the 1920s, there was widespread support for *swaraj*. In 1947, these and other efforts culminated in India's independence, which profoundly and permanently altered the relationship between Britain and India.

In terms of religion more particularly, from the late nineteenth century onwards there was exponential growth in religiously motivated political organisations and activism, including militancy. The Partition of Bengal in 1905 under Curzon (1859–1925), Viceroy of India, into predominantly Hindu West Bengal and Muslim-dominated East Bengal further divided and antagonised Hindus and Muslims across India. The following year, the All-India Muslim League was formed with the aim of safeguarding Muslim interests. In 1915, numerous Hindu organisations joined together to form the Hindu Mahasabha, a Hindu nationalist organisation set up in opposition to the League and whose politics focused on the advancement of Hindu unity in India.

The rise in political and religious division, and communal violence, particularly in northern India, contributed to the spread of ideas promoting the separation of communities along religious lines.[19] This complex maelstrom of ideas and activities permeated every part of Indian life, including the study of history. The three historians discussed here were living, working and writing in this socially and politically tumultuous context, and some were more actively involved than others.

Of the three historians, only Raychaudhuri stood aloof from active involvement in national political movements.[20] Mookerji and Majumdar, in contrast, were well known for the Indian nationalist and pro-Hindu sentiment in their work, and their association with political and religious institutions.[21] Mookerji, for example, had a fully fledged political career alongside his academic one. Between 1937 and 1943, he was Leader of the Opposition for the secular Congress Party in the Bengal Legislative Council. In 1957, Rajendra Prasad, the first President of the Republic of India, awarded him the Padma Bhushan, the third-highest civilian award established by the Government of India after independence. Majumdar, for his part, was appointed Honorary Head of the Department of History of the nationalist-leaning Bharatiya Vidya Bhavan ('House of Indian knowledge'). Mookerji and Majumdar had religious associations as well as political ones. Mookerji was a member of the Hindu Mahasabha, while Majumdar worked at BHU, a university founded to revive Hindu traditions among other purposes.[22] Each historian had his own particular take on Seleucid-Mauryan relations and, for this reason, they will be dealt with separately in this chapter.

Raychaudhuri

Raychaudhuri was known for his close focus on source material for his reconstruction and analysis of history.[23] In his *Political History of Ancient India* (1923), Raychaudhuri focuses closely on, and regularly quotes or cites, all the available Graeco-Roman and South Asian sources which contain information about Chandragupta and his reign. He also supplies translations or overviews of the Greek and Latin sources drawn from McCrindle's anthology, as well as from, for example, John Selby Watson's translation of Justin's *Epitome of Pompeius Trogus* (Watson 1886), and H. C. Hamilton and W. Falconer's translation of Strabo's *Geography*.[24] On the basis of his reading of the translated sources, Raychaudhuri introduces Chandragupta as the Indian Arminius or Charles Martel, both renowned as national unifiers: the 'Indian who was made of a different stuff' from the other Indian rulers of Punjab.[25]

Unusually, Raychaudhuri put forward the idea that Chandragupta 'thought of ridding his country' not only of the Macedonian 'tyrant', but also of the 'Indian' tyrant, specifically the Nanda dynasty, which he overthrew.[26] This vision of Indian tyranny is based on Plutarch's *Life of Alexander*, in which Plutarch reports that the Indian king contemporary with Alexander (that is, the ruler of the Nanda empire), was 'hated and despised'.[27] In relation to the encounter between Seleucus and Chandragupta, Raychaudhuri writes, 'It will be seen that the classical writers do not give any detailed record of the actual conflict between Seleukos and Chandragupta. They merely speak of the results', and continues, 'There can be no doubt that the invader could not make much headway, and concluded an alliance which was cemented by a marriage contract.'[28]

Concerning the specifics of the alliance, Raychaudhuri generally and explicitly follows V. A. Smith. For example, he agrees with Smith that the evidence 'testifies merely to a "matrimonial alliance"', thereby going against the 'current notion' that the alliance involved Seleucus' daughter marrying Chandragupta.[29] Similarly, Raychaudhuri accepts Smith's suggestion that the territories transferred to Chandragupta by Seleucus included the satrapies of Aria, Arachosia, Gedrosia and the Paropamisadae. Although he notes that Smith 'adduces good grounds' for proposing this, Raychaudhuri only provides one piece of evidence. In relation to the 'inclusion of the Kābul valley within the Maurya Empire', he notes the presence of Aśokan inscriptions in the north-western regions of the subcontinent. In relation to the elephants, Raychaudhuri assumes that Chandragupta received the lands from Seleucus for the 'comparatively small recompense of 500 elephants'.[30] He does not refer to the unique status and considerable military advantage that owning such a large number of elephants would confer on a Western ruler, nor does he mention the success at Ipsus that Seleucus owed to the possession of so many elephants. In other words, he is not at all interested in the significance of the treaty for Seleucid history: his focus is entirely on ancient India.

Majumdar

Raychaudhuri's careful, almost tentative, conclusions, based closely on the available sources, and his acceptance of some of Smith's conclusions, are strikingly different from either Mookerji or Majumdar's interpretations and representations of the contact between Seleucus and Chandragupta, and its outcome. For example, in the Preface to his first work, *Outline of Ancient Indian History and Civilisation* (1927), Majumdar uncompromisingly sets out his opinion of the way in which 'European' authors – singling out V. A. Smith as an example – write about aspects of Indian history. He notes:

> Those who cannot forget, even while writing the history of ancient India, that they belong to the imperial race which holds India in political subjection, can hardly be expected to possess that sympathy and broad-mindedness which are necessary for forming a correct perspective of ancient Indian history and civilisation. European scholars have rendered most valuable service by way of collecting materials for ancient Indian history and civilisation, and India must ever remain grateful to them for their splendid pioneer work. But they would hardly be in a position to write the history of India, so long as they do not cast aside the assumptions of racial superiority and cease to regard Indians as an inferior race.[31]

Instead, Majumdar writes that the '[t]ime has come when an attempt should be made to write the history of India purely from the historical standpoint, untrammelled by any Imperialistic or European point of view. I have constantly kept this in mind in writing this little book.'[32]

He notes that the 'details of the conflict between these mighty enemies are not yet known, but that it ended in a decisive and disastrous defeat on the part of Seleucus, is no longer doubted by any sane historian'. Seleucus 'had to buy peace by ceding Paropanisadai, Arachosia, and Aria, three rich provinces with the cities now known as Kabul, Kandahar and Herat respectively as their capitals, and also Gedrosia (Baluchistan), or at least a part of it'. Chandragupta was the 'proud victor' who 'probably married the daughter of his Greek rival, and made a present of five hundred elephants to his royal father-in-law'.[33] However, as we saw in Chapter 1, the available evidence does not point to, or even suggest, that Chandragupta defeated Seleucus, or that Seleucus had to purchase peace at the cost of the upper satrapies, or even that Chandragupta presented the elephants to Seleucus as a gift, or married Seleucus' daughter.

Majumdar uses this encounter between a European and an Indian as an opportunity to counter Smith's opinion of the 'inherent weakness of the greatest Asiatic armies when confronted with European skill and discipline'.[34] Majumdar argues: 'it may be said, with far greater logic, that the triumph of Chandragupta over Seleucus demonstrated the inherent weakness of the greatest Hellenic armies when confronted with Indian skill and discipline'. And yet, of course, there is no evidence for the 'crushing defeat inflicted upon the Greek hosts of Seleucus' by Chandragupta.[35]

One of Majumdar's stated aims in writing this book was to correct the bias introduced into the writing of Indian history by 'imperialist' 'Europeans'. However, Majumdar's presentation of Seleucus versus Chandragupta makes similar moves, albeit in the other direction, veering away from the available evidence, which was accessed via McCrindle's translations. Majumdar's 'historical standpoint' is located in an India in which Indian nationalism had taken its hold.

In *Ancient India*, published in 1952 – five years after independence and just a few years before Chandragupta's statue was erected in the Indian parliament complex – Majumdar treats the Seleucid-Mauryan encounter in much the same way as in his earlier work. Indeed, many of the sentences are identical. There are, however, some differences, and all emphasise Seleucus' defeat at Chandragupta's hands. For example, Majumdar writes, 'The otherwise inexplicable silence of the classical writers, as well as the net result of the expedition, however, clearly indicate[s] that Seleucus met with a miserable failure.' And 'Some Greek writers have represented this gift [of five hundred elephants] as the price of the rich provinces ceded by Seleucus, which is of course absurd. It is difficult to believe that Seleucus would have readily agreed to part with his rich provinces for such paltry gifts unless he were forced to do so. It is therefore legitimate to hold that Seleucus was worsted in his fight with Chandragupta.'[36] As in his earlier book, Majumdar neither refers to nor quotes specific sources for any of this information.

Mookerji

Where Majumdar's representation of Seleucus and Chandragupta's meeting and its outcome is influenced by his political leanings, Mookerji's position is even more extreme. The first two sentences in the first chapter of *Chandragupta Maurya and His Times* (1943) read, 'Chandragupta Maurya ranks as one of India's greatest rulers. There are many titles to his greatness which, in several respects, is found to be even unique.' He goes on to explain what he means by this and starts with the claim that Chandragupta was 'the first Indian king who established his rule over an extended India, an India greater than even British India'. In the same paragraph, he continues, '[Chandragupta] was again the first Indian leader who had to confront the distressing consequences of a European and foreign invasion of his country, the conditions of national depression and disorganisation to which it was exposed, and then to achieve the unique distinction of recovering his country's freedom from the yoke of Greek rule'.[37]

It is clear from the outset that Mookerji is consciously and overtly presenting Chandragupta as *the* great Indian champion who not only was the first to unify India – an India that was 'greater even than British India' – but also defeated the 'foreign' 'European' invasion of 'his' country, thereby freeing India from the 'distressing consequences' of alien rule. In this way, Mookerji makes his position on two points immediately clear. Firstly, the reader is left in no doubt of his opinion of British and European colonial rule in India. Secondly, Chandragupta and the Greeks are employed, none too discreetly, as a metaphor for contemporary India fighting off British colonial rule. Chandragupta is the historical champion of ancient Indian independence, providing both a precedent and an inspiration for those involved in the contemporary Indian struggle for liberty. In this context, the date of publication of this book is important: 1943, a mere four years before Indian independence was declared.

The image of Chandragupta as Indian hero par excellence permeates Mookerji's work, influencing his interpretation of the sources. For example, Mookerji uses 'Chandragupta as leader of revolution' as the heading for the section in which he cites Justin's *Epitome of Pompeius Trogus* for the overview it provides of Chandragupta's rise to power. He goes on, 'The Greek withdrawal from India was not an automatic process. It was forced by a revolution, a war of independence declared by Chandragupta as its leader.'[38] The use of the word 'withdrawal' is interesting because there is no reference to a Greek withdrawal in the passage of Justin – only to putting Alexander's governors 'to death' – whereas it is particularly apt given the contemporary British withdrawal from India.[39] Furthermore, in connection with Chandragupta's encounter with Alexander as noted in Justin, Mookerji writes: 'The hero [Chandragupta] of Indian independence must have impressed Alexander with the promise of his future and roused his suspicion and enmity. This only added a private cause to the national cause of Chandragupta's hostility to Greek rule.'[40] There is, here, a transformation from a personal cause – Chandragupta's desire to throw off Greek rule and unite India – to a national cause: now, all India is portrayed as wishing to throw off Greek rule. The reference to Chandragupta's own subjugation of the Indian population is conveniently overlooked, as is the anachronism of India itself as a united cultural entity.

Nor is there much nuance in Mookerji's reading of Seleucus and Chandragupta's encounter and its outcome: the section heading reads, 'Defeat of Seleucos [*sic*], 304 B.C.: Extension of Empire up to Persia.' Mookerji refers to all of the classical sources that mention this meeting or aspects of the subsequent treaty – Appian, Strabo and Plutarch – and accesses them through McCrindle's work. The first source that Mookerji presents, and the only one he quotes, is Plutarch, who writes, 'Not long afterwards, Androcottos [Chandragupta], who had at that time mounted the throne, presented Seleukos with 500 elephants and overran and subdued the whole of India with an army of 600,000.'[41] There is no reference to any military engagement between the two rulers, nor a treaty. Instead, the focus is on Chandragupta's Indian military achievements and accession to the throne, with a small note, taken out of its original treaty-based context, referring to a 'gift' of 500 elephants that he made to Seleucus. Mookerji himself contextualises this gift, writing, 'The present to Seleukos was the result of a war between the two.'[42] It is instructive to quote Mookerji in full in reference to this battle:

> Taking the route along the Kabul river, he [Seleucus] crossed the Indus (Appian, *Syr.* 55). But the expedition proved abortive and ended in an alliance. It was because he had to confront a new India, strong and united, under Chandragupta in command of a formidable army, and felt that discretion was the better part of valour.[43]

This reading of the military encounter is not found in the only source that mentions it. As discussed in Chapter 1, Appian does not explain who the victor (if any) was, nor does he paint a portrait of Chandragupta as the leader of a 'strong and united' India, or give any indication that Seleucus backed down discreetly. Mookerji's presentation of events is so different from Appian's that it is worth quoting Appian again here:

> The whole region from Phrygia to the Indus was subject to Seleucus. He crossed the Indus and waged war with Sandrocottus, king of the Indians, who dwelt on the banks of that stream, until they came to an understanding with each other and contracted a marriage relationship.[44]

This difference prompts the question: did Mookerji exclude this vital quotation from Appian, even though he was clearly aware of it, because it was so at odds with the way in which he wished to present the encounter between Seleucus and Chandragupta, as well as India? Given the overall context, it certainly appears that way. This suggestion is backed up by the way Mookerji goes on to present the treaty agreed in the aftermath of the battle.

There is a significant contrast between how Mookerji writes about the three constituent parts of the treaty between Seleucus and Chandragupta that have come down to us, and his reading of the treaty and of what Strabo and Appian actually wrote. As seen above, Appian only writes that the rulers 'came to an understanding with each other and contracted a marriage relationship'. Strabo provides the fullest, albeit still limited, overview of the treaty:

> The geographical position of the tribes is as follows: along the Indus are the Paropamisadae, above whom lies the Paropamisus mountain: then, towards the south, the Arachoti: then next, towards the south, the Gedroseni, with the other tribes that occupy the seaboard; and the Indus lies, latitudinally, alongside all these places; and of these places, in part, some that lie along the Indus are held by Indians, although they formerly belonged to the Persians. Alexander took these away from the Arians and established settlements of his own, but Seleucus Nicator gave them to Sandrocottus, upon terms of intermarriage and of receiving in exchange five hundred elephants.[45]

As can be seen, Strabo presents the treaty as an exchange of land for elephants, based on a marriage alliance. In contrast, Mookerji repeatedly writes that the elephants given by Chandragupta to Seleucus were a 'gift' or 'present', whereas Seleucus is said to have 'ceded' the land to Chandragupta, thereby allowing Chandragupta to 'add another glorious feather to his cap'.[46] Furthermore, it was Chandragupta's generous 'gift' that allowed Seleucus to defeat Antigonus at Ipsus and led to a Western demand for further elephants.

The marriage aspect of the alliance is dealt with briefly, and any personal aspect to it is essentially rejected. Mookerji acknowledges, basing his opinion on Appian, that there is a 'suggestion … that there was a marriage alliance between the two kings so that Seleukos became either the father-in-law or the son-in-law of Chandragupta'.[47] Mookerji follows Macdonald's suggestion in the *CHI* that there was 'a convention establishing a *jus connubii* between the two royal families. In that land of caste, a *jus connubii* between the two peoples is unthinkable.'[48] However, Strabo's wording allows not only this, but also the suggestions that Mookerji rejects. Mookerji does not provide the reasons behind his choice of interpretation. It is interesting that he chooses the interpretation (and quotation) that refers to the establishment of a 'convention', rather than any actual intermarriage taking place, and 'caste'. On his interpretation, it may be that his own Brahmanical caste, which does not permit marriage with others of a different caste, influenced his decision here. It must be noted that the available evidence for Chandragupta's caste, late, limited and problematic though it is, suggests that the Mauryans were of *Kṣatriya* (warrior aristocracy) rather than Brahmin caste.[49] Overall, there is no suggestion in Mookerji's book of the equitable outcome that is indicated by the sources.

In his 1944 review of this work, the British Indologist Lionel Barnett (1872–1960) considered Mookerji's picture of Chandragupta to be 'too credulous', drawing 'many details from romance which he [Mookerji] apparently retells as realities'.[50] To this assessment, I add that not only is Mookerji occasionally 'credulous', but his image of Chandragupta, and his analysis of the sources, is heavily influenced by contemporary events in India, more so even than Majumdar's. His approach to and idealisation of Chandragupta also influenced how his students interpreted this figure, and none more so than P. L. Bhargava.

Publication of the first book to focus on Chandragupta

One of Mookerji's students, Purushottam Lal Bhargava (1909–2002), went on to write the first book solely devoted to Chandragupta: *Chandragupta Maurya* (1935). This endeavour was encouraged by Bhargava's father, and the work was published and printed through his family's publishing house.[51] Bhargava wrote this book at an early stage of his career and it remains popular: it is regularly cited in books dealing with Mauryan history, and has gone through two editions (the second of which was published in 1996) and numerous reprints (the most recent being in 2014).

In his Preface, Bhargava expressed surprise that, before the publication of his book, there was 'not a single book in English describing exclusively his [Chandragupta's] achievements'. He goes further, writing, 'It is indeed strange that such a great personage should have passed almost unnoticed by historians.'[52] What is more 'strange' is that Bhargava considered him to be overlooked by historians: while it is true that there had been no biographies of Chandragupta, Chapters 3, 4 and 5 of this book show quite clearly that he was mentioned time and again by prominent historians in histories of ancient India from the late eighteenth century onwards. Given the limited evidence available for Chandragupta's life, it is not surprising that entire books were not dedicated to him. And, as Bhargava's own work shows, this lack of evidence means that any such book must, by necessity, be both short and highly speculative.

Bhargava holds Chandragupta up as an ideal ruler, writing, 'As a student of history I have always been fascinated by the career of Chandragupta Maurya, one of the greatest of kings, conquerors and administrators the world has produced.'[53] This opinion has a profound impact on how Bhargava portrays Chandragupta and leads to the often overblown language he employs to describe him and his achievements. For example, Bhargava describes Chandragupta as 'the mightiest ruler of his time and one of the most lustrous stars in the firmament of monarchy', and 'an uncommon genius'. He goes on: 'it would be worthwhile to compare Chandragupta with three of the world's greatest Kings – Alexander, Akbar and Napoleon.'[54] Bhargava's opinion of Chandragupta also influences his interpretation of the Graeco-Roman sources, accessed through McCrindle's translations, pertaining to the meeting between Seleucus and Chandragupta, and the treaty agreed between them.

He sets up the military engagement between the two rulers as an opportunity for Chandragupta to 'measure [his] strength' against that of Seleucus. He provides a brief summary of Seleucus' career to demonstrate Seleucus' previous experience and success in battle, noting that he was 'formerly a general of Alexander ... [who] conquered Babylon ...[,] assumed the title of king ... [and] also subjugated the Bactrians'.[55] He elevates Seleucus yet further, describing him as 'the most powerful foreign king'.[56] Given the context, Bhargava's aim is to set Seleucus up as a worthy opponent for Chandragupta to fight against; Seleucus' association with Alexander would make Chandragupta's victory all the more glorious. Any assumption of victory on either side is, of course, problematic. While Bhargava recognises that no 'account of the actual conflict has survived', the lack of evidence does not prevent him from stating that 'the results, as mentioned by the classical authors, clearly show that Seleucus recognized the superiority of Chandragupta and was obliged to conclude a humiliating treaty'.[57]

Bhargava unquestioningly accepts V. A. Smith's suggestion that Seleucus handed over to Chandragupta four satrapies: Aria, Arachosia, Paropamisadae and Gedrosia, even though there is no firm evidence for this assumption. His exploration of the marriage contract is likewise pure speculation. He suggests, for example, that 'the real explanation of the whole treaty seems to be that Seleucus married his daughter to Chandragupta, giving the territories of Afghanistan and Baluchistan as a sort of dowry'. In a footnote, Bhargava continues in this vein.[58] As shown below, Raychaudhuri picks up on this idea and expands it.

The elephants that Chandragupta gave to Seleucus are mentioned only briefly – 'We further learn that Chandragupta presented 500 elephants to Seleukos' – and nothing more is said on this matter.[59] If the tables were turned and Seleucus had handed over such a vast number of elephants to Chandragupta, one wonders if Bhargava would have accorded this event more importance. Bhargava concludes that, but for Chandragupta, India 'would have surely fallen a prey to the ambition of the successors of Alexander. He [Chandragupta] was solely responsible for the redemption of India.'[60] This is praise indeed. In a few short decades, scholarship moved from Dutt's presentation of Chandragupta as the unifier of northern India, to Chandragupta as the redeemer of all India.

New series of Indian history for a new India

There is a marked contrast between the representation of Seleucus and Chandragupta's meeting and its outcome included in the Oxford and Cambridge histories, and that in two post-independence histories that were supported by prominent members of the new Indian government. These volumes were *The History and Culture of the Indian People: The age of imperial unity* (1951) and *Age of the Nandas and Mauryas* (1952). Another difference relates to authorship: only British authors contributed to the Oxford and Cambridge histories, while the two historical series published in India were written entirely by Indian scholars.

Rajendra Prasad, later the first President of newly independent India, was a key figure in one of these projects. A lawyer by training,

Prasad was long involved in politics, becoming a member of the INC in 1916 and elected as its President in 1934. Prasad also had an interest in education, establishing a national college in Bihar (the state in which he was born) in *c.*1920 with the aim of transforming it, with Gandhi's support and encouragement, into a National University.[61] In 1937, he founded the Bhāratīya Itihās Prasad ('Indian Academy of History') for the purpose of producing the multi-authored *A New History of the Indian People* in 20 volumes.[62] This series was soon amalgamated with the 12-volume series on the history of India that had been proposed by the Indian History Congress at its annual meeting in 1940.[63]

The result of this merger was that only one volume of *A New History of the Indian People* was published: *Age of the Nandas and Mauryas*, which had originally been projected to be the fourth volume of the series. It was edited by Kallidaikurichi Aiyah Nilakanta Sastri (1892–1975). Sastri was a historian of South India known for his Indian nationalist viewpoint; in 1957, the President of India awarded him the Padma Bhushan in the field of Public Affairs. Printing commenced in 1945 but publication was halted almost immediately because of events associated with the Partition of India: the premises of Motilal Banarsidass, the publishing house responsible for publishing the volume, were destroyed during riots in Lahore. Motilal Banarsidass, a Jain-owned business, relocated to two premises in India, Patna in Bihar and Varanasi in Uttar Pradesh. This move delayed publication until 1952.[64] Once published, the book was well received and reviewed: the philologist Luciano Petech, for example, wrote, 'The work as a whole belongs to the best products of contemporary Indian scholarship.'[65]

H. C. Raychaudhuri contributed two chapters to *Age of the Nandas and Mauryas*; the one titled 'Chandragupta and Bindusara' is of particular relevance here. As in his *Political History of Ancient India* (1923), Raychaudhuri covers the full range of available source material. He uses McCrindle's translations more widely in this second work than in his first, and points out problems relating to different interpretations based on translations.[66] However, despite the commitment to basing his analysis firmly on the source material, Raychaudhuri is more generous to Chandragupta in his second than in his first work. For example, he describes Chandragupta as 'a man of heroic proportions', and 'the great liberator'.[67]

This more positive impression of Chandragupta seems to influence Raychaudhuri's assessment of the military engagement between Chandragupta and Seleucus, as well as the treaty agreed between them. He writes: 'while the war [between Seleucus and Chandragupta] itself received scant attention at the hands of the historians, the "understanding" seems to have attracted greater notice.' He goes on to say, 'The details of the "understanding" to which Strabo bears witness leave no room for doubt that Seleucus could not make much headway.' While in his earlier work Raychaudhuri had been more circumspect about the outcome of the battle between Seleucus and Chandragupta, here he writes that Chandragupta was the 'conqueror of … Seleucus'.[68]

In his first work Raychaudhuri generally followed Smith's arguments in relation to certain aspects of the treaty between Seleucus and Chandragupta. In this second work, he takes the opportunity to counter Smith. For example, he concludes: 'A lady of the Seleucid family probably graced the royal palace of the king of Prasii.'[69] This is contrary not only to Smith, but also to Macdonald in the *CHI*. It is based on Raychaudhuri's interpretation of Strabo, namely that the transfer of territories on terms of intermarriage 'implies that the marriage did take place, the lands in question being possibly treated as the dower of the Seleucid princess like the Kāśi village in the Buddhist story of Kosalā devī, and Bombay in the case of Catherine of Braganza'.[70]

Concerning the transfer of territories, Raychaudhuri uses the Graeco-Roman and Aśokan texts to argue against Smith's interpretation, and also that of W. W. Tarn.[71] Tarn (1869–1957) was a British scholar of the Hellenistic world who focused on Alexander (whom he admired greatly) and the Greeks in Bactria and India.[72] Tarn had suggested, drawing on Strabo, that Seleucus ceded only those satrapies that lay alongside the Indus, specifically Paropamisadae, Arachosia and Gedrosia. In contrast, Raychaudhuri presents a more nuanced, open approach based closely on the sources, which do not themselves allow any firm conclusions.[73] There is no difference in Raychaudhuri's interpretation of the transfer of elephants; indeed, he uses the very same sentence here as he does in his first work.

Overall, Raychaudhuri's interpretation of the sources and opinion of Chandragupta had changed between 1923 and 1952. He asserts more confidently and firmly his own arguments against those of Smith, and later those of Tarn and Macdonald. This is to be expected given that the chapter in *Age of the Nandas and Mauryas* was written during the height of his career as one of the most prominent historians of India, while the first book was a revised version of his doctoral thesis. Various factors may have resulted in his more positive impression of Chandragupta, and these must be unrelated to the available sources, which had not changed in the intervening 30 years.

It may, then, be that political changes, and also the views of the editor, Sastri, had had an impact on Raychaudhuri, who was the most politically neutral of his contemporaries. After all, the chapter published in 1952 was written in the years immediately preceding Indian independence. The shift in opinion relating to Chandragupta's encounter and relations with Seleucus goes unnoticed by Raychaudhuri's biographer, Harihar Panda. In relation to Raychaudhuri's perspective on Chandragupta and Seleucus, Panda writes, 'Chandragupta defeated Seleukas, a worthy successor of Alexander and cemented matrimonial alliance with the latter offering 500 war elephants and getting Ariā, Arāchosia, Gedrosiā and Parapanisadai (Herāt, Kandāhār, Makrām and Kābul, respectively) in return.'[74] Any nuance is gone. In terms of the presence of nationalism in Raychaudhuri's work, Panda writes, 'A careful examination of his works does not reveal any such marked influence [of nationalistic trends] as is seen in the writings of Prof. R. K. Mukherjee [also Mookerji] .... His [Raychaudhuri's] writings do not reflect nationalistic bias.'[75] On the contrary, the comparison made here between Raychaudhuri's earlier and later works dealing with Chandragupta, including an analysis of Chandragupta's meeting with Seleucus, suggests that contemporary events in India had influenced Raychaudhuri's impression of this more ancient event.

In 1938, just a year after the foundation of the Bhāratīya Itihās Parishad, a similar institution came into being, following the vision of its own founder. The Gujarati lawyer and politician Kanaiyalal Maneklal Munshi (1887–1971), who was closely involved in the independence movement, founded the Bharatiya Vidya Bhavan ('House of Indian knowledge'), an educational institution that aimed to promote Indian, especially Hindu, history.[76] As one part of its overall aim, Munshi envisioned the publication of a new history of India.[77] This series was funded by the industrialist and philanthropist Ghanshayam Das Birla (1894–1983), who was one of Gandhi's key supporters (see Chapter 6 for details about his role in the construction of the Birla Mandirs and the link with Chandragupta).

R. C. Majumdar was appointed General Editor of *The History and Culture of the Indian People*. The volumes of this series were published in quick succession from 1951 to 1969, and contributors included some of India's most prominent historians, including Mookerji. Munshi remained closely involved in the series, writing the Foreword to every volume, and his political vision is apparent from the very start. In the Foreword to the first volume, for example, he wrote, 'Generation after generation, during their school or college career, were told about the successive foreign invasions of the country, but little about how we resisted them and less about our victories.'[78]

The title of the volume on ancient India, *The Age of Imperial Unity* (1951), implies that India was unified during this period. This interpretation contrasts with, for example, Smith, who had written 50 years earlier:

> [T]he complete political unity of India under the control of a paramount power, wielding unquestioned authority, is a thing of yesterday, barely a century old. The most notable of her rulers in the olden time cherished the ambition of universal Indian dominion, and severally attained it in a greater or less degree. But not one of them attained it completely, and this failure implies a lack of unity in political history which renders the task of the historian difficult.[79]

Mookerji wrote the chapter that dealt with Chandragupta's reign, and here he briefly deals with Chandragupta's encounter with Seleucus. He presents a striking contrast between the India Alexander had to face and the India that Seleucus encountered: Alexander 'had to fight against a divided India, split up into a multitude of states', while Seleucus 'had to face a united and a much stronger India organised by an able leader [Chandragupta]'. Mookerji suggests that the reason the 'Greek writers [whom Mookerji accessed through McCrindle] do not give details of his [Seleucus'] conflict with Chandragupta' is that they would 'naturally' pass over 'his [Seleucus'] defeat and discomfiture at the hands of an Indian ruler'.[80]

Mookerji's interpretation of the treaty agreed between Seleucus and Chandragupta is clear: 'The terms of the peace leave no doubt that the Greek ruler fared badly at the hands of Chandragupta.' Seleucus, writes Mookerji, 'had to purchase peace by ceding to Chandragupta territories then known as Aria, Arachosia, and Paropanisadae, ... and probably also a part of Gedrosia'. In contrast, Chandragupta is said to have 'presented' Seleucus with 500 elephants. There is a marked difference between the status of these two aspects of the treaty. Any notion that 'Chandragupta' married a daughter of Seleucus is wholly rejected: 'this is not warranted by known facts', and nothing further is said about this part of the treaty.[81]

The combined factors of political changes connected with independence and involvement with projects aimed at writing new histories of India for an independent India influenced the interpretation and presentation of the encounter between Seleucus and Chandragupta.

Conclusion

The difference in the ways in which British and Indian historians presented the meeting between Seleucus and Chandragupta and its outcome is striking. The rise and fall of British rule in India is in evidence through the presentation of this encounter, as is India's growing sense of its own national, unified political identity, including the rise of religious communalism.

Of the British historians discussed in Chapters 3 and 4, Mill chose to raise Seleucus to victory, while, at the other end of the spectrum, Rapson, Thomas and Macdonald declined to see any military encounter at all. In stark contrast to them, only Smith presented Chandragupta as victor. Notably, he was also the only one of the group with personal experience of India, including first-hand knowledge of the exceptional ancient monuments there. This familiarity and understanding of the country appears to have influenced his interpretation of the Seleucid-Mauryan encounter.

Dutt takes up the idea of Chandragupta defeating Seleucus and ties it into his unification of northern India. This is a key moment in the understanding and presentation of this relationship. It is on this interpretation that later Indian scholars build their own ideas about Chandragupta and his importance to Indian unity. Historians such as Mookerji and Majumdar were not merely passive observers of the events surrounding independence, but actively involved in them. They found an ancient figure whom they helped to transform, through their work, into an idealised hero: Chandragupta. This figure and his achievements embody all of the qualities they could want: he was Indian, a Hindu, and he won a glorious victory driving off foreign invaders, unified India and founded a glorious dynasty that included his grandson Aśoka.

However, the fit is occasionally a little too perfect. As demonstrated in this chapter, different historians interpreted the very limited evidence about Chandragupta and his encounter in ways that matched their own political allegiances. The difference shows the conscious and conspicuous rejection by the second generation of Indian historians of India of Macaulay's hope, expressed long before, 'through English-medium instruction in the arts and sciences of Europe, to form an elite class that was "Indian in blood and colour, but English in taste, in opinions, in morals, and in intellect"'.[82]

Notes

1 Lal 2003, 62.
2 Masselos 2005, 37, 82, 86–7, 103, 126–7. There have been numerous studies on this subject, including Jaffrelot 2010.
3 Whitehead 2003, 5; Lal 2003, 31; Masselos 2005, 48. For a detailed study of the transmission of information in India from the late eighteenth to the late nineteenth centuries, see Bayly 1996.
4 Vasunia 2013, 23; Masselos 2005, 47, 48.
5 This was not McCrindle's only work on Megasthenes: he translated into English E. A. Schwanbeck's important collection of Megasthenes' fragments, as well as some of Schwanbeck's arguments about this material. This information came from Schwanbeck 1846. Alongside this information, McCrindle included extensive footnotes of his own (Stoneman 2022, 16).
6 McCrindle 1877, iii.
7 McCrindle 1877, iv.
8 McCrindle's collection of translations proved popular beyond the academy. In his review of McCrindle's work, the British army surveyor Sir Thomas Hungerford Holdich (1843–1929) highlighted the compact size of the volumes of translations. The small size meant they were easily transportable in 'an ordinary pocket' and therefore invaluable to those 'political, military, and commercial wanderers whose business leads them into the remoter regions of our Indian Empire [North-Western Frontier Province and Afghanistan]'. Holdich rated this work so highly that he recommended that it be a 'familiar addition to the personal equipment of the Indian frontier official' (Holdich 1901, 610).
9 In his review of Majumdar's compilation, J. G. de Casparis (1962, 152) rightly notes that Majumdar's introductory claim that his volume includes all classical texts pertaining to India is 'exaggerated'.
10 Lal 2003, 80.
11 Vasunia 2013, 11.
12 This is a very brief overview of a complex subject for which there is a considerable literature, including: Jaffrelot 1999, 2010; Metcalf 2008; Corbridge and Harriss 2000. Jaffrelot brings the story up to the present in his 2021 book *Modi's India: Indian nationalism and the rise of ethnic democracy*. Vasunia (2013, 9–20) provides more detail about the conceptual roots of this periodisation in classical scholarship in Europe during the eighteenth and nineteenth centuries.
13 See http://hansard.millbanksystems.com/commons/1908/jul/21/india-governor-generals-council (accessed 28 October 2022).
14 Like Dutt, Naoroji lectured at UCL. He was Professor of Gujarati at this university from 1856 to 1865. There are a number of new publications on Naoroji, including Dinyar Patel, *Naoroji: Pioneer of Indian nationalism* (2020).
15 Dutt 1900, 49.
16 Bhandarkar 1900, 2.
17 Bhandarkar 1920, iii.
18 Masselos 2005, 114, 150.
19 Masselos 2005, 128–9, 132; Bapu 2013, 2.
20 Raychaudhuri's biographer, Harihar Panda (2007, 8), put it thus: 'Prof. Raychaudhuri led an extremely uneventful personal life. In fact, besides his academic activities, very little remained in his life. ... He knew comparatively a few persons and of those only a few intimately. He had no taste for sports and social gatherings and hence he was usually taken as harsh or unsocial.'
21 Jaffrelot 1999, 288; Lal 2003, 142.
22 Jaffrelot 2010, 208. BHU was founded in 1916 by Madam Mohan Malaviya (1861–1946), Brahmin politician and member of Congress. The aim was both to preserve specifically Hindu tradition and learning and to revive it. Malaviya was also a key figure in strengthening the influence of the Hindu Mahasabha within Congress (Jaffrelot 2009, 61–62). For more information about BHU, see Renold 2005.
23 This aspect of his approach is mentioned by various authors, including Panda 2007, 5–6, 99, 176, and C. E. A. W. Oldham (1928) and C. A. F. Rhys Davids (1928), who reviewed the second edition of Raychaudhuri 1927.

24 Watson 1886; Hamilton and Falconer 1854–7.
25 Raychaudhuri 1923, 137. Arminius was a German tribal leader who routed the Roman invaders at the Battle of Teutoburg Forest in AD 9 (Wells 2004). During the unification of Germany in the nineteenth century, Arminius was transformed into a national symbol (Winkler 2015, 59). Charles Martel was an eighth-century Frankish ruler who reunited Francia and halted the Muslim invasion from Spain at the Battle of Tours in AD 732 (Fouracre 2000, 92).
26 Raychaudhuri 1923, 139. Interestingly, he referred to India as 'his [Chandragupta's] country' in relation to the period before Chandragupta had even embarked on his mission of unification (Raychaudhuri 1923, 139).
27 Plut. *Alex.* 61.
28 Raychaudhuri 1923, 142.
29 Raychaudhuri (1923, 142) citing Smith (1920, 15).
30 Raychaudhuri 1923, 142.
31 Majumdar 1927, v.
32 Majumdar 1927, v.
33 Majumdar 1927, 132, 133.
34 Majumdar (1927, 133–4) quoting Smith 1920.
35 Majumdar 1927, 134, 135.
36 Majumdar 1952, 105.
37 Mookerji 1943, 1, 3.
38 Mookerji 1943, 51; Just. *Epit.* 15.4.13–21.
39 Just. *Epit.* 15.4.12.
40 Mookerji 1943, 53.
41 Mookerji 1943, 58.
42 Mookerji 1943, 58–9.
43 Mookerji 1943, 59.
44 App. *Syr.* 11.55. Translation by Horace White.
45 Strab. 15.2.9. Translation by H. L. Jones.
46 Mookerji 1943, 60.
47 Mookerji 1943, 61.
48 *CHI* Vol.1, 431 quoted in Mookerji 1943, 61.
49 The Aśokāvadāna (36), for example, mentions that Chandragupta's son Bindusāra was of *Kṣatriya* caste, which implies that he was as well.
50 Barnett 1944, 417. Giuseppe Tucci's review of the third edition of this book, in which Mookerji's assessment and impression of Chandragupta's image and achievements remain unchanged, is also critical (1963).
51 P. L. Bhargava's father, M. B. L. Bhargava, established the Upper India Publishing House in Lucknow (Bhargava 2010, 22). The front matter of Bhargava 1935 reads: 'Printed by R. P. Bhargava, at the Oudh Printing Works, Charbagh, Lucknow.'
52 Bhargava 1935, iii.
53 Bhargava 1935, iii.
54 Bhargava 1935, 101, 104, 101.
55 Bhargava 1935, 37, 38.
56 Bhargava 1935, 100.
57 Bhargava 1935, 38.
58 Bhargava 1935, 39. The footnote (Bhargava 1935, 39n2) reads: 'This view is generally accepted and seems to be correct, as the marriage of Hindu kings with non-Hindu princesses was not unknown in ancient India, the Mahabharata mentioning the marriage of Arjuna with a princess of the Naga tribe. On the other hand, a vice-versa case does not appear possible in view of the evident success of the Indian King, besides the fact that in that event the Greeks would naturally have been more explicit, as they are about Alexander's Asiatic marriages.' References from the Mahabharata are anachronistic, while Bhargava's assumption that Graeco-Roman authors would 'naturally' mention a marriage between Seleucus and an Indian woman is faulty: evidence about Seleucus and his family is very limited, and it is not even certain how many children he had.
59 Bhargava 1935, 39.
60 Bhargava 1935, 100.
61 Prasad 1946, 55, 117–19; Kuracina 2010, Appendix B.
62 Lal 2003, 91.

63 Sastri 1952, iii; Sastri 1959, 95; Lal 2003, 91.

64 Lahore was the capital of Punjab. Under Partition, Punjab was divided between India and West Pakistan. Lahore was located in the Pakistani portion and is now the capital of Punjab Province, Pakistan. Large-scale violence and disorder associated with the mass migration of entire communities between East and West Punjab saw many thousands of people killed and the wholesale destruction of property.

The enforced delay because of conflict finds a parallel with that of the *CHI*, the publication of which was delayed by the onset of the First World War.

65 Petech 1954, 301.

66 Raychaudhuri 1952, 144. This is in relation to older rather than more recent translations of Justin's *Epitome*.

67 Raychaudhuri 1952, 133, 139.

68 Raychaudhuri 1952, 152, 156.

69 Raychaudhuri 1952, 157.

70 Raychaudhuri 1952, 154.

71 Raychaudhuri 1952, 153–4.

72 For example Tarn 1938, 1948a, 1948b. I did not include Tarn among the British scholars discussed in the previous chapter because he did not write a history of India.

73 Raychaudhuri 1952, 153–4.

74 Panda 2007, 30.

75 Panda 2007, 7.

76 Lal 2003, 91.

The Bharatiya Vidya Bhavan remains an active educational trust with over one hundred centres, including schools, across India. It also has international centres in London, New York, Sydney, Kuwait, Doha and Abu Dhabi. The centre in London holds regular courses in, for example, Indian dance, music and languages, as well as performances and exhibitions.

77 As outlined in his Foreword to the first volume of *History and Culture of the Indian People: The Vedic Age* (1951).

78 Munshi 1951, 9.

79 Smith 1904, 5.

80 Mookerji 1960 [1951], 60.

81 Mookerji 1960 [1951], 60.

82 Trautmann 1997, 111, citing Macaulay, 'Minute on Indian education', 1835 (Macaulay 1972).

Part III
Antiquity, art and contemporary popular culture

The four chapters of Part III look at representations of Chandragupta and the Seleucid-Mauryan encounter in artwork and popular culture from the early twentieth century up to the present day. When embarking on this study, I did not know just how wide-ranging the depictions would be or how little they would change over time. From the early twentieth century onwards, Chandragupta is a key figure in plays, films, television series, historical novels and even comic books aimed at children. He is also portrayed in sculptures installed in both secular and religious contexts and, in the mid-twentieth century, in paintings and murals.

Surprisingly, the first modern works of art to depict Chandragupta in sculpture, murals and paintings are found in a religious context, in the Birla Mandirs (temples built by the Birla family). The first of these temples, the Lakshmi Narayan Mandir in Delhi, was completed in 1939; it includes multiple representations of Chandragupta. These artworks, and many others in the temple complex, have labels (such as you would find in a museum) that share a narrative that accords with the Birlas' overall aims and message in constructing their temple. The second modern sculpture of Chandragupta is also found in a prominent location in Delhi: the Indian parliament. The story behind the production of this bronze figure by Hilda Seligman, humanitarian and author, and its installation in the parliament is told for the first time in Chapter 7.

As the nationalist movement picked up speed and moved inexorably towards independence from colonial rule, Chandragupta was embraced as the original Indian hero who could fend off European incursions into the subcontinent. By having Chandragupta versus Seleucus stand in for the contemporary fight between Indians and the British, playwrights and filmmakers aimed to circumvent colonial censors. This was not always successful, as H. M. Reddy, director of the Tamil film

Mathru Bhoomi (1939), was to find. He used his film adaptation of Dwijendralal Ray's 1911 play *Chandragupta* as a vehicle for nationalist songs, and it was soon banned by colonial censors for this reason (see Chapter 8).

Two posters of films about Chandragupta that were made on either side of 1947 exemplify the difference that independence made to artistic expression. They had similar storylines because they were based on Ray's play. However, the poster for the earlier film, Jayant Desai's *Samrat Chandragupta* (1945), had to underplay Chandragupta's victory over Seleucus. In contrast, Babubhai Mistry's *Samrat Chandragupt* (1958) shows Chandragupta holding Seleucus on the floor at spearpoint. The vital importance of the founder of the Mauryan empire and his battle with his Seleucid counterpart in narratives that promoted nationalism and freedom is shown in the absence of movies about him from 1958 onwards. This is after the release in quick succession of four films about Chandragupta between 1934 and 1945, the peak of independence activity.

After this, it took more than 50 years for Chandragupta to return to the screen, this time the small screen. The focus was no longer on his battle with Seleucus, but on his rise to power in India. Where Greeks entered the scene, for example in the person of Chandragupta's wife Helena, whom he married as part of his treaty with Seleucus, their portrayal was cartoonish, prejudiced and disturbing to watch. It would be considered wholly unacceptable to depict minority-ethnic characters in this fashion here in the UK. But, disturbingly, it appears to be generally accepted in India, including in relation to children of mixed heritage.

Another troubling development comes through the Amar Chitra Katha comic book about Chandragupta. *Chandragupta* was released in 1978 and has yet to be updated. It purports to share a historically accurate version of Chandragupta's life and rise to power but is actually based on a work of fiction rather than on any historical evidence. The result is a wholly fictious storyline. And yet, this faulty, inaccurate narrative is the one that is shared with millions of children. This state of affairs comes to the heart of why it is vital to assess how historical figures and encounters are shared in popular culture: popular culture, far more than history books, shape public perception. Once an idea or narrative, however problematic or plain wrong, is inculcated in us, it is extremely difficult to change.

6
A national project of a different sort: representations of Chandragupta in the Birla Mandirs

The Birla Mandir project

Representations of Chandragupta are found in a rather unexpected setting: in five Birla Mandirs located in Delhi, Patna, Mathura, Bhopal and Varanasi. Birla Mandirs are Hindu temples constructed at multiple sites across India by members of the Birla family between the 1930s and the 1990s, sometimes in partnership with other organisations. The Birla Mandir project was initiated by Baldeo Das Birla (1863–1956) and continued by his son Jugal Kishore Birla (1883–1967) and his grandson Ganga Prasad Birla (1922–2010).

The Birla family, from Pilani in Rajasthan, began their meteoric rise to becoming an Indian industrial colossus in the nineteenth century, through their involvement in the opium and cotton trades. Over the generations, their businesses expanded into numerous other industries, from motorcar manufacturing to media interests, and much else. Alongside these business concerns, the family have long channelled their wealth into extensive philanthropic work in India. Through a series of trusts, the family build schools, universities, research institutions, libraries, museums, planetariums and hospitals across the country, while funding religious and cultural heritage work, including the renovation and foundation of temples. The newly founded temples are known as Birla Mandirs.

The Lakshmi Narayan Mandir in Delhi was the first Birla Mandir to be built. It provided a template for future Birla Mandirs in its physical manifestation of the underlying ideology through aspects of architectural style, artistic decoration, inscriptional narratives, and the inclusion of a spacious garden ornamented with carefully chosen and newly produced sculptures. It is here that the first representations of Chandragupta in sculptural and pictorial form are found. For these reasons, this temple will be the primary focus in this chapter.

The original foundation of the Birla Mandirs, and the ideals that they expressed, must be understood within the wider context of the family's staunch adherence to Hinduism and their support for those working towards Indian independence. Gandhi, in particular, looms large in this picture because of his close association with the Birla family. By taking a holistic approach to reading the decoration of these temple complexes, we can determine the vision that B. D. Birla, and his descendants, wanted to share with worshippers and visitors. Furthermore, and which is of particular relevance here, a careful investigation of the ideology that underlies the construction and decoration of these temples helps to reveal the reasons behind Chandragupta's inclusion in them.

Magadha in New Delhi: shaping a narrative through architecture

The Lakshmi Narayan temple, completed in 1939, was designed by Sris Chandra Chatterjee (1878–1966) in his composite Modern Indian Architecture style (Figure 6.1). Chatterjee was an architect, a civil engineer in the Public Works Department in India, and a member of the National Planning Committee. His appointment, and the style of architecture that he espoused, represented a particular, albeit short-lived, moment in India's architectural history in the early part of the twentieth century. His selection showcases the Birla family's political ideals as well as their hopes and aspirations for their temple project and India's future.

During the 1930s and 1940s, Chatterjee was at the helm of the Modern Indian Architectural Movement, which had an explicit political and aesthetic agenda.[1] Chatterjee believed that Modern architecture had no place in India because, according to him, Indian architecture should be based on traditional Indian styles.[2] So, through an understanding and amalgamation of indigenous architectural traditions, Chatterjee aimed to develop a national architecture for modern, independent India. Ancient India, particularly Magadha, which was the heartland of the Mauryan empire, inspired his approach, as did contemporary movements such as the *Swadeshi* movement.

The *Swadeshi* movement was part of the independence movement and Indian nationalism, involving the boycott of foreign goods in favour

Figure 6.1 Exterior of the Lakshmi Narayan temple, New Delhi designed by Sris Chandra Chatterjee. This temple was completed in 1939 and was the first Birla Mandir to be conceived and constructed. Source: Dan Lundberg. Shared under a Creative Commons Attribution-ShareAlike 2.0 International licence (CC BY-SA 2.0), Wikimedia Commons, bit.ly/3R9mFr7.

of locally produced Indian goods. For Mahatma Gandhi, it was a fundamental part of the journey to *swaraj* ('self-rule'): for example, Gandhi was a proponent of Indians making and buying homespun cotton ('khadi') rather than Lancashire mill-made cotton. Images of Gandhi wearing clothing made from khadi cloth while sitting and spinning cotton or agitating for independence have become iconic.

The impact of *swadeshi* was wide-ranging and influential. For Chatterjee, who was, like the Birla family, a keen supporter of Gandhi, it was a valuable tool, because he believed that gaining political independence was linked to achieving cultural freedom.[3] *Swadeshi* had practical applications in architecture, such as the use of traditional Indian methods and materials for constructing buildings. Chatterjee advocated this approach, and the Birla family put it into practice by commissioning primarily local artisans to work on their temples.[4]

As cultural and political changes swept through India during the march towards independence, artists increasingly looked to India's past for inspiration. This approach is perhaps most famously encapsulated by the work of the Bengal School of Art, led by Abanindranath Tagore

(1871–1951) and supported by others, including the art historian and teacher E. B. Havell (1861–1934). These architectural and artistic networks were interlinked, and ideas passed fluidly between them. Tagore, for example, admired Chatterjee's aims and methods, while Chatterjee agreed with many of Havell's ideas about using local materials and methods, and Havell, in turn, acknowledged that Chatterjee was 'working on the right lines and has a grasp of the problems to be solved that is, to adopt the living traditions of Indian building to present needs by a real co-operation between the designer and the builder'.[5]

As he explored ancient Indian architecture and design through extensive travel in order to develop the idea of Modern Indian Architecture, Chatterjee was 'inspired by a vision of ancient India resplendent with fortresses, palaces, residences, temples and gardens of the kings and people'.[6] He was especially captivated by the ancient surviving buildings from Magadha, a region and ancient kingdom located in what is now southern Bihar. This area formed the core of the Mauryan empire and it is here that their capital city, Pataliputra, was found, alongside other important historic and religious sites such as Bodh Gayā and Nālānda.

In his book *Magadha: Architecture and culture* (1942), Chatterjee extols the virtues of this region, writing, 'what made the deepest impression on my happiest dreams was a colourful and ever-moving kaleidoscope of the well-organised and progressive, yet artistic, life of the people of pre-historic ages who settled in the fertile valleys of the mighty Ganges and the Sôn along the picturesque regions of the great empire of Magadha subsequently governed by Chandragupta and Aśoka.'[7]

Chatterjee noted that while Alexander the Great's invasion brought Greek influences to the art of north-western India, Chandragupta 'successfully checked the Greek invasion and established a kingdom of his own'.[8] In the context of his book, the implication here is that Chandragupta prevented Greek influence on the art and architecture of Magadha. Instead, 'The art of Town Planning which found distinction in ancient Rājagṛiha, was considerably developed with the splendid civic reform and progressive administration of Pataliputra by Chāṇakya' (Chandragupta's 'illustrious Brahman minister').[9] The architectural and artistic purity of the region was thereby preserved and would be an invaluable part of a future national architecture for India.

These manifold ideas and sources of inspiration coalesced in Chatterjee's architectural designs, finding expression in such buildings as the Lakshmi Narayan temple in Delhi. For Chatterjee, the basis of a national architecture was the renaissance and synthesis of ancient styles, using both traditional and modern building techniques.[10] However, he was not able to realise this ambition, and a clear and coherent national style of architecture did not emerge through his work. Instead, his designs brought together an array of styles primarily derived from ancient rather than mediaeval or modern buildings. His focus on the ancient meant that elements from Hindu, Buddhist and Jain structures were included and represented in Chatterjee's work, while those derived from Islamic buildings were mostly, although not entirely, absent.[11]

In this specific sense, his designs ran counter to the Indo-Saracenic style which drew inspiration from Indo-Islamic architecture combined with European Gothic revival and Neo-Classical styles. Indo-Saracenic designs had been widely used for public buildings in India during the late nineteenth and early twentieth centuries. Chatterjee generally admired this style but was less keen on Lutyens's and Baker's interpretation of it for the new imperial capital in New Delhi, built between 1912 and 1931. In his view, their version of Indo-Saracenic architecture was stylistically inconsistent.

This is a rather ironic take on Chatterjee's part, because his own designs were highly eclectic: he combined disparate architectural elements from different periods, styles and buildings. Indeed, his work has been described as 'more of a pastiche than a synthesis of ideas'.[12] One of Chatterjee's most important commissions was the Lakshmi Narayan Mandir, and it sits right next to Lutyens's Delhi with Rashtrapati Bhavan, the official residence of the President of India, within easy walking distance. The temple comprises a mix of styles, much like the Indo-Saracenic architecture which surrounds it.

Designing and decorating the first Birla Mandir

Each architectural element that Chatterjee included in his designs was selected for its symbolic value and meaning. In the overview that he wrote of the Lakshmi Narayan temple, he outlined the religious stories and ancient architectural features that underpinned his plans for the building. These details are drawn from various regions, periods and styles, including the Mahābodhi temple in Bodh Gayā, Bihar (in ancient Magadha), and the Sūrya temple at Konarak, Odisha. His aim was for the temple to 'represent a chariot with Visṇu-Sūrya as World Conqueror'. However, not all of his ideas came to fruition: 'such important items as Sūrya, sun-window and wheel-carvings on plinth were omitted in course of construction without any knowledge or consent of the architect.'[13]

Nonetheless, he notes that the 'experiment has been appreciated' and, in this way, he has been able to move closer to his architectural ideal.[14]

One might assume that there would be some cross-over between architect and artist when it came to the internal decoration of the temple, but Chatterjee's scathing remarks indicate that there was not. He writes, 'the interior has been affected by garish over-ornamentation and cheap oil painting .... Much better result would have been achieved had simpler, congenial elements been introduced in decorating the interior and in places of the exterior.'[15] In relation to the 'places of the exterior', Chatterjee is presumably referring to the statues and smaller structures such as pavilions that dotted the complex. And yet, these 'discordant' elements were vital to the success of the project: they enabled the Birlas to share their vision and message with temple visitors.

Deities as well as religious, legendary and historical figures are depicted in pictorial and sculptural form within the numerous temple buildings and monuments as well as in the garden. Many of these artworks have descriptive inscriptions and there are also stand-alone text panels dotted around the compound. One of these panels provides a clear explanation for the guiding principle by which the art and inscriptional content were chosen for this project: 'In this temple Vedmantras, Upnishadas [sic], Shlokas, Bhajans and artistic life pictures have been inserted with a view to awaken the Aryadharami Hindus to regain their ancient glory and power and there after preach the message of peace and true happiness to the whole world. We hope all Aryadharami Hindus (including Sanatanists, Aryasamajists, Buddhists, Jains, Sikhs etc.) will accede to our humble prayer.'[16]

'Aryadharami Hindus' are followers of the *Ārya dharma*. These are complicated, multi-layered and multi-faceted words to translate and extensive scholarship has resulted in a lengthy bibliography spanning centuries. However, a careful evaluation of the use of the term *Aryadharami* in a range of inscriptions at the Delhi temple by Marta Kudelska and her team reveals that it meant something specific in the Birla Mandir enterprise. Here, the term was used to express the sanctioning and incorporation into Hindu tradition of 'all Indian religions that could strengthen the mainstream of tradition, and support the building of a community (a new nation and state)'.[17] This represents a universal understanding of the word which was also emphasised by the fact that, from its very inception, the flagship Birla Mandir has been open to all regardless of their social status or religion. The same is true of all the Birla Mandirs constructed subsequently, and panels at the entrances of these temples highlight this message of openness.

In this case, the immediate inspiration for this openness came from Gandhi, who agreed to be involved in the temple opening on the condition that it was open to everyone, regardless of caste or religion.[18] However, the caveat to this stated universality is most clearly expressed through the historical and legendary figures who are and are not included in the temple complex.

Presence and absence: statues in the temple garden

The figures represented in the paintings and sculptures that decorate the Lakshmi Narayan temple and gardens in Delhi can be broadly divided into six main groups: deities, religious people, legendary figures from epic poetry, historical rulers, culturally significant people, and contemporary individuals.

The primary deities of this temple are Lakshmi Narayan (the goddess Lakṣmī with her consort Viṣṇu). As is usual in a Hindu temple, other deities and their avatars are also included here. More unusually, figures from other religious traditions are present as well, including the Buddha, Ṛṣabhadeva (the first Jain *Tīrthaṅkara*) and Guru Nanak (founder of Sikhism). An important commonality is that all of the religious figures represented are associated with religions that originated in the subcontinent, as are the rulers whose statues stand in the temple garden. This trend brings further explanation of the vision that the Birlas aimed to share with worshippers and other visitors to the temple.

Individual statues of the following legendary and historical rulers were included in the temple garden: Yudhiṣṭhira (legendary king from the *Mahābhārata*), Chandragupta Maurya, Aśoka Maurya, Vikramāditya (legendary king), Prithviraj Chauhan (*c.*1166–92), Pratap Singh I (*c.*1545–96), Chhatrapati Shivaji (*c.*1630–80), Surajmal of Bharatpur (1707–63), and Ranjit Singh (1780–1839). It is immediately apparent that only a partial history is being shared here: all of these kings are Hindu, with one Buddhist and one Sikh ruler represented, and there are no Jain or Muslim kings among them. Another commonality is that all but two of the kings – Yudhiṣṭhira and Aśoka – were involved in resisting either foreign invasion or foreign rule already established in India.

Chandragupta, for example, fought off Seleucid power, and the legendary king Vikramāditya was believed to have seen off the Śaka (Scythian) invaders.[19] Prithviraj Chauhan resisted the initial invasions of Mu'izz ad-Din Muhammad (also known as Muhammad of Ghor), Sultan of the Ghurid Empire, but was later defeated by him at the Second Battle of Tarain in 1192. Pratap Singh I successfully fought against the expansion of Mughal power in India. Chhatrapati Shivaji expanded Maratha power against a backdrop of the declining Adil Shahi Sultanate, while alternately agreeing alliances with and fighting against Mughal forces, as well as other neighbouring sultanates and the nascent European presence in India. Similarly, Surajmal of Bharatpur fought against the Mughals, while Ranjit Singh repeatedly defeated incursions from Afghanistan. All of the rulers can be seen as enforcing *Ārya dharma*. In addition, all were located in northern India and experienced foreign invasions from the north-western corridor into the subcontinent. Given the choice of rulers depicted, the emphasis is on Indian rulers resisting Islamic power.

By the time the first Birla Mandir was consecrated in 1938, there had been and still were numerous Muslim rulers across India whose families had settled there many generations before. They were unquestionably now part of the fabric of India and India's history. However, in the Delhi temple garden, this complex, multi-faceted inheritance is set aside in favour of an appeal to a highly selective past in which rulers practising religions indigenous to India took up arms against those invading India. Internal warfare, which was always part of the reality of Indian history, is also carefully put to one side. Indeed, all of the kings depicted in sculptural form fought internal battles against fellow Indians, as did Yudhiṣṭhira and Aśoka. According to the *Mahābhārata*, the legendary ruler Yudhiṣṭhira led the Pāṇḍava to victory against their cousins the Kurauva. Aśoka's war against the Kaliṇga in eastern India was so bloody that he went on to renounce violence and convert to Buddhism.

Representations of Indian rulers who fought colonial powers during the eighteenth and nineteenth centuries are also noticeably absent. This story was not only pertinent given the period of the temple's construction, but would also have provided an opportunity to include a wide range of rulers who played a prominent role in such activities, for example Tipu Sultan (1751–99), a ruler of Mysore who was eventually defeated by the British at the Battle of Sririgapatna in 1799 during the Fourth Anglo-Mysore war. Instead, Rani Lakshmibai of Jhansi (1828–58), who fought the British and became a symbol of resistance to the British Raj, appears to be the only ruler famous for fighting the British represented in the complex. She is depicted in bas relief on a *kīrti stambha* ('pillar of fame') in the garden alongside such as Chhatrapati Shivaji, Baji Rao Peshwa and Maharaja Ranjit Singh.

It can only be surmised that a decision was taken to focus on earlier rulers (with the exception of Ranjit Singh) who practised indigenous Indian religions and to avoid selecting prominent anti-British figures.

Given the prominence and significance of large-scale statues placed in the garden, this choice would have had to be ratified at the highest levels, specifically, by the Birlas themselves in conjunction with prominent historians, archaeologists and other cultural figures (see Chapter 5 for G. D. Birla's funding of the history series *The History and Culture of the Indian People*). After all, this was a project that they themselves initiated at great expense in India's capital city, and which was endorsed by influential figures, including Gandhi. Had they misjudged a key aspect of the temple design and decoration, the potential ramifications for their social and political standing, and hence their business-related activities, could have been significant and damaging. So it is inevitable that they would draw on their network to ensure their project fulfilled their objectives. Unfortunately, documents that might shed light on the purpose and meaning behind the construction and embellishment of the Birla Mandirs are not available for study.[20]

Chandragupta: a close-up

This section takes a closer look at the iconography of Chandragupta's statue and the inscriptions carved into its large plinth (Figure 6.2). The aim is to better understand the vision and aspirations underpinning the creation of the first Birla Mandir through the prominent inclusion of Chandragupta and the message the Birla family wished to share through it.

In his statue, Chandragupta's face is idealised and clean-shaven with half-closed eyes, recalling sculptural representations of Hindu deities or the Buddha in meditation. He wears a helmet with a circular disc at the front, perhaps recalling the moon after which he is named. He is depicted barefoot and wearing traditional Indian unstitched clothing, as are the other ancient rulers standing around him. The decorative edging on the upper cloth around his chest is covered in small circles, while the lower garment is edged with geometric patterns. Beneath the thicker strap draped over his left shoulder is a smaller thread that runs diagonally down to his waist. This represents the *yajñopavītā*, or sacred thread, worn by the men of the Brāhmin, *Kṣatriya* and *Vaiśya* castes. In Chandragupta's case, it marks him out as a *Kṣatriya* or member of the warrior caste.

Chandragupta is bedecked with jewellery, wearing heavy earrings, necklaces, armlets, bracelets and an intricately made *kamarband* comprising strings of beads (or pearls) draped across his hips. In his right

Figure 6.2 Statue of Chandragupta Maurya in the grounds of the Lakshmi Narayan temple, New Delhi. Source: Ashish Bhatnagar, Wikimedia Commons, bit.ly/3flJzhK.

hand he holds a mace that rests on the ground, and he carries a book in his left hand. Curiously, this book does not resemble a palm-leaf manuscript as might be expected given traditional Indian sculptural conventions. Instead, it is a European style, hard-cover book. The letters carved into the book cover are worn and now difficult to make out but the words may refer to one of the texts carved into the plinth below.

The statue is carved from what looks like buff-coloured sandstone and it stands on a red stone plinth, similar to the plinth on which Seligman's bronze sculpture of a young Chandragupta rests. Framing the figure is a large back panel, also carved from sandstone although the edges are coloured red. The panel resembles a full-body halo, albeit without the radiating elements, of the kind that is sometimes found in stone sculpture from the Sarnath workshop. Among all the kings, only Chandragupta and Yudhiṣṭhira are honoured with a *chattra* ('parasol'), an ancient emblem of Indian kingship, and this is carved in red stone. Red stone *chattras* are also found on some large sculptures at Sarnath. These aspects may well have been inspired by the exceptional Buddhist sculptures found in Sarnath.

However, it is difficult to pinpoint the inspiration for the rest of Chandragupta's imagery. The statue brings together a disparate variety of styles and motifs, none of which can easily be attributed to a specific period, region or genre, which is much like Chatterjee's architectural style. Broadly speaking, sculptures in this type of buff-coloured stone are found at large temple sites in Madhya Pradesh, such as Khajuraho, but they are also found at Sarnath and elsewhere. However, as with Chatterjee's Modern Indian Architecture, the impression given by the sculptural style is particularly important and relevant: here it gives the overall impression of 'ancient Indian ruler'. In this way, the sculptures serve their purpose by imparting this message to visitors.

The inscription on the plinth reads:

> *Ārya* king Chandragupta Maurya, who defeated the Greek king Alexander's commander-in-chief and later successor, King Seleucus, and married his daughter Helena and brought her to India. During Chandragupta Maurya's time his Mauryan Army consisted of 20 lakh[21] infantry, 10 lakh cavalry, 1 lakh elephants and 1 lakh charioteers.[22]

In Graeco-Roman literature, the marriage alliance is at the heart of the peace treaty that Seleucus and Chandragupta agreed. This detail is little known outside academic circles. Its inclusion here therefore suggests that historians were consulted as part of the process to decorate the Delhi Birla Mandir.[23] It is more difficult to ascertain which these might have been, although the Indian historians discussed in Chapter 5, particularly the politically active individuals, are the most likely candidates. For them, as depicted in the temple, Chandragupta is an important ruler who stands out in the history of ancient India.

Beneath this inscription is a map showing the whole Indian subcontinent and greater India with place names inscribed onto the different regions. In this way, the whole Indian cultural sphere is associated with Chandragupta. The text and map explain why Chandragupta was selected to stand in the Birla Mandir garden. According to the text, Chandragupta defeated a foreign power, assimilated a specific foreign element – Helena – into his life and empire, and raised a great army. Furthermore, the inclusion of the map links him to the burgeoning Indian influence that was later to spread not only across South Asia but also into South East Asia.

The presence of five quotations, in Sanskrit and translated into Hindi, on either side of the plinth reveal that there are other messages associated with Chandragupta. The first śloka ('verses') are from the *Mānava-Dharmáśāstra* (also known as the *Manu Smṛiti* or Manu's Code of Law) and three passages are from the *Cāṇakya Nīti* (aphorisms of Cāṇakya). It is not clear whence the remaining text derives. Surprisingly, Cāṇakya's most famous text, the *Arthaśāstra*, is not included.

The core text of the *Mānava-Dharmáśāstra* is likely to have been written in the second to third century AD by a single author – probably a Brahmin in northern India whose name is unlikely to have been 'Manu' – with later additions by others.[24] Patrick Olivelle describes it as a 'blueprint for a properly ordered society under the sovereignty of the king and the guidance of Brahmins'.[25] According to tradition, Chandragupta had a Brahmin advisor named Cāṇakya, and Megasthenes' *Indica* notes that Chandragupta ruled over a well-ordered State. Additionally, there are parallels to be drawn between Chandragupta and Manu. In the temple garden, Chandragupta is presented as a Hindu founder emperor of India while Manu was believed to be the first human being and, according to at least one tradition, the first king.[26] The inclusion of a quotation from the *Mānava-Dharmáśāstra* on Chandragupta's plinth makes sense in light of these points.

As Olivelle's work shows, the section devoted to the king, statecraft and law in the *Mānava-Dharmáśāstra* is 'disproportionately large in comparison to Manu's predecessors within the expert tradition of *dharma*'.[27] However, the quotation from the *Mānava-Dharmáśāstra* does not come from the *Rājñaḥ Karmavidhiḥ* (Rules of action for a king) section of this text, but from the preceding one, *Brāhmaṇasya Caturvidhaḥ Dharmaḥ* (Fourfold dharma of a Brahmin). The central section of the ten-point Law *śloka* (6.92) is found on the plinth. I include the full *śloka* (6.91–3) here with the inscribed section in italics:

> Twice-born men belonging to all these four orders [student, householder, forest hermit and ascetic] must always observe the ten-point Law diligently. *Resolve, forbearance, self-control, refraining from theft, performing purifications, mastering the organs, understanding, learning, truthfulness, and supressing anger: these are the ten points of the Law*. Those Brahmins who learn the ten points of the Law and, after learning, follow them, attain the highest state.[28] (Inscription 1)

Inscribing only the core section of this verse removes the qualifications for those who should follow these laws in living their lives, namely the four orders and Brahmins. In this way, the attributes are made universal and not even confined to one religion (Hinduism).

Of the remaining four quotations, three are from the *Cāṇakya Nīti*. *Nīti* texts are collections of aphoristic verses of practical, everyday wisdom; those contained in the *Cāṇakya Nīti* are attributed to Chandragupta's minister Cāṇakya. Numerous different manuscripts of this text have come down to us and there is no definitive collection or version. Instead, there exist multiple compilations comprising a range of maxims. Whether or not the verses can in fact be linked to Cāṇakya is debatable.[29] Unlike Inscription 4, Inscriptions 3 and 5 are not directly linked to the *Cāṇakya Nīti* on the plinth. However, slight variations of these quotations are found in the paintings at the Birla Mandirs in Delhi, Bhopal and Mathura and, in these cases, are attributed to this text. For this reason, they can be associated with the *Cāṇakya Nīti*. Inscription 2 has proved difficult to track down. While it may have come from one of the many available compilations of the *Cāṇakya Nīti*, it may equally have come from another text entirely.[30]

The content of these inscriptions reveals the lessons that the Birla's were keen to impart to temple worshippers and visitors. They read:

> A clever and intelligent man always propagates his religion like the wealth he accumulates and with urgency as if death has taken hold of his hair and [is] pulling it apart. (Inscription 2)

> If killing one evil person saves a number of lives from oppression and danger, then that act of killing brings virtue to the killer. When killing that evil person, you do not need to judge him beforehand. Performance of *dharma* is the core reason for happiness. (Inscription 3; *Cāṇakya Nīti*)

> The person who is deeply addicted to something, he can never succeed. If controlled by passions then he can easily be destroyed even if he has a large, well-formed army. If you are truly committed to any work, then it will most certainly be achieved. The work that is done with complete focus is always successful. You can only be successful in your work if you are aware of the time you live in, and can understand which way the wind is blowing. If you believe in luck then you will not be successful. A completely honest man cannot achieve anything. You need to start your work playing to your strengths (and avoiding your weaknesses). *Cāṇakya Nīti.* (Inscription 4)

> If a child is giving you sage advice, heed it. But do not believe in anyone more than they deserve to be believed in. An evil man always brings you pain and hurt even if you have behaved well with them and treated them well. The impatient do not belong to this world or the next. Do not consider yourself immortal. Only believe in the *Vedas*, there is no religion beyond them. Your success or failure depends on this. It is not wise to enrage an elephant by misusing your senses. Controlling your senses will bring you *Moksha*, the ultimate healing from all diseases. The one who is destroyed is destroyed because of the needs of injustice. The one who knows the scriptures by heart but does not understand the core meaning and can live by them are fools and are destroyed. Only the light of knowledge can dispel the darkness and fear of this *Sansar*. (Inscription 5; *Cāṇakya Nīti*)

Many different ideas jostle for position in these maxims and, overall, they serve to provide general examples of how best to approach life. As seen in Inscriptions 2 and 4, religion is the central component to living a successful life. Other aspects, such as self-control, playing to one's strengths and distrust of others are also important factors according to the aphorisms. In this context, Inscription 3 comes as something of a surprise: it explains that if killing one person saves more lives, then that is essentially fine and in accordance with *dharma*. Only within the wider context of the Birla Mandir and the pervasive influence of the *Bhavagad Gītā* in the temple complex does the core message become apparent.

Scenes from the *Bhavagad Gītā* ('song of god'; part of the *Mahābhārata*) predominate at this Birla Mandir. In numerous paintings, Arjuna is shown alongside Kṛṣṇa (an avatar of Viṣṇu) as they survey the battlefield and engage in their famous dialogue. Arjuna despairs about the horrors of the bloodshed that is to come when he and the other *Pāṇḍava* fight their own kin, the *Kaurava*. Kṛṣṇa counsels Arjuna to fulfil his duty as a *kṣatriya* (person belonging to the warrior class) by defeating his enemies and upholding the *dharma* – as Viṣṇu did time and again.

While obviously an important religious text through the ages, the *Gītā* also had contemporary resonance: prominent figures involved in India's independence movement cited it as their spiritual inspiration. For Gandhi, the *Bhavagad Gītā* was not about physical violence but 'described the duel that perpetually went on in the hearts of mankind', and, the author of the *Mahābhārata* 'has not established the necessity of physical warfare; on the contrary he has proved its futility. He has made the victors shed tears of sorrow and repentance, and has left them nothing but a legacy of miseries.' Gandhi continues, 'instead of teaching the rules of physical warfare, [the *Gītā*] tells us how a perfected man is to be known. In the characteristics of the perfected man of the Gita, I do not see any to correspond to physical warfare.'[31] This interpretation also fed into his approach to obtaining independence, specifically through *Satyagraha* ('holding firmly to truth'), a form of non-violent resistance.

The key difference between Gandhi's message and that inscribed on Chandragupta's plinth in the Birla Mandir relates to violence: for Gandhi, violence in the *Gītā* was metaphorical; in this inscription, the message is straightforward: if actual violence begets freedom from oppression and danger then it is a performance of *dharma*.

These are extraordinary words to find in a religious compound, as is the inclusion of statues of kings *because* they engaged in violence, specifically against foreign invaders. The placement of the statues on tall plinths is also significant: it ensures that the texts are in visitors' sightlines and that the statues tower above them. The result is twofold: firstly, one must literally look up to these rulers; secondly, reading the inscriptions becomes part of the experience when visiting the complex. In this way, the religious complex is transformed into a space that resembles a museum. The placement and context of the other artworks depicting Chandragupta reinforce this impression.

A Graeco-Indian marriage in the wedding *maṇḍapa*

There are two further representations of Chandragupta in the Birla Mandir complex. This section focuses on his depiction in the wedding *maṇḍapa* (a pillared hall or pavilion used for ritual purposes) which is located in the gardens (Figure 6.3). There are numerous pavilions of

Figure 6.3 The wedding maṇḍapa in the grounds of the Lakshmi Narayan temple, New Delhi. © Agnieszka Staszczyk.

Figure 6.4 Frieze inside the wedding maṇḍapa depicting the marriage of Chandragupta and Helena. The maṇḍapa is in the grounds of the Lakshmi Narayan temple, New Delhi. © Agnieszka Staszczyk.

different sizes and for different purposes in the gardens of the Lakshmi Narayan temple. The pavilion used for wedding ceremonies has painted friezes running round the top of the interior walls, along with explanatory inscriptions. One of the friezes runs the full length of one wall; it depicts Chandragupta, his queen and his army in a marriage procession (Figure 6.4).

It is quite dark in the upper recesses and consequently it is difficult to make out the words, which are written in small characters and positioned at the very top of the walls. The Hindi inscription here is identical to the text found on the plinth:

> Ārya king Chandragupta Maurya, who defeated the Greek king Alexander's commander-in-chief and later successor, king Seleucus, and married his daughter Helena and brought her to India. During Chandragupta Maurya's time his Mauryan Army consisted of 20 lakh infantry, 10 lakh cavalry, 1 lakh elephants and 1 lakh charioteers.

The painting illustrates this text, depicting a procession of soldiers, chariots drawn by horses, horsemen, elephants and their riders, and a group of young women holding a flywhisk, a fan, a tray of flowers, and tall-necked vases, one of which has a spout. At the back of a group of Indian soldiers are two figures wearing a strange assortment of clothing: Roman-style plumed military helmets, nineteenth-century belted military jackets with large epaulettes, and sandals with criss-crossed straps running from ankle to knee. Both men hold in their right hand a sword pointing towards the floor. One is obscured by the Indian soldiers standing in front of him. Above them is a short label that reads 'Greeks', indicating that they represent Seleucus' soldiers. The two figures are placed in such an unobtrusive position that were it not for the descriptive label they could easily be missed.

The central section of the frieze shows Seleucus' daughter Helena carried on a palanquin. Dressed in white clothing and bedecked with jewels, she holds a lotus flower in her left hand and her eyes are demurely cast downwards. In case there should be any doubt as to who she is, the words 'Maharanī Helena' are included in brackets next to her head. In front of Helena is her new husband, labelled 'Samrāṭ Chandragupta'. He wears a crown, heavy jewellery and a dhoti, and sits cross-legged on a large horse-drawn chariot, the front of which is shaped like a peacock, a clear reference to 'Maurya'. The chariot has a throne-like back and a parasol extends over his head. The inscription that describes the whole scene is placed above this central section.

Many famous marriage stories are found in Hindu mythology and Indian history. So, it is curious to find a scene for which there is no evidence for one that is not so well-known and may not have taken place. Furthermore, this marriage is referenced twice in inscriptions and once in pictorial form in the temple. So it was clearly a significant event within the scope of the project. A closer look at the inscription and the way the marriage procession is represented is revealing.

The reference to Chandragupta's marriage to Seleucus' daughter Helena is sandwiched between a reference to Chandragupta's victory in war and a description of his army. It was on the basis of this victory that he went on to marry Helena. The depiction of Chandragupta with Helena therefore represents his victory over Seleucus, and Seleucus as Alexander's general, no less. In the work of Indian historians who were writing during the period in which the temple was being constructed, the Mauryan defeat of Greek forces represented India's throwing off the colonial yoke. In the same way, this scene and the accompanying text could easily stand in for ideas about the desired relationship between India and Britain. To extend this metaphor, the image of Chandragupta could also be interpreted as India independent and strong on the back of a glorious victory, keeping what was good and useful from Britain (represented by Helena), and marching on towards a rosy future.

Inside the temple with Cāṇakya

The third and final representation of Chandragupta in the Delhi Birla Mandir is in a painting on the wall of the main temple hall alongside Cāṇakya (Figure 6.5). Below it, there is a polished brass plaque which reads 'Emperor Chandragupta and Chanakya' in Hindi.

Chandragupta, dressed in traditional Indian unstitched clothing – a blue upper garment and a yellow lower garment – sits on a dais. Cāṇakya sits to his right on a lower seat wearing the saffron robes, sacred thread and shaved head with single lock of hair of a Brahmin priest. Their names are written above them. On the floor before them are placed Chandragupta's shield, arrows and sheathed sword. Two architectural elements are included at the back of the painting and one in the foreground.

The element immediately behind Chandragupta is heavily embellished with intricate floral carving and resembles a stūpa gateway. Similar examples can be found at the Great Stūpa at Sanchi. The architectural feature at the back on the left-hand side looks like a stūpa railing pillar, while the one at the front on the right appears to be an imagined amalgamation of a stūpa railing pillar, cross-bars and a gateway. This structure is also covered in floral patterns, some of which emanate from the mouths of *makara* (mythical sea monster often with the head of an elephant and body of a crocodile). The horizontal bars on the element in the foreground as well as those on the one behind Chandragupta are embellished with rows of elephants. The bar above Chandragupta's head is carved with a row of hares. This type of animal decoration encourages

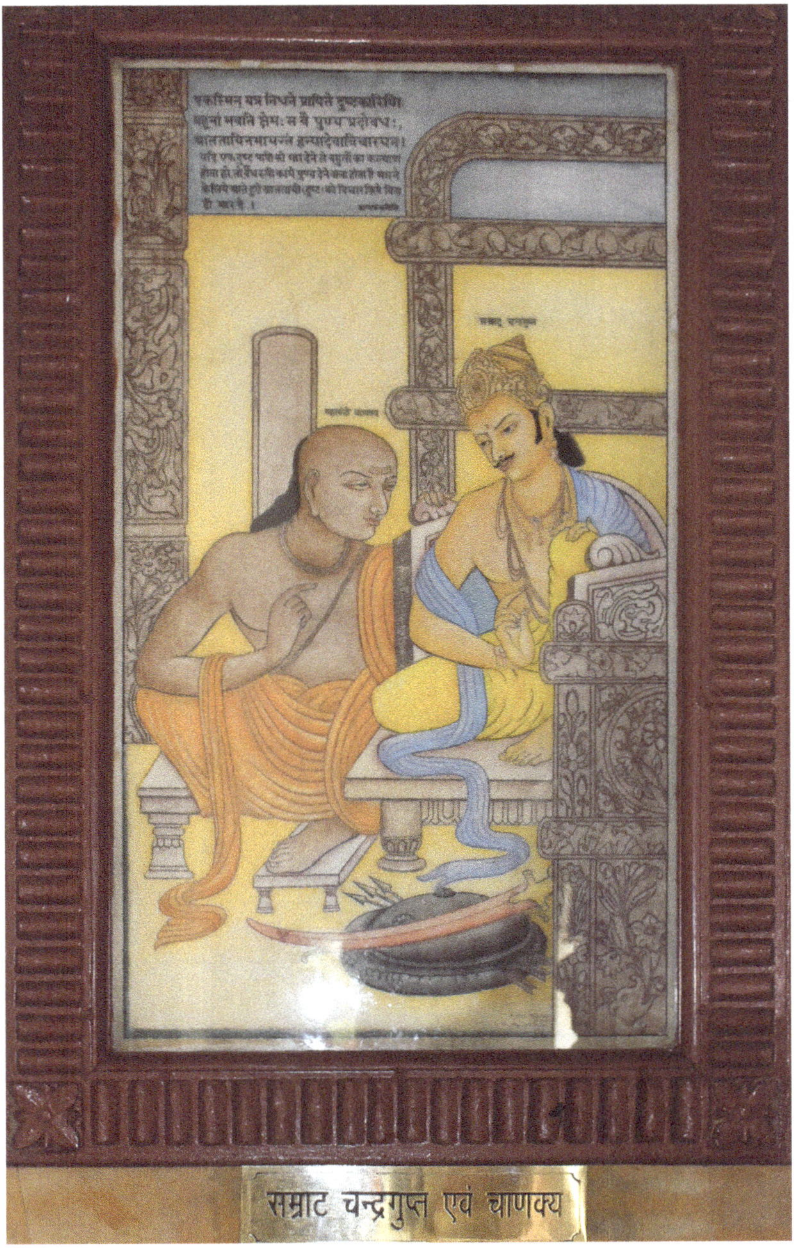

Figure 6.5 Painting of Chandragupta and Cāṇakya in the main temple hall of the Lakshmi Narayan temple, New Delhi. © Agnieszka Staszczyk.

further connection with Buddhist architecture, including Sanchi and Bharhut stūpa railings and gateways, and the abacuses atop some Aśokan pillars. There is a high yellow wall in the background of the painting that is punctuated by an empty doorway or window. Above this wall is a horizontal band of blue sky on which is written a quotation from the *Cāṇakya Nīti*.

The proportions of this painting and the inclusion of a text in this position are reminiscent of Indian miniature painting. Early eighteenth-century *Barahmasa* ('songs of the seasons') paintings produced in Amber, Rajasthan, have a similar band of colour across the top for text.[32] Miniature paintings of the same period from the Rajasthan School provide a close comparison in terms of the composition. One in particular bears a striking resemblance to the image of Chandragupta and Cāṇakya: a gouache painting of Yaśodā holding the infant Kṛṣṇa in her lap with a female attendant to her right (Figure 6.6). There is a building behind Yaśodā on the right-hand side of the composition.[33] I am not suggesting that this specific painting was the inspiration for that of Chandragupta and Cāṇakya in the Birla Mandir, rather that the artist drew on examples from Amber and the Rajasthani School as a model for this artwork.

The text is a slight variation of Inscription 3 from the statue plinth. It reads:

> If killing one evil person can bring peace and tranquillity for the subjects, then the act of killing that person is an act of virtue. If anyone comes into your house to attack you (or just attacks you), you are justified in killing that person without remorse or seeking the intervention of the court.[34]

As noted above, this is an unexpected message to find on a temple wall and can be interpreted in different ways. Given the location of this painting in the main hall, the words may suggest that any violence brought into this temple precinct will be met with violence. Or, in a wider historical context, particularly in association with the message conveyed by the statues in the garden, the 'house' may relate to 'India'. So those coming 'into your house to attack you' might refer to foreigners entering India. These suggestions must remain just that unless and until documents concerning the building and decoration of the Birla Mandirs are made available for study.

Figure 6.6 Rajasthan School painting of Yaśodā holding the infant Kṛṣṇa, attended by a woman. Registration Number 1880,0.2372. © The Trustees of the British Museum. Shared under a Creative Commons Attribution-NonCommercial-ShareAlike 4.0 International (CC BY-NC-SA 4.0) licence.

Representations of Chandragupta in Birla Mandirs at Patna, Mathura, Bhopal and Varanasi

Representations of Chandragupta are found in four other Birla Mandirs: Deva Mandir in Patna, opened in 1942, Srimadbhagavadgita Mandir in Mathura, opened in 1946, Lakshmi Narayan Mandir in Bhopal, opened in 1964, and the New Vishwanath Mandir in Varanasi that opened in 1966. The paintings are located in the main halls of the temples at Bhopal and Mathura, in the upper gallery of the main hall in Patna, and on the ground floor of the temple at Varanasi. All have short titles naming the two individuals depicted therein, for example 'Maurya Emperor Chandragupta and his Prime Minister Chanakya'.

All of these paintings are based on the original example installed in the Delhi Birla Mandir, although there are minor differences between them. This similarity of composition indicates that the artists involved in decorating the different temples were given clear instructions and images to work from.

The paintings at Delhi and Varanasi are almost identical (Figures 6.5 and 6.7). The main differences are that the Varanasi version has a wholly blue background and the vertical window or doorway in the wall has been transformed into a structure that resembles a sandstone pillar. An Aśokan pillar was discovered at the Buddhist site of Sārnāth, near Varanasi, in 1905 by F. O. Oertel (1862–1942), a civil engineer, architect and amateur archaeologist. This pillar was discovered broken but its well-preserved four-lion capital – later chosen as the symbol of the Indian Republic – was unearthed a little distance away from it. The importance of the Sarnath pillar may have inspired the transformation of the window into a pillar in the Varanasi painting.

The text included in the Varanasi artwork is the longest found in any of the paintings and is mostly derived from the *Cāṇakya Nīti*. The first section begins with the first half of Inscription 4 from Chandragupta's statue plinth and ends with additional material from elsewhere. The next three sentences are also from the *Cāṇakya Nīti* but not found on the plinth, and the last paragraph contains part of Inscription 5. The list at the end comes from the *Mānava-Dharmáśāstra*, which is also included in the plinth Inscription 1. The translation is:

> The person who is deeply addicted to something can never succeed. If controlled by passions then he can easily be destroyed even if he has a large, well-formed army. If you are truly committed (without distractions) to any work, then it will most certainly be achieved. The work that is done with complete focus is always successful.

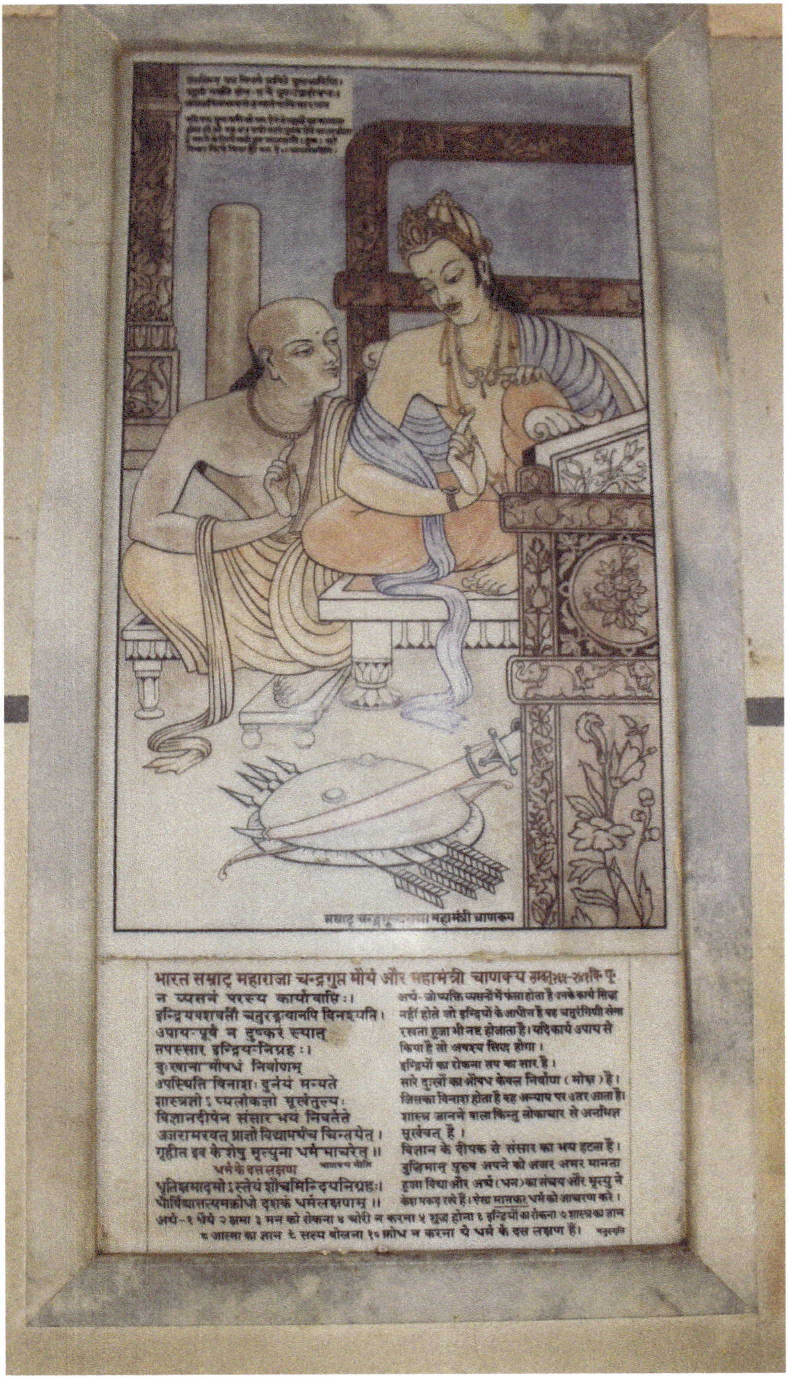

Figure 6.7 Painting of Chandragupta and Cāṇakya in the central hall of the New Vishwanath temple, Varanasi. © Agnieszka Staszczyk.

> You can only control your senses through yoga practices.
>
> Attaining *Nirvāṇa* (*Mokṣa*) is the cure for all sorrows.
>
> If someone chooses a path of cruelty and evil, then they will be destroyed.
>
> Even if you know the *Sastras* by heart but are not aware of how to behave in public in accordance with traditions, then you are nothing but a fool.
>
> Only the light of knowledge can dispel the darkness and fear of this *Sansar*. An intelligent person knows that time is limited and they are not immortal. So, they spend their time in acquiring the light of knowledge and in pursuit of wealth, because they know that death is always clutching their hair. Remember this, and act wisely. This is your *Dharma*.
>
> *Cāṇakya Nīti*.

The paintings at the temples in Mathura and Bhopal are very similar to one another (Figures 6.8 and 6.9). The architectural feature to the left-hand side of the painting, for example, has been transformed into a pillar with a lotus-style band near the top. The sky at the back has been removed entirely and the doorway filled in with floral motifs. The text has been moved to a separate panel at the bottom of painting. The colours in the Mathura painting remain bright, while those in Bhopal are faded.

As regards quotations, the Bhopal painting has the same text as the one in Delhi. The text in the Mathura example is in two parts: at the top, there is the same first sentence as found in Delhi and Bhopal; underneath this, there is a compilation of Inscriptions 4 and 5 from Chandragupta's statue plinth:

> Do not trust anyone more than they deserve. You can only be successful in your work if you are aware of the time you live in, and can understand which way the wind is blowing. If you believe in luck then you will not be successful. A completely honest man cannot achieve anything. You need to start your work playing to your strengths (and avoiding your weaknesses).
>
> *Cāṇakya Nīti*.

The modern city of Patna sits atop the earlier Mauryan capital city of Pataliputra. This being so, one might expect the connection between

Figure 6.8 Painting of Chandragupta and Cāṇakya in the central hall of the Srimadbhagavadgita temple, Mathura. © Agnieszka Staszczyk.

Figure 6.9 Painting of Chandragupta and Cāṇakya in the central hall of the Lakshmi Narayan temple, Bhopal. © Agnieszka Staszczyk.

Chandragupta and this site to be emphasised through numerous artistic depictions and quotations. Instead, the Patna Birla Mandir contains only one painting and it is the plainest of all of them (Figure 6.10). It focuses entirely on the two figures and the only additional detail is the

Figure 6.10 Painting of Chandragupta and Cāṇakya in the upper gallery, main hall of the Deva temple, Patna. © Agnieszka Staszczyk.

architectural feature in front of Chandragupta. The painting includes a single line of text naming the figures; these words are placed above the figures on the left-hand side. They are 'Emperor Chandragupta and Kautilya Chanakya'.

An important point about all of these paintings is that without the labels it is not clear that the figures represent Chandragupta and Chanakya. This is because, as with the statue in the New Delhi temple garden, there are no visual clues to identify them. So unless the viewer reads the labels identifying the figures and knows this period of Mauryan history, the key message visually imparted by the artwork is that a non-specific Indian ruler has a Brahmin advisor. The heavy jewellery worn by the king and the beautifully carved architectural elements surrounding the two men suggests opulence. The laying down of arms indicates that there is currently a peaceful interlude, although the weapons are available at a moment's notice. These additional layers to the visual language convey the idea that by listening to his advisor, a king becomes successful and strong enough to, temporarily at least, put down his weapons, and yet maintain his authority and a wealthy, secure kingdom. These, then, are the main messages imparted to the temple visitors.

Conclusion

The discussion of the Birla Mandirs presented in this chapter is the first detailed investigation of the elements associated with Chandragupta. It is apparent that Chandragupta's life and achievements formed an important component of the wide-ranging messages that the Birlas wished to convey through their temples. Furthermore, the original temple in Delhi was a key source of inspiration for later Birla Mandirs.

The decoration of these temples moves beyond the religious imagery expected in such complexes, and into the sphere of museums, not least through the inclusion of explanatory labels. For the Birla family, the temples were not solely religious constructions, but vehicles for their own ideas about Hinduism, as well as about India's past, present and future. The inclusion of representations of martial rulers who engaged in bloody warfare against foreign invaders makes sense in this context, but it is jarring to see them within a religious complex.

Many people have seen, and indeed continue to see, the multiple representations of Chandragupta at all of these sites. To what extent and how readily the messages are understood, let alone adopted and put into practice, by visitors and by devotees, is less certain. This is because only a small proportion of people stop in front of works of art to look closely at them. An even smaller number take the time to read any text associated with them. These detailed aspects are important to those involved in developing, designing, building and decorating these temples, as well as scholars later researching them. It is no easy matter to interpret and translate them successfully into the displays and fabric of a building or outdoor space so that visitors easily recognise and understand them.

More of this type of interpretation work is needed to ensure that the messages, particularly the more nuanced ones, contained within the Birla Mandirs are shared more clearly with worshippers and visitors alike. At present, for most people, it is the overall impression imparted by the architecture and decoration that is most easily recognised. In Delhi, the overarching idea presented by the statues in the garden is of India's great past, with powerful, martial rulers able to maintain its boundaries against the threat of foreign incursions. In this context, the heroic, Hindu, unifying king Chandragupta is a central part of the storyline.

Notes

1 Lang, Desai and Desai 1997, 131.
2 Lang, Desai and Desai 1997, 132.
3 Kudelska et al. 2021, 29.
4 Kudelska et al. 2021, 31.
5 Chatterjee 1942, 104; Gupta 1991, 194, 196.
6 Chatterjee 1942, xvii.
7 Chatterjee 1942, xviii.
8 Chatterjee 1942, 27.
9 Chatterjee 1942, 27.
10 Gupta 1991, 191–3.
11 In his book *Magadha* Chatterjee mentions the tomb at Sasaram, Bihar, of Sher Shah Suri (1472–1545), governor of Bihar under Mughal Emperor Humayun (1508–56) and later founder of the Sur Empire, which spanned northern India. He also refers to the Taj Mahal and is full of praise for both buildings, describing Sher Shah Suri's tomb as a 'masterpiece' and an 'epic poem in Chunar stone', while the Taj Mahal was a 'unique example of exquisite, feminine grace and beauty' (Chatterjee 1942, 57; pl. XIII).
12 Lang, Desai and Desai 1997, 132.
13 Chatterjee 1942, 83.
14 Chatterjee 1942, 83.
15 Chatterjee 1942, 83.
16 Kudelska et al. 2021, 287, fig. 48.
17 Kudelska et al. 2021, 294. See also 41, 290–303.
18 Kudelska et al. 2021, 39. Naturally, the inspiration for the construction, ethos and decoration of the Birla Mandir came from many sources, as would be expected given G. D. Birla's wide social and business circles. There is a lengthy chapter in Kudelska et al. (2021, 99–144) that discusses the manifold ideas and influences in more detail. The authors trace the spark of inspiration to four key individuals: Swami Vivekananda (1863–1902), a Hindu monk, philosopher and reformer who founded the Ramakrishna Mission; M. M. Malaviya (1861–1946), scholar, social reformer and politician who was closely involved in the Indian independence movement and co-founder of Benares Hindu University; B. G. Tilak (1856–1920), an Indian nationalist and independence activist who was one of the first advocates of *swaraj* ('self-rule'), famously declaring, '*Swaraj* is my birthright and I will have it!'; and Gandhi.
19 A number of early Indian rulers had the epithet 'Vikramāditya', including the Gupta Emperor Chandragupta II (r.376–415). In this case, 'Vikramāditya' refers to a legendary king who was believed to have defeated the Śaka (Scythians) and to have established in *c*.57/58 BC the Vikrama Saṃvat (the Vikrama Era), which is still used in India (Kudelska et al. 2021, 326–7; Singh 2004, 376).
20 Despite repeated efforts, Kudelska and her colleagues were unable to access Birla family archives and documentation relating to the construction of the Birla Mandirs (Kudelska et al. 2021, 12). My attempts were similarly unsuccessful.
21 A 'lakh' is one hundred thousand.
22 My thanks to Tathagata Neogi for translating into English all of the inscriptions from the Birla Mandirs that are included in this chapter.
23 G. D. Birla's involvement in the book series founded by K. M. Munshi, *The History and Culture of the Indian People*, did not start until 1945. So, attempting to connect the expertise necessarily required for the temple decoration and the volumes of this series does not quite fit.
24 Olivelle 2005, 5–7, 20, 22, 24.
25 Olivelle 2005, 65. Fitzgerald (2004, 120–1) and Olivelle (2005, 37–41) suggest that the *Mānava-Dharmásāstra* was written in the post-Mauryan period as a reaction against 'the historical reality and especially the historical memory of two or three centuries later of the Maurya state and especially of the Aśokan political, social, and religious reforms' (Olivelle 2005, 38). This was because Aśoka's reforms displaced Brahmins from their privileged position in the social structure, thereby breaking the relationship between political power and the religious establishment. As Olivelle (2005, 38–9) notes, the 'Sanskrit compound *śramaṇa-brāhmaṇa* used frequently by Aśoka in his inscriptions indicates that his social philosophy envisaged a dual class of religious people worthy of respect and support: the newly formed

ascetic communities and the old Brahmin class'. More than this, Aśoka's prohibition of Brahmanical animal sacrifice 'undercut the very raison d'être of Brahmanical privilege: the Brahmin's ability to perform sacrifices for the well-being of society and for the furtherance of royal power symbolized principally in the royal horse sacrifice' (Olivelle 2005, 39). So while it seems reasonable to include a quotation from the *Mānava-Dharmáśāstra* on this plinth at a high-level reading and understanding of the text, its deeper meaning and the context in which it was written renders it rather less appropriate. However, it is important to reiterate that these are newer understandings of the text that were not available to those working on the Birla Mandir sculptures and inscriptions at the time they were selected.

26 Olivelle 2005, 19.

27 Olivelle 2005, 13.

28 Olivelle 2004, 105.

29 In the Foreword to the *Cāṇakya-Rājanītī-Śāstram* (Sastri 1926, iii), Johan van Manen, Librarian at the Imperial Library, Calcutta, noted, 'Cāṇakya Nīti collections in various forms were very popular in India and have been printed and reprinted so often that of some collections the editions may be counted by the dozen'. Ludwik Sternbach (1963, 40) notes that there is a 'great amount and variety of Cāṇakya MSS', and new ones continue to be discovered. In terms of authorship, some scholars suggest that an original collection of aphorisms came from a treatise on polity attributed to Cāṇakya and that, in subsequent generations, more maxims were added (Sternbach 1963, 6). However, a detailed study of the multitude of manuscripts and editions available has not yet been completed, which makes it difficult to associate any of the aphorisms with Cāṇakya with any certainty.

It has not been feasible to track down and check all of the different versions and compilations of this text, many of which remain untranslated into English or Hindi, within the confines of this project.

30 I checked the *Mānava-Dharmáśāstra* and *Arthaśāstra* as well as some versions of the *Cāṇakya Nīti*, but the three quotations were not found in these texts.

31 Desai 1946, 123, 124.

32 An album at the British Museum, for example, contains eleven *Barahmasa* paintings with this type of text-bearing band (Registration Number 1999,1202,0.1.2–12).

33 This painting is at the British Museum; the Registration Number is 1880,0.2372.

34 My thanks to Tathagata Neogi for providing this translation.

7

Wimbledon to New Delhi: a statue of Chandragupta in the Indian parliament

Enduring symbols

The Mauryan dynasty provided newly independent India with some of its most enduring symbols. The Aśokan lion capital from Sārnāth, for example, was adopted as the symbol of the Republic of India on 26 January 1950, the very day India became a republic. This symbol is found on all government documents, including passports, as well as on stamps and currency. The 24-spoke Aśoka *cakra*, which depicts the *dharmacakra* ('wheel of *dharma*'), on the lion capital base was selected to sit at the heart of the *Tiraṅgā*, the Indian national flag. The *Tiraṅgā* was adopted as the official flag of the Dominion of India on 15 August 1947.

Given the importance of Aśoka's symbols in newly independent India, it is not surprising that Chandragupta, Aśoka's grandfather and the founder of the Mauryan dynasty, was also prominently represented in India's capital city during this period. In the years following independence, the first sculpture installed in the Indian parliament complex was a representation of a youthful Chandragupta. Unexpectedly, this sculpture was created by a little-known author, humanitarian and sculptor based in Wimbledon, named Hilda Seligman (1882–1964).

This chapter explores, for the first time, the circumstances surrounding the creation, installation and meaning of this artwork in the Indian parliament in the wider context of this period. The influence of earlier historical texts, as well as that of the work of British and Indian scholars, on the way in which Seligman chose to represent Chandragupta is also discussed.

Art for a new nation

There is a long-standing tradition of including in the Indian parliament complex works of art that depict important figures in India's struggle for independence, as well as contemporary politicians. This practice began less than a fortnight after Indian independence with the installation of a life-size oil-on-canvas portrait of Mahatma Gandhi in Parliament's Central Hall. This work was painted by the prominent British artist Sir Oswald H. J. Birley (1880–1952). Birley was known for his portraits of the British royal family, the great and the good of British and American society, and wartime leaders such as Winston Churchill and General Eisenhower. Gandhi's portrait was acquired from the artist by Sir Prabhashankar Pattani (1862–1938), Diwan of Bhavnagar and Gandhi's close friend. On his death, Pattani bequeathed the painting to the nation. Almost a decade later, on 28 August 1947, when Indian independence was finally achieved, Gandhi's portrait was unveiled in parliament by Rajendra Prasad (1884–1963), the first President of India.[1] It still holds pride of place in the Central Hall of Parliament House in New Delhi.

The portrait captured Gandhi at a frustrating moment in his life's work of bringing about India's independence. Gandhi was in Britain at the end of 1931 for the Second Round Table Conference to discuss constitutional reform in India. While the conference failed to achieve real political reform in India, Gandhi was enthusiastically received by the British public, including those who might not have been expected to have any sympathy for his cause: photographs record his warm welcome by unemployed mill workers in Darwen, Lancashire, who had lost their jobs as a result of Gandhi's *Swadeshi* movement but still supported his mission.[2]

Birley's decision to paint Gandhi was a personal one rather than the result of a commission and Gandhi did not sit for the portrait. Instead, Birley based the work on several sketches he made of Gandhi when he saw him in person during the 1931 visit. It was a painting that Birley regarded highly enough to submit it along with two others to the Royal Academy Summer Exhibition of 1932. At this point, politics appears to have intervened in the art world. While Gandhi's portrait was initially approved by the Selection Committee, the decision was reversed by the Royal Academy's Council. The President of the Royal Academy, Sir William Llewellyn, claimed 'there was no political motive behind the rejection [and] repudiated any notion that Government influence had anything to do with the Academy's decision'. Given the increasingly fraught political situation at the time, and the move from acceptance to rejection at such a high level, this statement is not wholly convincing.[3]

While Birley took care not to overtly criticise the committee, in a statement he said: 'The reason given for the rejection is that the portrait was the least important of the three I sent in. … That does not agree with my own view, which is, however, neither here nor there, for the selection committee had a perfect right to do what they have done. … I think that it is a very excellent portrait.'[4] It must be noted that the committee did accept Birley's portrait of Lord Irwin (1881–1959; later 1st Earl of Halifax), Viceroy of India (1925–31). After its display at the Summer Exhibition, Irwin's portrait was sent to India and hung in the newly constructed Viceroy's House, New Delhi.[5] Irwin was the first Viceroy to occupy this building on its completion, so it was fitting that his portrait should be displayed here in his official home at this time.

The presence of Birley's portrait of Irwin in Rashtrapati Bhavan and his portrait of Gandhi in the Central Hall of the Indian parliament tell two sides of a moment in the tumultuous history of and changing political relationship between Britain and India. As noted above, Irwin's portrait was accepted and displayed at the Summer Exhibition and went on to be installed in the Viceroy's House. However, the building has since been renamed Rashtrapati Bhavan and is now the home of the President of India, not the British Crown's Viceroy. Irwin's portrait does not feature in the online catalogue of the Rashtrapati Bhavan Museum, whereas the portrait of his wife is included. Indeed, it is not even clear where Irwin's portrait currently hangs.[6]

In contrast, and in another of the monumental buildings designed by Herbert Baker and Edwin Lutyens in New Delhi, Gandhi's portrait represents the flip side of this history: the success of decades of agitation for Indian self-rule and ongoing recognition of this figure's contribution to Indian history. Gandhi's portrait was rejected by the establishment in London only to be acquired by one of his closest friends and supporters. Sir Prabhashankar purchased the painting with the aim of donating it to the nation after independence from colonial rule. The portrait still hangs where it was originally placed in the Central Hall at the heart of the Indian parliament building where the Indian Constitution was framed. In addition, Gandhi retains his profound importance to the people of India and freedom fighters the world over. The difference in meaning, past and present, between Birley's portraits of Irwin and Gandhi could not be greater.

This example shows just how significant the choice of artwork for inclusion within such a context during the mid-twentieth century is. It serves, therefore, to highlight the importance of Chandragupta's representation in the parliament complex as well. Interestingly, Gandhi's visit to London in 1931 provides a link to the artist responsible for creating and donating the first sculpture to be installed in the Indian parliament complex.

Hilda Seligman

Hilda Seligman was an author, humanitarian and sculptor who lived in Lincoln House, Wimbledon. It was here that she entertained Gandhi and provided a temporary home for Haile Selassie, Emperor of Ethiopia (r. 1930–74) and his family, during his exile.[7] Seligman had previously visited India and developed an abiding interest in India's ancient past. In 1943, while the Second World War raged, she set up the Skippo Fund in London using royalties from the sale of her children's book *Skippo of Nonesuch* (1943), about an adventurous goat named Skippo. The Fund, to which others in Britain, India and New Zealand contributed, financed Ashoka-Akbar mobile health vans to provide medical care for those living in isolated villages in India and, after Partition, in Pakistan as well. These vans were maintained and operated by the Village Mobile Health Van Committee of the All-India Women's Conference (initially known as the 'Skippo Committee').

In the Skippo Fund leaflet, Seligman explained that she named the vans after Aśoka and Akbar because they recalled 'two golden ages in the long history of India' and that it was 'in India that the first hospitals ever known were built, during Aśoka's reign ... for "the welfare of man and beast"'. Seligman had hoped to provide vans for veterinary work in order to 'carry out Aśoka's ideals to the full' but this aim was not realised.[8]

The epigraph in Seligman's book *When Peacocks Called* (1940) suggests a deeper reason for naming the vans after both the Mauryan Emperor Aśoka and the Mughal Emperor Akbar. It reads:

> The story of the Peacock Kings who, in the third and fourth centuries B.C., built an empire at the foot of the Himālayas and, discarding armed force, maintained and developed it by moral force alone.

Here, 'the Peacock Kings' refers to the Mauryan rulers. The reference to 'discarding armed force' and the maintenance of an empire by 'moral force alone' is specifically associated with Aśoka, the third Mauryan emperor. After seeing the results of the bloody campaign that he waged against the Kaliṇga in eastern India (modern-day Odisha), Aśoka explains in Rock Edict 13 that he chose to reject violence and embrace Buddhism.

When Peacocks Called was published in 1940, the year that followed the outbreak of the Second World War and which saw the evacuation of Dunkirk, the Battle of Britain and the start of the Blitz. In this context, the words with their longing for 'discarding armed force' and the maintenance of an empire by 'moral force alone', are especially resonant.[9] Given the establishment of the Skippo Fund at the height of all-out war, it is easy to see how Seligman would have been inspired by Aśoka's renunciation of warfare in favour of peace and named her vans accordingly. Similarly, as religious tensions between Hindus and Muslims ratcheted up on the path to independence during the early to mid-twentieth century, Seligman's selection of Akbar (1542–1605), a ruler who encouraged religious toleration among his subjects, was also fitting.

Seligman's interest in Aśoka and the Mauryan dynasty was not confined to the naming of the health vans. *When Peacocks Called* was published three years before she founded the Skippo Fund. It was a work of historical fiction and, unlike her later books, it was aimed at a general adult audience rather than at children. It was while researching and writing this book that Seligman shaped and refined her ideas about Chandragupta and his grandson Aśoka. They were to prove enduringly influential, not only in the naming of the Skippo Fund vans and the humanitarian aims of this project, but also for Seligman's sculptural depiction of Chandragupta.

Chandragupta as a shepherd boy

In the Author's Note at the beginning of *When Peacocks Called*, Seligman recalls hearing Indian shepherds playing their pipes when she first visited India.[10] Drawing on the trope of an eternal, never-changing India that was so vehemently rejected by V. A. Smith, she continues, 'After a lapse of years I have wandered back to India through records of ancient writers of the third and fourth century B.C. and find the shepherd prince, Chandra Moriya [Chandragupta], playing on just such pipes as I used to hear.'[11] This depiction of Chandragupta as a shepherd boy is a core element of Seligman's story. It is also the basis for her sculptural representation Chandragupta. As such, it warrants closer examination.

Seligman's bibliography reveals that she drew on the work of numerous prominent Indian and British scholars, including D. R. Bhandarkar, P. L. Bhargava, R. C. Dutt, R. Mookerji, V. A. Smith and E. J. Rapson (see Chapters 4 and 5).[12] At the time she was writing, these authors represented the most up-to-date, mainstream scholarship pertaining to Mauryan history. Of this group of people, only Bhargava, Smith and Rapson wrote at any length about Chandragupta's early life. Smith and Rapson mentioned his 'inferior social rank' and 'low-born' status by virtue of his mother's 'lowly origin' or 'caste'.[13] In contrast, Bhargava skirted around the thorny issue of Chandragupta's apparent 'low' birth or caste by mentioning that his family had 'lost all its previous rank' and that he was born 'in humble life' and leaving it at that.[14] None of them made any reference to Chandragupta as a shepherd boy.

Bhargava does mention the *Mahāvaṃsa-ṭīkā* as a source for Chandragupta's early life. This is important: the *Mahāvaṃsa-ṭīkā* is the only ancient source which states that Chandragupta was found and raised by a herdsman when he was a baby. The *Mahāvaṃsa-ṭīkā* is the commentary to the *Mahāvaṃsa*, the Sri Lankan Buddhist 'Great Chronicle' written in Pāli (see Chapter 1). A reading of this text reveals that Seligman's presentation of Chandragupta's birth, the circumstances surrounding his abandonment and discovery, as well as his being raised by a herdsman, closely mirror the core elements in it.

In both versions, for example, Chandragupta's father, the Peacock king, is killed in battle. The queen, who is pregnant with Chandragupta, flees to Pataliputra with members of her family. While the *Mahāvaṃsa-ṭīkā* states that the queen left her son at the door of a cattle pen, Seligman writes that she left him in a disused trough. In both accounts, a bull named Chando was standing guard over the baby when he was found by a herdsman, and the child was named after this animal.[15] The child grows up as a herdsman, although Seligman occasionally uses the words 'shepherd' and 'herdsman' interchangeably.

Information derived from the *Mahāvaṃsa-ṭīkā* is included in the work of J. W. McCrindle, an author Seligman consults, albeit not in the volume of his work that she includes in her bibliography. McCrindle's *Ancient India as Described by Megasthenês and Arrian* (1877), which does not contain information from the *Mahāvaṃsa-ṭīkā*, is listed in her bibliography. His *The Invasion of India by Alexander the Great* (1896), which is not listed in Seligman's bibliography, does include information about Chandragupta's early life, including the reference to him as a young shepherd. However, Seligman does not access the *Mahāvaṃsa-ṭīkā* via McCrindle. While McCrindle draws on the *Mahāvaṃsa-ṭīkā* for a basic summary of Chandragupta's early life, this text does not include some of the details that Seligman includes in her book, for example how Chandragupta came by his name.[16] So we must turn elsewhere.

Seligman includes W. L. Geiger's and M. H. Bode's translation of the *Mahāvaṃsa* (1912) in her bibliography, but this book does not refer to Chandragupta's early life. However, Geiger had included this information in his earlier work *The Dīpavaṃsa and Mahāvaṃsa and Their Historical Development in Ceylon* (1908), which Seligman does not list in her bibliography. Notably, in his 1908 book, Geiger refers the reader to G. Turnour's *Mahāwanso* (1837) for 'the history of the youth of Candagutta'.[17] And, indeed, the information Seligman derives from the *Mahāvaṃsa-ṭīkā* to shape the story of Chandragupta's youth in her own work is found here in Tournour's work. The close similarity between Seligman's youthful Chandragupta and the description found in Turnour suggests this is the source of Seligman's artistic vision – literary and sculptural – of the young Chandragupta.

'Dreaming of the India he was to create'

Unlike Birley, Seligman was not a particularly well-known or celebrated artist either in her lifetime or today. Of her sculptural work, only one of her pieces, titled 'Innocence', is held by a UK art gallery or museum.[18] She is best known for her portrait bust of Haile Selassie. Seligman had the opportunity to sculpt this work from life in 1936 when Selassie stayed with the Seligman family for a time during his exile from Ethiopia. Originally, this bust stood in the garden of Lincoln House, Seligman's family home in Wimbledon. When Lincoln House was demolished in 1957, she donated the work to Cannizaro Park, a public park in Wimbledon. It stood there until June 2020 when it was toppled off its pedestal and destroyed by a group of protestors.[19]

Much of Seligman's known surviving sculptural work features children. It includes 'Innocence', a small bronze of Haile Selassie's daughter, and, of course, the bronze of a youthful Chandragupta.[20] However, beyond this broadly contextual information, little is known about the circumstances surrounding Seligman's production of the Chandragupta figure, such as what inspired its creation or even when it was made. Correspondence with Seligman's grandson, Lincoln, a prominent British artist well known for his large-scale sculptures and paintings, has proved revealing.[21]

During his early childhood, Lincoln Seligman (b.1950) lived in a cottage in the extensive grounds of his grandparents' home in Wimbledon. During these years, he recalls seeing a version of the sculpture of Chandragupta. It is not clear if this was the original sculpture in bronze or another iteration of it. Given that it was installed outside in the gardens, it is unlikely to have been a plaster sculpture and more likely of a durable material such as stone or bronze, materials with which Seligman worked. Lincoln and his family moved away from the cottage when he was four years old. This means that Seligman had already expressed her literary vision of Chandragupta in sculptural form by *c.*1954. I suggest that this sculpture may have been created around the time she was writing, or had published, *When Peacocks Called*, that is, in the late 1930s or early 1940s, when this particular conception of Chandragupta was prominent in her mind. The sculpture was moved away from Lincoln House between 1954 and 1957, when the house was demolished.

Just before this time, in 1953, the 'Report of the Planning Sub-Committee on a scheme of decorating the Parliament House, New Delhi' was published. The Report was the brainchild of G. V. Mavalankar (1888–1956), Speaker of the Provisional Parliament (1949–52) and, later, after the first general elections in independent India, he was elected Speaker of the first Lok Sabha (1952–6). In 1950, Mavalankar visited different parliament buildings in Europe and was struck by the way in which the history of these countries was represented in their parliaments. He recognised that this particular aesthetic served to create an inspirational atmosphere for MPs and others to work in and for the general public, including children, to visit. Mavalankar noted that these buildings were decorated 'with a view to create a national historical atmosphere. As one gets into the building, one sees on canvas or in statuary, the great heroes who had fought the battle of independence, the great events in their national history. ... For obvious reasons, our Parliament House is devoid of all these.'[22]

In his farewell address to parliament on 5 March 1952, Mavalankar expanded on his reasons for instigating this work. It is worth quoting in full because it is here that we find the reasons for the later presence of Chandragupta's statue in the Indian parliament complex.

> The building that we occupy is undoubtedly a stately and magnificent building: but unfortunately does not touch our hearts, as the surroundings are entirely Western and do not reflect our indigenous philosophy of life and action, in which we are soaked through centuries and which alone can inspire us to the further effort, to build up the future of our State to its legitimate heights, on the basis of our ancient culture. The House does not bring to our eyes a vivid picture of our ancient, medieval and recent life, history and philosophy nor does it give us, in the form of pictures, paintings

> or statues, the inspiration that we can derive through art, of our ancient national life and our struggle for independence during the last hundred years or more. I have therefore set up a Committee, who will advise and prepare plans of decorations for the Parliament House, which, when executed, will go a great way to create a very inspiring atmosphere. However, I know the greatest difficulty in our way will be the finances. I am in no hurry to achieve this all at once. All that I am anxious for is that an overall plan be made which may be executed by bits from year to year by our successors.[23]

In 1951, following his trip to Europe, Mavalankar set up the Planning Committee mentioned in his speech to initiate discussions on the decoration of Parliament House. The Committee comprised five members and two associate members. The members included those with extensive museum and archaeological experience, such as N. P. Chakravarti, Archaeological Adviser to the Government of India, and V. S. Agrawala, Superintendent, Central Asian Antiquities Museum. The academic S. N. Sen, Vice-Chancellor of Delhi University, was also brought in.[24] Interestingly, Indira Gandhi, future Prime Minister of India and daughter of Jawaharlal Nehru, was also a member of this panel.[25] The Committee met five times at the end of 1952 and their suggestions about the decoration of Parliament House fed into the 1953 Report.

Through the Report, the Committee expressed the wish that 'carefully selected subjects of mural and plastic art, executed by the well known artists and sculptors of India, would … help them [visitors to parliament] to purify their thought, advance their knowledge of the glorious past of their country and mould their life to a loftier reality according to the best traditions of India.'[26] The Report focused on developing and bringing to fruition ideas for a large mural comprising carefully selected themes that depicted what the Committee believed to be the 'outstanding episodes in the nation's history'.[27]

Fifty-nine panels were eventually commissioned and fifty-four of them were completed and displayed in the outer corridor of the ground floor of Parliament House. The mural begins with panels depicting Indus Valley objects and symbols, including a range of stamp seals, bronze 'dancing girl' and 'priest king' figures, and the as yet undeciphered Indus script.[28] Further panels include scenes from the epic Sanskrit poems the *Rāmāyaṇa* and the *Mahābhārata*, followed by representations of religious figures, rulers, philosophers, trading relations between India and the world, and numerous other moments in time up to and including Indian independence.[29]

Chandragupta Maurya was included in the Report's list of proposed subjects for this mural, but was not represented in the final mural panels.[30] Instead, Cāṇakya (also known as 'Kauṭilya') is depicted alongside Pāṇini in Panel 12. This mural was painted by Pratap Chandra Sen under the supervision of Barada Ukil. Cāṇakya is traditionally believed to have been Chandragupta's advisor and the author of the *Arthaśāstra*, a treatise on statecraft, while Pāṇini was a Sanskrit grammarian and philologist. Alexander the Great is shown alongside Porus in Panel 13, while Chandragupta's grandson Aśoka is included in Panel 14.[31] In this context, Chandragupta's omission is curious, especially given his prominent profile in histories of ancient India published in the first half of the twentieth century by influential Indian historians, many of whom had political interests and connections.

However, Chandragupta was represented in a different medium. The entrance to the outer corridor where the mural is installed is located at Gate Five of the parliament complex. From here, the visitor begins their journey of circumnavigating select moments and personalities in the history of India. It is also here, next to Gate Five, that Chandragupta's statue stands.

The Planning Committee mentioned statues only briefly in their Report. They 'considered the important question of erecting statues of national leaders to fill up the 50 or more niches on the ground and first floors of the Parliament House'. According to them, 'some space should be left for the future and for the present the ground floor should be filled up. ... Some of the leaders could also be shown in oil paintings in the Central Hall and elsewhere in the Parliament House.'[32] At this point in the Report, the Committee returned to the murals and nothing more is said about statues or portraits.

And yet statues and portraits of key figures in India's history formed an important component of the parliament's decoration. As we have seen, Birley's portrait of Gandhi was installed in 1947, while the statue of Chandragupta was the first to be installed in the complex. So while Chandragupta is not among the great and the good selectively represented in the mural, he is prominently positioned where visitors will see him before they view the painted scenes (Figure 7.1).

In this location and context, the wording carved into the red sandstone plinth that the figure rests on takes on an added importance. The words, inscribed in Hindi written in Devanāgarī script (above) and English (below), read:

> Shepherd boy Chandragupta Maurya dreaming of the India he was to create

Figure 7.1 Bronze statue of Chandragupta by Hilda Seligman. Source: Parliament of India. Shared under a Creative Commons Attribution-ShareAlike 4.0 International licence (CC BY-SA 4.0), Wikimedia Commons, bit.ly/3SAl6DI.

These words fulfil a dual purpose. Firstly, they interpret the sculpture for visitors. There are no surviving images of Chandragupta from antiquity for artists to draw on for inspiration and Seligman's sculpture is among the earliest contemporary sculptures of Chandragupta known to have been produced. Taken together, these factors mean that a visual language, with all its symbols, postures, colours and other attributes, had not been established for representations of this figure. Secondly, the words express the idea that Chandragupta was instrumental in laying the foundations not merely of his empire but of India itself. Given the location of the plinth, the message has much deeper resonance and meaning: Chandragupta's dream of India was ultimately fulfilled in modernity by the establishment of the Republic of India in 1950 and its supreme legislative body, the Parliament of India. Thus, the statue is perfectly placed at the entrance to the parliament which housed the newly elected Indian government and, of course, the mural which depicts key moments and objects in the history of India.

It is not possible to state conclusively that Seligman wrote these words. However, they certainly accord with her romantic ideal of Chandragupta and bear a close resemblance to her style of writing. The underlying sentiment is present in the Author's Note at the beginning of *When Peacocks Called*.[33] Here, Seligman talks about hearing Indian shepherds playing their pipes when she visited India. She writes, 'After a lapse of years I have wandered back to India through records of ancient writers of the third and fourth century B.C. and find the shepherd prince, Chandra Moriya [Chandragupta], playing on just such pipes as I used to hear. These records tell of the ancestors of the Bhotiyas I saw, who ... witnessed the meeting of Chandra Moriya and the magician Kautilya, a coincidence which led to the founding of the first great empire of Ind.'[34]

From Wimbledon to New Delhi

The circumstances leading to the transfer of the statue from Wimbledon to New Delhi are shrouded in mystery. As mentioned above, the figure was in Seligman's garden during the early 1950s and removed by 1957 when the house was demolished and the family relocated. Archives in the UK, including Seligman's papers held at the Women's Library, Wimbledon Museum and the Merton Heritage Service, do not hold any information about the movement of this sculpture from Lincoln House.[35] Seligman's family are also unsure about the events that surrounded the sculpture's movement. Unless papers come to light in India, it is unlikely that the mystery will be satisfactorily resolved or the date of its installation by Gate Five known. However, something that may shed some light on the turn of events is information about Seligman's contacts among prominent figures in Indian society and politics, as well as her humanitarian work in India.

Seligman's network of connections reads like a Who's Who of mid-century Indian literary, social and political giants. She was not a passive collector of these contacts but actively used them to further her aims. None other than Rabindranath Tagore (1861–1941), author, artist and winner of the Nobel Prize for Literature (1913), penned the Foreword to Seligman's book *When Peacocks Called*. Seligman's introduction to Tagore came via Sarvepalli Radhakrishnan (1888–1975), Indian philosopher and the second President of India (1962–7). Seligman was in contact with Radhakrishnan during his tenure at Oxford University as Spalding Chair of Eastern Religion and Ethics (1936–52). Radhakrishnan's letter to Tagore reveals that the impetus for the request came from Seligman: 'she believes – and I agree with her – that a few lines from you by way of a foreword will give it the necessary push.'[36]

For the advancement of her humanitarian work through the Skippo Fund Seligman drew upon and further developed her extensive network among the elite of British and Indian society. She secured Lady Runganadhan, wife of the High Commissioner of India, as President of the Skippo Fund, along with a number of other prominent patrons. This circle of supporters helped her to secure donations and gifts that enabled the project to thrive, while further expanding her network. Illustrious patrons of the Fund included: the Earl of Clarendon (Lord Chamberlain of the Household, previously Governor-General of South Africa); the Earl of Halifax (Foreign Secretary, previously the Lord Irwin, Viceroy of India) and the Countess of Halifax; Diwan Bahadur Sir Samuel Runganadhan (High Commissioner for India); Maj.-Gen. Sir Frederick Sykes (formerly Governor of Bombay); and Mr Shamaldhari Lall (Deputy High Commissioner for India) and Mrs Lall. This is not to say that Seligman was solely reliant on the great and the good for fund-raising towards and the building of this project: royalties from the sale of her children's book, *Skippo of Nonesuch*, supported the vans and Seligman went on to raise additional money by holding a children's fete in her garden in 1948.[37]

Through the Skippo Fund, Seligman became closely associated with the All India Women's Conference (AIWC) and, through this organisation, with a number of prominent Indian women. The AIWC was founded in Poona (Pune) in 1929 by Margaret Cousins (1878–1954), the Irish-born suffragette and social reformer. Her aim was to promote and advance women's and children's education and social welfare. It remains active and is one of the oldest women's organisations in India. The aspirations of this organisation and those of Seligman coincided. The result was that, in 1946, Seligman presented the first Ashoka-Akbar Mobile Health Van to the Bombay branch of the AIWC and work began to provide medical assistance to those living in rural areas. On 15 May Mr B. G. Kher (1888–1957), Prime Minister of Bombay, presided over a public reception that inaugurated the van. The success of and support for this venture were such that by 1953 there were six vans in operation in different parts of the country.[38]

As the annual reports show, the project quickly became an important component of AIWC work and, in December 1946, Seligman attended the nineteenth session of this organisation in Akola, Berar. She was thanked for her endeavours by the AIWC President, Lady Rama Rau (1893–1987), founder and president of the Family Planning Association of India, who emphasised 'that this humanitarian piece of work had been undertaken by Mrs Seligman and all her helpers for a distant country at a time when their own homes and cities were being bombed in the course of a total war.' Lady Rama Rau conveyed 'to Mrs Seligman and the other organisers and donors of the Skippo Fund the deep appreciation and thanks of the Women's Conference for their substantial gesture of good will which, she was sure, would have far-reaching beneficial results.'[39]

When Lady Rama Rau invited her to speak at the conference, Seligman explained that she had originally been in touch with Kamaladevi Chattopadhyay (1903–88), independence activist and social reformer, when she first had the idea of mobile health vans for India. Chattopadhyay supported this venture, writing to Seligman that the AIWC would be prepared to maintain and operate such a van. With this backing in place, Seligman set about fund-raising.

Other friends and acquaintances acquired during her trip to India included the Princess Dürrüsehvar of Berar (1914–2006), whom she met at the AIWC and who invited her to stay in Hyderabad upon the conclusion of the conference. Seligman and the Princess shared a number of interests, including the provision of healthcare to the wider population. While Seligman was the driving force behind the Skippo Fund in the 1940s, in later life Princess Dürrüsehvar established a children's and general hospital at Purani Haveli. Their friendship was to last many years.[40]

Following her interlude in Hyderabad, Seligman returned to New Delhi where she resided with Mr and Mrs Lall. During this eventful period in Indian history, Seligman also spent time with Lady Wavell, penultimate

Vicereine of India, at the Viceregal Lodge.[41] A note sent by Lady Wavell to Seligman reveals that she was aware of Seligman's work with the Skippo vans. This note was reproduced on Skippo Fund letterheaded paper alongside numerous other supportive messages that Seligman had received from people such as Kulsum Sayani, Honorary Secretary of the AIWC. Sayani mentioned that an anonymous donor had given Rs12,000 to Lady Rama Rau to run the van for a year. A note from the Vice Chancellor of Patna University revealed that all of these messages were sent in response to letters Seligman herself had posted to prominent people across India who might be interested and supportive of her project; indeed, these responses and the wider support she garnered reveal that the people were encouraging and helpful.[42]

Conclusion

Clearly, Seligman had the useful ability to make and keep a wide circle of influential friends and acquaintances and leverage these relationships for the benefit of her humanitarian work. Naturally, this focused on the Ashoka-Akbar mobile health vans, but it extended to her literary output, especially *When Peacocks Called*. This was no straightforward historical novel: Seligman believed it was her duty to share as widely as possible an alternative way of life as demonstrated by Aśoka. In her Author's Note, she wrote, 'never was it more necessary that the world should learn the lesson Asoka taught than it is today. … Hand in hand the races of Britain and Hindustan, with their complementary characteristics, will once again prove the strength, wisdom, and workableness of the law of non-violence.'[43] It was for this reason that, aspiring towards peace and unity, she reached out, via Radhakrishnan, to Tagore. The Foreword reveals that Tagore understood and supported the contemporary relevance of the message Seligman was trying to disseminate through her book. He wrote about the 'perennially modern significance' of ancient India and the 'great humanism which came with King Asoka', particularly in 'an age of fratricide, aided by intellectual dehumanization in large areas of the world'.[44]

Given the nature of Seligman's long-standing benevolent involvement with India and her contact and support for prominent Indian figures working towards Indian independence, the presence of the figure of Chandragupta in the Indian parliament becomes less surprising. With this wider understanding of her life and achievements, the statue becomes much more than a depiction of a historical figure. Her representation of

Chandragupta as a shepherd boy also encapsulates her interest in helping those living in rural parts of India. Thus it can be seen as symbolic of her humanitarian work.

It may well transpire that the impetus for the installation of her sculpture in this location came from Seligman herself, and that she harnessed her extensive network to make this vision a reality. Seligman's grandson Lincoln suggested that she probably donated the bronze because she 'seldom, if ever, took money for her work'.[45] Given parliament's financial constraints at the outset of independence, including in relation to the decoration of the building it inhabited, a donation rather than an expensive purchase would have been welcome.

Wisdom and valour: depicting Chandragupta on India's stamps

In 2001, India Post released 58 commemorative postage stamps. As in preceding years, the people and themes represented on these stamps were wide-ranging. They included Maharaja Ranjit Singh, Yuri Gagarin, Raj Kapoor, temple architecture and Cancer Awareness Day. Most were priced at the standard ₹4. One of these, released on 21 July, depicted Chandragupta; three million of this issue were printed (Figure 7.2). The text released with the stamp reads, 'Owing to his remarkable military successes and insight into state craft, Chandragupta Maurya stands out as one among the most colourful personalities of Indian history. The Department of Posts is proud to issue a postage stamp on this great monarch of ancient India.'[46]

The Chandragupta stamp was designed by one of India's most prominent and prolific stamp artists, Sankha Samanta. The golden stamp shows Chandragupta seated on a lion throne with his right hand resting on a sword hilt and his left hand raised in Abhayamudrā. This mudrā or 'gesture' represents protection and the dispelling of fear in Hindu, Jain and Buddhist iconography. He wears jewellery and traditional unstitched Indian clothing, and has a halo around his head. Around him are four symbols that will be familiar to numismatists, because they are from silver punch-marked coins traditionally, although not accurately, ascribed to the Mauryan period.[47]

This depiction of Chandragupta differs in many respects from the two sculptures installed in New Delhi during the mid-twentieth century. When I asked Samanta what impression of Chandragupta he was trying to convey through his work, he explained that because this ruler came

Figure 7.2 Postage stamp illustrating Chandragupta, designed by Sankha Samanta. © Government of India, licensed under the Government Open Data License – India (GODL). Photograph: Ali Mackie.

from a humble background, he wanted to focus on Chandragupta's 'wisdom and valour' in the design. For this reason, Samanta kept the design simple and included the 'gesture of his hand and his sword'.[48]

In relation to his broader inspiration for the stamp, the artist noted that it was a challenging assignment because he couldn't find any images of Chandragupta from the Mauryan era, only the silver punch-marked coins. So he incorporated the most common punch-mark symbols he found into the stamp design and these – not Chandragupta – formed the basis of the design. Indeed, as Samanta explained, the 'illustration of Chandragupta Maurya had to be from imagination and blend well with the punch mark symbols'. In this artistic context, he thought 'a minimalist line art in silhouette would be best'. Aśoka and his lion capital inspired the throne that Chandragupta sits on, while the jewellery was drawn from 'Ajanta cave paintings and other sculptures of that period'. Lastly, Samanta painted the background in such a way that it would resemble old parchment with a 'glowing look to express time and also power'.

It was fascinating to gain an insight into how Samanta approached this commission, because there are no ancient representations of Chandragupta upon which he could draw. Instead, he pulled together a variety of images and motifs to create a composite idea of this ruler. In this way, he emulates the anonymous artist who created the sculpture in the Lakshmi Narayan temple in Delhi, and Seligman, the sculptor of the bronze in the Indian parliament complex. However, most people will not have the opportunity to visit these buildings in Delhi and so to see the two sculptures of Chandragupta contained in them. They are more likely to see depictions of Chandragupta through media such as the ACK comics (see Chapter 9), television series, or these stamps. Together, these three formats serve to shape an impression of Chandragupta in popular culture. So Chandragupta is presented to, and preserved in, the Indian national consciousness through these widespread forms of artistic representation.

Notes

1 There remains some confusion about the impulse behind the creation of this portrait and even about how it came to be hung in the Indian Parliament. For example, the catalogue that accompanied a recent exhibition of Birley's work noted that Sir Prabhashankar commissioned this portrait. Its author went on to write that Sir Prabhashankar intended to present the painting to Gandhi himself but died before he was able to do so (Black 2017, 31). However, Sir Prabhashankar's son, Mr A. P. Pattani, gave a different account when he addressed parliament during the presentation and unveiling of the portrait. Pattani noted that Birley had painted the portrait for himself and he had agreed to sell it to Sir Prabhashankar. Once this painting arrived in India, Sir Prabhashankar stored it in its original packaging at his home. It was only after the Government of India Act of 1935 was passed that he told his son that he intended to present it to the nation when the new Government of India was inaugurated. This did not come to pass during his lifetime and so it fell to his son to ensure that his wishes were enacted (Constituent Assembly Debates: Official Report, vol. V, 14.8.1947–30.8.1947, 285–6: https://eparlib.nic.in/bitstream/123456789/762982/1/cad_28-08-1947.pdf#search=null%201947 (accessed 31 October 2022).

2 Gandhi's visit to Darwen forms part of the new displays in the Manchester Museum South Asia Gallery in partnership with the British Museum (opened 2023). He had been invited to Darwen by the Davies family, who owned the Greenfield Mill there. The family wanted Gandhi to see the hardship caused to the unemployed mill workers in Darwen by his *Swadeshi* movement and its boycott of Manchester-made textiles. Because of the impact on local families, it had been assumed that Gandhi's visit would cause trouble. However, he received a warm and rapturous welcome from the local population.

3 Black 2017, 14.

4 Charles A. Selden, 'Academy rejects Gandhi's portrait; British royal institution holds Birley's painting undesirable for exhibit. …'. *New York Times*, 21 April 1932: https://www.nytimes.com/1932/04/21/archives/academy-rejects-gandhis-portrait-british-royal-institution-holds.html (accessed 31 October 2022); 'Refuse to hang Gandhi portrait', *Winnipeg Tribune*, 21 May 1932: https://www.newspapers.com/clip/44497452/oswald-h-birley-portrait-of-gandhi/ (accessed 31 October 2022).

5 Black 2017, 96.

6 Rashtrapati Bhavan E-Art Catalogue: https://presidentofindia.nic.in/eartcategorydetail.htm?4&type=cat (accessed 31 October 2022).

7 Obituary of Hilda Seligman's son, Adrian Seligman (1909–2003) in the *Telegraph*: https://www.telegraph.co.uk/news/obituaries/1439346/Adrian-Seligman.html (accessed 29 November 2022.

8 Skippo Fund leaflet among the Hilda Seligman papers held at the Women's Library Archive, LSE. Ref. GB 106 7HSE.

9 Tragically, Hilda's son Oliver was killed in Normandy in 1944 aged just 28 and she made the trip to France to identify his body (correspondence with Dominic Seligman, October 2022). This horrific experience must surely have contributed to her dedication to continue the work of the Skippo health vans and enduring belief that war must be avoided.

10 Hilda was sent to India by her parents to 'distract her from the romantic overtures' of Richard Seligman (correspondence with Lincoln Seligman, February 2018). This attempt at separation failed and they were married in 1906. Their marriage lasted for almost sixty years until Hilda's death in 1964.

11 Seligman 1940, 13.

12 Seligman 1940, 295–6.

13 Smith 1908, 115; Rapson 1922, 223.

14 P. L. Bhargava 1935, 30–1.

15 Turnour 1837, xxxix–xl.

16 McCrindle 1896, 408.

17 Geiger 1908, 39.

18 This small plaster sculpture is held by Huddersfield Art Gallery. It measures H 19 cm × W 22 cm × D 16cm; the registration number is KLMUS 1983.727. Grant Scanlan, Huddersfield Museums Manager, confirmed that their files do not contain any information about this sculpture (email dated 17 June 2021).

19 Matthews 2018, 232. For more details about the destruction of the sculpture see BBC News, 'Haile Selassie: Statue of former Ethiopian leader destroyed in London park', 2 July 2020: https://www.bbc.co.uk/news/uk-53259409 (accessed 1 November 2022).

20 The bronze portrait sculpture of Haile Selassie's daughter is in Lincoln Seligman's collection (L. Seligman, pers. comm., February 2018). Hilda Seligman sculpted this piece when Selassie and his family stayed with her briefly.

21 This fortuitous contact came about after a chance conversation with my colleague Isabel Seligman, Monument Trust Curator of Modern and Contemporary Drawing at the British Museum, who sits in the office next to mine. Because of her surname, I asked if she was related to Hilda Seligman. It transpired that Hilda was Isabel's great-grandmother and Isabel kindly put me in touch with her father, Lincoln, and her uncle, Dominic, who generously shared their knowledge about their grandmother and her work with me.

22 'Report of the Planning Sub-Committee on a Scheme of Decorating the Parliament House, New Delhi', 1953, 1–2. My thanks to Shirin Rai for generously sharing this document with me.

23 Fifth Session of Parliament of India, vol. I (1952), 2044–2045.

24 Rai 2014, 903.

25 Planning Sub-Committee Report 1953, 4.

26 Planning Sub-Committee Report 1953, 3.

27 Planning Sub-Committee Report 1953, 1.

28 The 'dancing girl' and 'priest king' statuettes were excavated at the Indus Valley site of Mohenjo-Daro, previously in British India and now in Pakistan. After Partition, the 'dancing girl' was allocated to India and is now held at the National Museum, New Delhi. The 'priest king' also remained in New Delhi until the Simla Agreement between India and Pakistan in 1972, when it was transferred to Pakistan; it is now in the National Museum, Karachi. So the meaning of these objects as depicted in a mural in the Indian parliament building has changed since it was painted: now, it relates not only to the history of India, but also to the post-colonial, post-Partition relationship between India and Pakistan.

29 For detailed discussion of the background to and meaning of these murals in their wider political context, see: Rai 2014; Johnson and Rai 2016.

30 The full list of the mural paintings can be found on the Rajya Sabha website: https://rajyasabha.nic.in/Gallery/GalleryView?catid=42&year=Mural%20Paintings%20at%20Parliament%20House (accessed 1 November 2022).

31 Jatin Das's vast mural painting, *The Journey of India: Mohenjo-Daro to Mahatma Gandhi*, was commissioned by the Parliament Secretariat in 1998 to celebrate the fiftieth anniversary of India's independence. Unveiled by the Prime Minister Atal Bihari Vajpayee in 2001, it, too,

includes a representation of Aśoka but not Chandragupta. A panoramic video of this mural can be viewed online at https://www.jatindas.com/copy-of-murals-sculptures-v2?pgid=kdlsgmqh-4ae49a52-d263-4244-b4f3-d57e2688dc8e (accessed 22 November 2022).

32 Planning Sub-Committee Report 1953, 7–8.
33 Seligman 1940, 13–14.
34 Seligman 1940, 13.
35 My thanks to Pamela Greenwood at Wimbledon Museum and Sarah Gould at the Merton Heritage Service for their help. Unfortunately, the Covid-19-related travel restrictions from 2020 onwards meant that I was not able to travel to New Delhi to consult archives there.
36 Bagchi 1990, 50.
37 *The News: Morden, Malden, Wimbledon, Merton*, 24 September 1948; Hilda Seligman papers held at the Women's Library Archive, LSE, ref. GB 106 7HSE.
38 Jhabwala 1953, 51–4.
39 Rama Rau 1946, 25.
40 Letter to Mrs Paddon dated 28 January 1947; Hilda Seligman papers held at the Women's Library Archive LSE, ref. GB 106 7HSE. Seligman's grandson Dominic recalled a visit by the Princess of Berar to see some pearls at Sotheby's, where he was working at the time. In an email dated February 2018, he noted, 'When she [Princess of Berar] learnt that Hilda Seligman was my grandmother, she was thrilled as they had been inseparable childhood friends.'
41 Letter to Mrs Paddon dated 28 January 1947; Hilda Seligman papers held at the Women's Library Archive LSE, ref. GB 106 7HSE.
42 Printed notes (unnumbered) among the Hilda Seligman papers held at the Women's Library Archive LSE. Ref. GB 106 7HSE.
43 Seligman 1940, xx–xi.
44 Seligman 1940, vii.
45 L. Seligman, pers. comm., February 2018.
46 iStampGallery, 'Chandragupta Maurya', 24 October 2015: https://www.istampgallery.com/chandragupta-maurya/ (accessed 1 November 2022).
47 Bhandare 2012.
48 Sankha Samanta, email correspondence, January 2020.

8
Chandragupta on stage and screen

A story ripe for creative interpretation

Filled with dramatic tension, heroic action and endless scope for adaptation, Chandragupta's story has long provided the creative arts with inspiration. The earliest known play to feature Chandragupta Maurya is *Mudrārākṣasa* (literally 'Rākṣasa's signet ring' and more commonly known as 'Rākṣasa's ring'). This *nāṭaka* (heroic drama) was written in Sanskrit by Viśākhadatta during the reign of Gupta Emperor Chandragupta II (*r.*376–415).[1] While Chandragupta features in the play, he is not the main character. Rather, he is presented as a fun-loving ruler who has handed the reins of power to Cāṇakya, to whom he is subservient. Greeks are referred to only along with other foreign invaders, such as the Scythians and the Huns. Chandragupta's battle with Seleucus and their treaty, including the marriage alliance, are not mentioned at all. Given that Chandragupta is a supporting character in the play, the absence of this particular storyline is not surprising.

In *Rākṣasa's Ring*, the drama focuses on the tension between Cāṇakya/Kauṭilya (the names are used interchangeably) and Rākṣasa, the exiled Chief Minister of the deposed Nanda king. The main storyline involves Cāṇakya manoeuvring to bring Rākṣasa over to Chandragupta's side so that Rākṣasa can become the new king's Chief Minister and Cāṇakya can retire from politics. The implication is that Chandragupta is unable to maintain his rule without an able minister by his side. Interestingly, this image of Chandragupta with Cāṇakya advising him has endured over the millennia and is reflected in the paintings found in the Birla Mandirs (see Chapter 6) as well as in plays written during the twentieth century.

As Upinder Singh notes, the 'noble idea of kingship takes a back seat' in *Rākṣasa's Ring*. Instead, the emphasis is on realpolitik to such an extent that the play resembles an 'ancient Indian version of the *House of Cards*' with its 'relentless political strategy and counter-strategy'.[2] Viśākhadatta's own experience is likely to have been a significant factor in his presenting such a politics-heavy storyline in which the king himself is a peripheral character. His father's and grandfather's titles, as given in the play, indicate that they belonged to a princely family who may have ruled as subordinates of the Gupta kings.[3] He would therefore have had ample opportunity to observe and even participate in courtly intrigue. Similarly, the drama's sophisticated courtly audience would have understood the machinations at play.[4] The play is thus very much of its time, as was the more modern play *Chandragupta* by the noted Bengali playwright Dwijendralal Ray (also known as Dvijendralal Ray/Roy and D. L. Ray, 1863–1913), published in 1911, two years before his death.[5] After a gap of some fifteen hundred years, Ray's play was the first to present this ancient story to a modern audience in twentieth-century Bengal.

Enter stage left: reshaping an old story for a new audience

Abhijit Sen contextualises the emergence of Bengali theatre during the nineteenth century in relation to – and in reaction to – the presence of British theatres in Calcutta that catered to local residents. From the eighteenth century onwards, the British staged productions in English. Wealthy Bengalis set up their own theatres following the European model and many of the first plays they staged were English-language productions of Shakespeare with Indian actors. By the mid-nineteenth century, however, things were changing: Shakespearean plays were translated into Bengali, Sanskrit plays were revived, and stories from Indian epics and myths were staged in European style.[6]

Soon, playwrights and others associated with theatres recognised that this medium was a valuable channel through which they could disseminate their reforming ideas. In 1859, for example, the Metropolitan Theatre staged *Bidhaba Bibaha*, Umesh Chandra Mitra's play which highlighted the problems faced by widows. Three years previously, the Widows' Remarriage Act legalised the remarriage of widows in those parts of India under East India Company authority. By the late nineteenth century, the staging of overtly political plays critical of colonial practices had become a major trend in Bengal Renaissance theatre. The national theatre, for example, was launched in 1872 with *Nildarpan*, a play that recounted the horrors of oppression by European indigo planters.[7]

Historical plays were soon added to the mix. Sen notes that, since it was not prudent to criticise the ruling government directly, 'The historical framing sought to provide a sense of remoteness; yet it was more often than not obvious that they were commentaries upon the unwelcome presence of the colonizer.'[8] During the second half of the nineteenth century, playwrights substituted the British with, for example, Mughals, and contemporary Indians with Rajputs and Mahrattas in plays about invaders of India versus the Indian defenders of India. In this way, Hindu nationalism came to the fore in Bengali theatres.[9] This genre of plays proved popular with the theatre-going public, not least because of the increasingly overt nationalist messages contained in them. Unsurprisingly, the colonial authorities did not welcome these plays with their rebellious narratives. In response, the authorities invoked the Act of Dramatic Performances Control (1876) to prohibit those plays which they considered seditious or libellous, including Kshirode Prasad Vidyavinode's *Pratapaditya* (1903) and Girish Chandra Ghosh's *Chhatrapati Shivaji* (1907).[10]

The early part of the twentieth century saw a continuation of this subject matter in the theatre but with a change in political emphasis. The patriotism and nationalism that infused the work of Bengali playwrights was joined by a desire for communal harmony. The shift was precipitated by the Partition of Bengal in 1905 by Lord Curzon, Viceroy of India, and Andrew Fraser, Governor of Bengal. This territorial reorganisation divided Bengal into West Bengal (with a Hindu majority population) and East Bengal (majority Muslim population).

All of these different ideas and ideals jostled for position with sometimes confused and contradictory results in the historical plays written at this time. In addition, the more religiously conservative elements in society pushed back against scenes and words that they believed cast a slur on revered historical Hindu rulers.[11] This, then, was the milieu in which Ray was writing and the context in which his play *Chandragupta* was first staged.

Chandragupta takes the stage

Ray studied agriculture in England before returning to India and embarking on a career in colonial administration in his native Bengal. Alongside this work, he had a flourishing literary career as a celebrated

Bengali poet, playwright and songwriter. Historical and mythological themes featured prominently in his output. His plays included *Sita* (1904), *Nur Jahan* (1907), *Mewar Patan* ('The fall of Mewar', 1908), *Shahjahan* (1910) and, of course, *Chandragupta* (1911). A deep sense of Indian national feeling and ideas about communal harmony permeated his work, as did his strong beliefs about matters such as the empowerment of Indian women, the reunification of Bengal after its partition in 1905, and concerns about high-caste Hindu social dominance. The situation of the time influenced his writing to such an extent that his works have been described as 'steeped in nationalism and patriotic feelings'.[12]

Like his contemporaries, and indeed Viśākhadatta before him, Ray took artistic liberties with historical details in his plays. He skilfully reshaped narratives, brought in a range of supporting characters to develop subplots, and included songs which proved popular in their own right. The result was that his plays were not only a vehicle for his social and political standpoint but also well received by the general public, with the result that he became one of the best-known playwrights of his age.

Ray was the first modern playwright to successfully resurrect Chandragupta's story for the stage. In his play, Chandragupta is Nanda's half-brother; when exiled, he joins Alexander's army, where Seleucus proceeds to teach him the art of warfare. Eventually, Chandragupta leaves the Greek army and, with Cāṇakya's help, overthrows his half-brother and takes power in Magadha. After Alexander's death, Seleucus takes over his possessions in Asia and proceeds to attack Magadha but is defeated by Chandragupta. Cāṇakya negotiates the peace treaty between the two kings and, as part of the treaty, ensures that Chandragupta marries Seleucus' daughter Helena. The love story between Chandragupta and Helena runs through the play.

The relentless power struggle between the king Chandragupta and the philosopher Cāṇakya is an important aspect of the play. The tension is only resolved when Cāṇakya relinquishes his authority on discovering his long-lost daughter.[13] The storyline concerning his wife and child is one of numerous subplots of the play. Another explores the futile love of Chhaya, an Indian woman, for Chandragupta. Yet another focuses on a Greek soldier named Antigonus, who also falls in love with Helena. When both Helena and her father refuse his request to marry her, Antigonus returns home westwards. Here, he learns that Seleucus is actually his father, which explains why Seleucus rejected him as a suitor for Helena.

Within this narrative, there are numerous allusions to life under colonial rule and Ray's hopes for India's future. One of these references is the plotline that concerns Chandragupta's gaining knowledge of warfare when he joins Alexander's army, and going on to employ this knowledge in rebuffing Seleucus' advance on Magadha. In the play, Chandragupta can be seen to represent contemporary Indians while Alexander and Seleucus stand in for the British rulers of India during the period in which Ray was writing. This being the case, contemporary Indians are depicted making full use of the understanding they have gained from long association with the British in order to resist and overthrow the colonisers. Their aim is to establish *swaraj* in place of the Raj.

Other aspects are less straightforward to interpret, including one of the most iconic moments in the *Chandragupta*. At a key moment in the play, Alexander stands with Seleucus on the banks of the Indus. They are looking across at the land of India laid out before them, which Alexander seeks to conquer. At this point Alexander says, 'Really Seleucus, this is a wondrous country.' Cue a conflict of emotion for the audience watching this scene. On the one hand, Alexander should be applauded for his admiration of India; on the other hand, this very admiration leads him to want to conquer the country. One can imagine the audience's cheers and jeers at these words when the play was performed.[14]

The agency ascribed to Helena and Chhaya in the play reflect Ray's reforming ideas about the role of women in early twentieth-century Indian society. This perspective is not surprising given that Ray imbues his plays with his own thoughts about society. However, the prominence he gives to the marriage between Chandragupta and Seleucus' daughter Helena in the play is unexpected. This is because the event entails the rejection of an Indian woman, Chhaya, in place of the European Helena. Multiple interpretations of this storyline within the context of early twentieth-century India are possible.

Prathama Banerjee, for example, suggests that the marriage reflected the philosophical questions raised by increasing scholarly interest in the newly rediscovered *Arthaśāstra*. Against this background, the union 'explicitly stands for the joining of Greek and Indic philosophy'.[15] Furthermore, the other union – that of Chandragupta and Chhaya – is almost sacrificed on the 'altar of this philosophical union'.[16] This interpretation may well have been understood by members of the audience familiar with scholarship pertaining to this text, but it is a niche area of knowledge. Most of the theatregoers are unlikely to have been aware of the intricacies of Greek and Indian philosophy, so any reading must necessarily be multi-layered.

Another way to interpret this relationship is that, by marrying Seleucus' daughter, Chandragupta is shown to be the more dominant of the two rulers. This is because Chandragupta is shown to both acquire and keep what he wants, and on his own terms. Thus, with Chandragupta standing for an independent India in the storyline, India is the dominant force in the relationship with the British. As such, India can gain something precious from the British, and on her own terms. The marriage between Chandragupta and Helena clearly took on significance in Indian consciousness during this period because, some years later, it is referenced twice in the first Birla Mandir in New Delhi, which opened in 1939 (see Chapter 6).

Ray's resurrection of Chandragupta's story proved enduringly influential: not only was it successful among theatregoers in Bengal, but it enjoyed considerable success elsewhere in India, and numerous translations were produced. It also served to encourage playwrights beyond Bengal to take up this subject, especially in the first half of the twentieth century. The plays include: N. C. Kelkar's (1872–1947) *Chandragupta* (1913) in Malayalam; Badrinath Bhatia's (d.1932) *Chandragupta* (1915) in Hindi; Balkrishna Kar's play written in Oriya in 1926; and Hindi plays by Udayshankar Bhatta (d.1979) and Jaishankar Prasad (1889–1937), released in 1931. Prasad's script was influenced by that of Ray and he even included fictitious characters – Philip and Cornelia – modelled on Antigonus and Helen from Ray's play. Like Ray's *Chandragupta*, Prasad's version proved popular with the public.[17]

The influence of Ray's *Chandragupta* was not limited to the stage. Novelists such as A. S. Panchapakesa Ayyar (1899–1963) (see Chapter 9) as well as screenwriters and directors were inspired by his work. In 1940, it was transferred to the silver screen in a Tamil version of the play, *Chandragupta Chanakya*, directed by C. K. Sachi. The widespread adoption of this topic during this period is easily understood: the story of Chandragupta fending off a Greek invasion of India took on added importance at a time when anti-colonial feeling was rising. As Sisir Kumar Das notes, *Chandragupta* 'presented a new hero, patriotic and noble, and a glorious Indian past built by the military prowess of the warrior class and the vision and pragmatism of Chanakya'.[18]

Setting the scene

Cinema arrived in India early: within six months of the Lumière brothers first moving-picture screening in Paris in December 1895, their films were being shown in Bombay.[19] The new technology was quickly adopted by Indians in India. In 1899, the first film was shot by the photographer H. S. Bhatavdekar (1868–1958), and in 1912 and 1913 the first two full-length Indian films were released. The second of these was the silent film *Raja Harishchandra* by Dhundiraj Govind Phalke (1870–1944), founder of the Phalke Films Company. This movie focused on the life of the legendary king Hariścandra, who appears in numerous religious texts, including the *Mahābhārata*, and the film followed the version from the *Mārkaṇḍeya Purāṇa*.

Many of Phalke's subsequent films, and those of his contemporaries, were also religious, mythological or historic in nature. They proved popular with Indian audiences, not least because they were part of a familiar repertoire for storytellers and viewers alike. There was already a long-standing precedent for presenting religious and historical stories through a visual medium. Pata paintings (cloth-based scroll paintings), for example, have been used over millennia by itinerant storytellers to tell mythological stories and folk tales. The tradition is not

Figure 8.1 Scene from the Gazi Scroll, probably depicting the Muslim saint Gazi Pir. Registration Number 1955,1008,0.95. © The Trustees of the British Museum. Shared under a Creative Commons Attribution-NonCommercial-ShareAlike 4.0 International (CC BY-NC-SA 4.0) licence.

confined to Hinduism: illustrated scrolls such as the Gazi Scroll are used to share stories of Muslim Pirs ('saints') (Figure 8.1).[20] Similarly, shadow puppets have long been used in south-eastern India, particularly the region that is now Andhra Pradesh, for sharing religious stories as well as those about contemporary events. For example, an almost life-sized shadow puppet representing Mahatma Gandhi that dates from the 1900s was used in Andhra Pradesh to disseminate information about his life and work to the broader populace (Figure 8.2).[21]

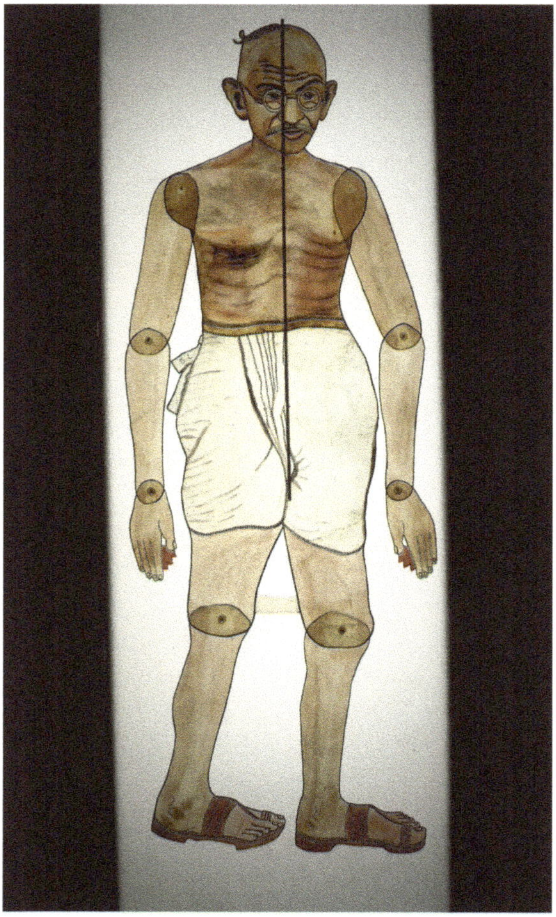

Figure 8.2 Shadow puppet depicting Mahatma Gandhi made in Andhra Pradesh. Registration Number As1972,13.3. © The Trustees of the British Museum. Shared under a Creative Commons Attribution-NonCommercial-ShareAlike 4.0 International (CC BY-NC-SA 4.0) licence.

From the end of the nineteenth century onwards, film-making provided an innovative medium through which to tell a broad range of stories, including those set in the past. Four main cinema industries producing films in four languages have grown up in India: Hindi-language cinema in Mumbai, known as 'Bollywood', probably the best known outside India; Tamil-language cinema in Tamil Nadu; Telugu-language cinema in Andhra Pradesh; and Kannada-language cinema in Karnataka. Among the many and varied subjects tackled by Indian cinema over the last century, historical themes have been – and remain – integral to its output.

The popularity of this new medium, and the interest it inspired, can be seen in the numerous film-related publications that sprang up alongside it. From the 1920s onwards, such publications proliferated, and they were produced in different languages and regions, especially Calcutta, Madras, Delhi and, of course, Bombay. While there were earlier periodicals and journals that included articles and other pieces about films, the first Indian periodical devoted entirely to cinema was J. K. Dwivedy's Gujarati-language *Mouj Majah* ('have fun'), launched in Bombay in 1924.[22] Widely regarded as the most influential of all of these was the English-language *filmindia*. It was founded in Bombay in 1935 by Baburao Patel (generally known by his first name; 1904–82), director, screenwriter, publisher and writer, who went on to become a member of the Indian parliament.

Chandragupta on the silver screen: a vehicle for revolutionary songs in the south

Films about the Mauryans were a key part of the historical genre – generally referred to as 'historicals' – from the earliest decades of cinematography in India.[23] As is true of the plays discussed at the start of this chapter, the context in which the films were produced is key to understanding the symbolism and meaning inherent in their storylines and visual repertoire, including publicity materials.

Six black-and-white movies released between 1923 and 1958 feature Chandragupta as a leading character. The earliest of these is a silent movie titled *Chandragupta* released by Star Film. The director of this film is unknown and the film does not appear to have survived. *Chandragupta* (1934), a Hindi and Urdu movie, was directed by A. R. Kardar (1904–89) for East India Film. Two Tamil-language films were released: *Mathru Bhoomi* (1939), directed by H. M. Reddy, and

Chandraguptha Chanakya (1940), directed by C. K. Sadasivam (more popularly known as C. K. Sachi). The Hindi film *Samrat Chandragupta* (1945) was directed by Jayant Desai (1909–76) for his own company Jayant Desai Productions. Finally, *Samrat Chandragupt* (1958), also in Hindi, was directed by Babubhai Mistry (1919–2010) for Mukti Films.[24]

Of the two Tamil films, it was Reddy's film, *Mathru Bhoomi* ('motherland'), released in 1939, that garnered more attention, including that of the film censors. Against an unsteady background, with a second world war looming and political deadlock in India, Reddy chose to adapt Ray's play *Chandragupta* for the silver screen. In the film, Seleucus is renamed 'Minander', while Chandragupta is called 'Ugrasena'. With Alexander's invasion of India representing the British colonial presence, and Ugrasena/Chandragupta's successful repulsion of Minander/Seleucus' attack on the nascent Mauryan empire, the film provided an allegorical take on the contemporary freedom movement. Reddy hoped that by using an ancient tale to reflect concerns about current events, the film would escape a ban by censors. However, it was because Reddy used the film as a vehicle for nationalist songs that it came to their notice.

In his earlier movies, such as the first Tamil-language 'talkie', *Kalidasa* (1931), Reddy included songs that were influenced by pro-independence sentiments. One of these was the hit *Ratina maam Gandhi kai baana maam* ('The charka is an arrow/weapon in Gandhi's hand').[25] His new film was no different. A number of songs in *Mathru Bhoomi* highlighted the strong Indian national feeling that was prevalent at the time, including 'Namadhu Janmabhoomi' ('land of our birth'), 'Annayin Kaalil vilangugalo' ('fetters on mother's feet') and 'Bharatha desam' ('the country of Bharat'). Of these songs, 'Namadhu Janmabhoomi' proved especially popular: thousands of gramophone records were sold and it was adopted as a song of morning prayer in south Indian schools.[26]

The nationalist emphasis of these songs was heightened by the character who sang them. All three were sung by Kumudhini, a fiercely patriotic figure who cast away her husband, the courtier Jayapala, upon learning he was a Greek spy. The songs attracted the attention of film censors, who briefly banned the film. The banning of a film because of its songs was not unique in India at this time, nor was the use of songs to spread nationalist messages a new phenomenon. From the early twentieth century, leaders of the *Swadeshi* movement recognised that they needed a variety of ways to share their message as widely as possible. Initially, they disseminated their ideas through newspapers and pamphlets, but these were regularly banned by the colonial authorities.

In his famous speech, 'Swadeshi Samaj' ('our own society'), given at the Minerva Theatre, Calcutta, in July 1904, Rabindranath Tagore offered another approach. He exhorted the Bengali middle classes to abandon English-style urban politics, including the emphasis on writing pamphlets. Instead, he urged them to concentrate their efforts on travelling to villages to share their ideas with the masses through traditional means. These initiatives included folk dramas, talks illustrated with magic-lantern slides and, of particular relevance here, songs.[27] Tagore himself set an example by writing numerous patriotic songs, including two that were later adopted as the national anthems of India and Bangladesh respectively: 'Jana Gana Mana' and 'Amar Shonar Bangla'.

The following year in south India, C. Subramanya Bharati (1882–1921), a Tamil author, poet and independence activist, translated Bankim Chandra Chatterjee's Bengali poem and song 'Vande Mataram' ('Mother I bow to you') into Tamil. This song was eagerly adopted by those associated with the Indian freedom movement and soon banned by the colonial government. Bharati's own collection of patriotic songs, *Swadesa Geethangal* ('Songs on Swadeshi'), was published in 1908 and met the same fate, as did his other publications. However, his songs were in such high demand that his supporters printed them in Sri Lanka and smuggled them into south India. In 1922, after his death, Bharati's songs were banned from classrooms, and in 1928 the Madras Presidency called for a blanket ban on all of his works, which included the seizure of his books on sale.

Despite this ban, directors and screenwriters continued to use his songs in movies. It was thanks to the efforts of Sundara Sastri Satyamurthi (1887–1943) that the ban was overturned by the provincial legislative assembly and Madras High Court in 1928.[28] Satyamurthi, an influential politician committed to *swaraj*, was one of the leaders of the Indian National Congress and, by 1939, a member of the Imperial Legislative Council and Mayor of Madras. It was in this year that, according to T. V. Kumudhini (1916–2000), who played the part of Kumudhini (hence the stage name), Satyamurthi intervened to ensure that the ban on *Mathru Bhoomi* was lifted.[29] Alongside his extensive political work, Satyamurthi had an abiding interest in music and was involved in setting up the Music Academy of Madras and the All India Music Conference, for example.[30] His politics, combined with his interest in music, ensured his support for songs and films that expressed the values he held himself.

Mathru Bhoomi was not the only film about Chandragupta that included nationalist songs. Desai's *Samrat Chandragupta*, for example, had 'Mata ki jai, Janani ki jai ho' ('Victory for mother, victory to the mother') among its songs. These songs, with their depth of feeling and strongly patriotic words, complemented and emphasised the storylines of the films they were part of. They ensured that the content, meaning and purpose of the movies were raised beyond the level of pure entertainment. So while it is certainly possible to watch the films as escapist historical fiction, the inclusion of these songs ensured that the audience was, at intervals, confronted with stridently anti-colonial, pro-freedom messages as well.

The songs included in the films about Chandragupta made before and after independence are strikingly different in character. While the pre-independence films incorporate rousing patriotic songs, Mistry's *Samrat Chandragupt* has none. By 1958, when this film was released, there was no longer any need to carefully embed pro-*swaraj* sentiments in a movie through song in order either to inculcate nationalist feeling in the audience or to avoid censorship or an outright ban: independence had already been achieved. Mistry replaced those types of tracks with love songs such as 'Mujhe dekh chand sharmaye' ('The moon feels shy seeing me'). That song and the others were sung by none other than the iconic playback singers Lata Mangeshkar (1929–2022) and Mohammed Rafi (1924–80). Playback singers pre-record songs for film soundtracks and actors lip-sync the songs, meaning that the singers themselves do not appear in the films, only their voices. As shown below, there was also a notable difference in the posters created for films made about Chandragupta before and after independence.

Chandragupta reigns victorious

India had changed dramatically in the period between the release of the first film about Chandragupta in 1923 and the last one in 1958. After decades of anti-colonial agitation and in the aftermath of two world wars, India gained independence in 1947. After this date, just one film about Chandragupta was released, as film-makers embraced other topics more relevant to India's new status and place in the world. Two films that straddle Indian independence are Desai's *Samrat Chandragupta* (1945) and Mistry's *Samrat Chandragupt* (1958). With their big budgets and all-star casts, these films represented the high point of depictions of Chandragupta on the silver screen in Bollywood and both enjoyed popular success. The two films had different scriptwriters but the storylines were broadly similar, not least because both were based on Ray's 1911 play.[31]

Despite the similarity between the narratives, there is a stark contrast in the posters produced to advertise the films.

In Desai's film, Chandragupta is shown to be a great Indian ruler who is friends with Seleucus, Alexander's general. He is aided and abetted by the wily politician Cāṇakya. Antigonus is portrayed as the villain of the piece. Chandragupta saves the lives of Seleucus and Seleucus' daughter Helen from Antigonus and from rampaging elephants. In return for his bravery, Seleucus permits him to marry Helen. The conquest of the Nanda empire and the establishment of the Mauryan empire are represented as resulting from this marriage. Following the conquest there are several attempts to overthrow the king, all of which are foiled, and only after this final success does happiness reign supreme.[32]

In Mistry's film, Chandragupta is deprived of the throne of Magadha by his stepbrother Nanda. At this point, Cāṇakya advises Chandragupta to join Alexander's army in order to learn the art of Greek warfare, so that he can both prevent Alexander's invasion of India and topple Nanda. Chandragupta enters Alexander's camp and goes on to save Helen, Seleucus' daughter, from being crushed under the feet of an elephant. Helen falls in love with her rescuer and persuades her father to teach Chandragupta the art of warfare, which he does. Chandragupta convinces Alexander not to invade India, and instead Alexander returns home while Chandragupta captures Magadha. On Alexander's death, Seleucus invades India but is defeated and captured by Chandragupta. The ending also takes inspiration from Ray's production: Cāṇakya negotiates a treaty between the two rulers which includes the marriage of Chandragupta and Helen.

The posters created to advertise the films condense the storylines to their key elements. The black-and-white poster for Desai's film has a man dressed in richly embellished clothing standing centre right.[33] The position of the film title beneath him shows that this is Chandragupta. Behind him stands a male figure in profile, silhouetted by a sunburst. This man is bald except for a single lock of hair – identifying him as the Brahmin priest Cāṇakya – and in outstretched arms he holds a sword. A small photograph of a beautiful woman, Helen, is placed to Chandragupta's right. She wears a combination of European- and Indian-style clothing and has a serious expression. At the very bottom of the poster is a panoramic image of an army, perhaps engaged in battle. The superimposition of the film title onto this scene reinforces Chandragupta's connection with warfare. Overall, the poster is framed by violence, but subtly: it is implied through the sword that Cāṇakya raises up and by the inclusion of the army below.

The messages expressed through the poster artwork for Mistry's *Samrat Chandragupt* are similar but more explicitly presented.[34] Here, violence and Indian supremacy in battle are presented front and centre. Chandragupta stands dressed in auspicious red and gold with a purple cloak, and holding a long wooden spear with the metal point at the throat of a Greek soldier, presumably Seleucus. The Greek man lies on the floor, the sword having fallen from his grasp and out of his reach, and with an expression that seems to beseech Chandragupta for mercy. Beneath these two figures, written in red, are the words 'Samrat Chandragupt' ('Emperor Chandragupta'), so that it is immediately clear who the man in red is. Just behind the two warriors an elephant holds aloft a woman; also the colour of her clothing links her to Chandragupta, so this must be Helen. To either side of the tableau, Greek and Indian soldiers fight on foot and on horseback, and white tents frame the action at the back.

Prominently placed above all of these scenes is the face of a beautiful woman, wearing heavy pearl jewellery and looking away from the scene into the distance. Evidently, it is a close-up of the woman in red. It is only when you look carefully that you realise there is another figure in the background. His face is in profile and shaded a bluish-green colour which blends into the indigo sky behind him. He wears the sacred three-lined white tilak horizontally across his forehead and is bald-headed, suggesting that he is a Brahmin. While he also looks into the distance, it is in a different direction from the woman.

In both posters, Chandragupta is the active military figure, with his supporting army in the background, and Helen is the romantic interest. Shaping events in the background is the shadowy figure of Chandragupta's Brahmin advisor, Cāṇakya. However, it is the poster for Mistry's film that emphasises Chandragupta's achievement as the great Indian emperor who brings down the foreign invader and now holds him at spearpoint. Film-makers no longer have to resort to surreptitiously including nationalist songs in their productions in order to promote a message of nationalism and freedom. Instead, after independence, the archetypal Indian hero Chandragupta and his European enemy Seleucus can be presented in such a fashion without fear of censorship. Chandragupta and India are victorious.

From the silver screen to the small screen

Chandragupta Maurya retains his hold on India's imagination. Recent decades have seen a surge in interest in television series. With an ever-increasing number of channels and streaming services available, and growing audiences eager to consume new serials as well as the latest episodes of old favourites, there has never been a better time to make television shows. And it is through this medium that the latest stories about Chandragupta have been shared on-screen. Between 2011 and 2019, three separate television serials focusing on his life were aired on Indian channels.[35]

The first of these series was *Chandragupta Maurya*, which was shown on Imagine TV. This series ran for 105 episodes in 2011–12, after which it came to an abrupt end with the closure of the channel. The second was *Chandra Nandini*, which ran for 286 episodes on Star Plus in 2016–17. The latest series, *Chandragupta Maurya*, saw the production of 208 episodes, which aired on Sony TV from 2018 to 2019. Compared with film and the stage, television allows for richer and more complex storylines extending across multiple episodes. Scriptwriters and directors harnessed this potential for the three series. The storylines for each of them varied, highlighting different aspects of Chandragupta's life and times.

The first series, for example, begins with Alexander the Great approaching the subcontinent. A male voice, which represents India, says, 'I was eagerly waiting for the person who would save me [India] from the danger posed by Alexander.' At this point, the camera turns to a male figure, Chandragupta, wielding a sword and silhouetted against the sun, which is emblazoned with a peacock. The voice then reveals, 'To carve these golden moments of my history the great Acharya ['teacher'] of Taxila, Chanakya, was chosen.' This opening sequence sets the scene for the series, which sees Cāṇakya taking a young Chandragupta under his wing and training him so that he can defeat Dhana Nanda, ruler of the Nanda empire, and Alexander.

Chandra Nandini takes a completely different approach to Chandragupta's story. As in Hilda Seligman's book *When Peacocks Called*, the story of Chandragupta's early life is inspired by the account found in the ancient Sri Lankan source the *Mahāvaṃsa-ṭīkā*. However, at this point, the series veers off in a wholly new direction. At the heart of the series is the convoluted love story between Chandragupta and Nandini, the daughter of king Nanda. Chandragupta has three wives: Nandini, Durdhara, mother of his heir Bindusāra, and Helena, Seleucus' daughter. At one point in the series, Chandragupta is about to be attacked by two of his fathers-in-law, Nanda and Seleucus. He succeeds in persuading Seleucus not to fight against him because his army is not as big as that of Seleucus, so Seleucus is at a significant advantage. It is at this point that Helena becomes his chief queen.

Helena is cast as the wicked and jealous principal queen of Magadha who plots against her fellow queens, particularly Nandini, sometimes with the aid of her mother Apama. All three queens bear Chandragupta children; those of Helena are named Alice and Adonis (yes, really). At the end of the series, and at Nandini's request, Chandragupta forgives Helena for her endless villainy against Nandini and sends her and their children back to Greece. Cāṇakya has an integral role in this series as Chandragupta's advisor.

The latest series, *Chandragupta Maurya*, which aired in 2018–19, is different again. It follows on from a previous, award-winning series, *Porus*. *Porus* was the most expensive show ever produced for Indian television and focused on the epic battle of the Hydaspes between Porus and Alexander. At the end of the show, Porus is assassinated by Ambikumar, son of Ambiraj (one of Alexander's vassals in India), and Seleucus. As Porus lies dying, he entrusts the future of India to Cāṇakya, his prime minister. *Chandragupta Maurya* continues seamlessly from this point. At the start of the new series, Cāṇakya travels to Magadha to ask the Nanda king to unite the country and drive Seleucus and his Macedonian army out of India. Dhana Nanda reveals that he supported Seleucus financially to assassinate Porus so that Seleucus would not attack Magadha. Cāṇakya vows to replace Dhana Nanda with another ruler and it transpires that this is Chandragupta. A complex storyline commences.

Cāṇakya raises Chandragupta from slave to warrior, and he eventually unites Macedonian and Paurava armies to defeat Nanda's forces. After this victory, he brings the Paurava and Taxilan forces together to fend off Seleucus. Eventually, Chandragupta kills Nanda and captures Seleucus, who had supported Nanda in revenge for his defeat at Chandragupta's hands. Chandragupta frees Seleucus on the understanding that Chandragupta will marry Seleucus' daughter Helena and that Seleucus will return the wealth he stole from India. At the very end there is a parallel with *Rākṣasa's Ring*: Rākṣasa, Nanda's former prime minister, takes Cāṇakya's place as Chandragupta's prime minister. This enables Cāṇakya to retire and write the *Arthaśāstra*.

Politics, warfare and family drama are woven together in compelling storylines that have attracted huge audiences to hear new tales about Chandragupta. As with the ending of the 2018–19 series *Chandragupta Maurya*, there are certain strands in each series that take inspiration from earlier plays and films. And as in previous productions there is little that is based on historical sources, for the simple reason that surviving material is limited and problematic. However, all of the television series retain Chandragupta's main identity as unifier and defender of India against foreign enemies. The rest of his story is built around this central theme, with Cāṇakya guiding Chandragupta to his destiny. The artwork created for the final *Chandragupta Maurya* series is very similar to the posters for Desai's and Mistry's films. Cāṇakya is in the background, shaping events, while Chandragupta is positioned in an active stance at the front, his enemies around him.[36]

A new aspect of the story that is not found elsewhere comes in *Chandra Nandini*. This series retains the enduring idea of foreigners as evil intruders and Chandragupta as the emperor who rebuffs them, but moves this storyline beyond Alexander, Seleucus and their soldiers and into the character of Helena. In this series Helena is not merely Chandragupta's wife, but a central figure with her own agency and motivation. Her endless manipulations to the detriment of Nandini result in her being sent back to her 'own country' with her and Chandragupta's children. Chandragupta is left with his devoted Indian wife Nandini, and his and Durdhara's son and heir Bindusāra. Whereas Seleucus' daughter was Chandragupta's primary and faithful love interest in previous plays and films, she is now the consummate foreign 'baddie' who is cast out of India with her mixed-heritage children. This is quite some transformation, and a disturbing one at that. What led to the development of Helena's character in this particular direction is unclear (see Chapter 9 for a similar presentation of Helena in a volume of contemporary historical fiction). An understanding of what the target audience was willing to accept may have featured in the decision-making process that underpinned it.

It is also interesting to see the more prominent role given to the female characters more generally in this television series compared with the other shows, films and plays about Chandragupta. This is part of a wider trend in contemporary Indian television, which has tended to depict women in the context of extended families. However, in shows such as *Masaba Masaba* (2020), which is based on the life of fashion designer Masaba Gupta, women are increasingly shown as independent characters with their own agency. Concurrent with this change is an increase in the number of women working in senior roles within the industry. *Chandra Nandini*, for example, was created by two women, Ekta Kapoor and Shobha Kapoor, and co-written by Neha Singh, and one of the creative directors was Sujata Rao. It was produced for Balaji Telefilms, an Indian company that produces television content, which was founded by Ekta and Shobha Kapoor.

A notable difference between the films and these television shows is their audience reach. The films were created for an Indian audience in India and few people living outside the country would have had the opportunity to see them. In contrast, Indian television channels and series are available to a global audience, and they particularly target the South Asian diaspora. While this was previously confined to cable and satellite, more recently the offering has extended to streaming services. For example, Disney launched India's largest OTT channel,[37] Hotstar, in the UK in 2018, and in other international markets in the following year, specifically aiming at the forty-million-strong South Asian diaspora. In 2021, the Indian broadcasting giant Zee followed suit, launching Zee5 in the United States in the hope of attracting the attention of the more than five million South Asians living there.[38]

Conclusion

Television series as well as film, fashion, music and much else besides not only generate an idea of Indian culture within the diaspora, but they are culture as well as showing it.[39] Nowadays, conversations have moved from 'Have you seen the latest film?' to 'Have you watched the latest episode of this series?' While family-based dramas such as *Baa Bahoo Aur Baby* ('mother, daughter-in-law and baby'; 2005–10) have long been popular, increasingly there is an appetite in the diaspora for historical dramas. *Dharti Ka Veer Yodha Prithviraj Chauhan* ('Prithviraj Chauhan, brave warrior of the land'; 2006–9) proved popular with diaspora families in the UK, as have other historical serials. It is often primarily through these serials that the diaspora, particularly the second and third generations, learn about the history of their ancestors and their ancestral homeland. This enables them to form a link with a country they may not have visited but with which they have a cultural affinity.

My earliest memory of watching a Hindi-language television serial is of gathering with the family at my Nanima's house in Leicester every weekend to watch the epic *Mahabharat*. Happily, the show had subtitles in English: my family spoke the East African dialect of Gujarati and were less fluent in Hindi. This show, with its dramatic tension, sound effects and wobbly chariots, ran for 94 episodes between 1988 and 1990, and we devoured all of them eagerly. The experience not only taught me about the intricacies and high drama of this epic poem, but introduced me to the visual world of Indian cinema and television.

Few studies have been undertaken on historical films about India's ancient past (compared with the mediaeval and early modern periods), and even fewer on television series on the same topic.[40] And yet this is a rich area for research, especially in relation to how such series are received and understood by diaspora communities.

Many members of the second and third generations of the South Asian diaspora in the UK consider themselves to be both British and, for example, Indian or Pakistani. In addition, increasing numbers in the diaspora are marrying out of their ethnic communities and have children of mixed heritage, or are of mixed heritage themselves. It would be interesting to understand the impact on them when they watch productions that have Indian nationalist strands running through them, including the fight against foreigners, which is a recurring theme. Similarly, it would be interesting to know what they make of storylines that automatically cast foreigners and those of mixed heritage, such as Helena and her children with Chandragupta as the 'baddies'. This cannot be easy viewing and may profoundly affect how these viewers think of themselves in terms of 'Indianness' and in relation to the country or countries of their ancestors. Indeed, storylines like that may well cause feelings of alienation from their South Asian heritage.

As historical television series become more and more readily available to a multi-generational global South Asian diaspora, the reception of these shows inevitably becomes more complex.

Notes

1 The date is based on the reference to 'Chandragupta' in the play's final benedictory verse. This Chandragupta is likely to be Chandragupta II, of the Gupta Empire, rather than Chandragupta Maurya. The dating makes Viśākhadatta contemporary with the famous Gupta-era playwright Kālidāsa, who wrote *Śakuntalā*.
2 Singh 2017, 219.
3 Coulson 2005, 15; Singh 2017, 219.
4 It is interesting to note that there was a resurgence of interest in this play in India during the second half of the twentieth century, particularly because of its political focus. Banerjee (2012) discusses the restaging of *Rākṣasa's Ring* in 1964 by Habib Tanvir (1923–2009), the playwright, director, poet and actor, and by others, including Vijaya Mehta (b.1934), director, in 1975, and B. V. Karanth (1929–2002), director, actor and musician, in 1978.
5 Kesavan and Kulkarni 1962, 121.
6 Sen 2022, 14.
7 Sen 2022, 18.
8 Sen 2022, 21.
9 Chattopadhyay 1989, 221–2.
10 Sen 2022, 21.
11 Chattopadhyay 1989, 222.
12 Chattopadhyay 1989, 221.
13 Banerjee 2012, 39.
14 A journalist recalls this play being a set text at his school and the enduring significance of this line in contemporary India (*New Indian Express*, 'A strange kind of brew', 6 April 2014: https://www.newindianexpress.com/lifestyle/books/2014/apr/06/A-Strange-Kind-of-Brew-594944.html, accessed 2 November 2022).
15 Banerjee 2021, 54.
16 Banerjee 2012, 39; Banerjee 2021, 54.
17 Das 1995, 113–14, 653, 693; Banerjee 2012, 38; Chattopadhyay 1989, 224.
18 Das 1995, 113.
19 Bose 2006, 38–9.

20 The Gazi Scroll dates from *c.*1800 and was produced in Bengal. It is held at the British Museum and the Registration Number is 1955,1008,0.95. Pata paintings are still being produced and used, albeit in smaller numbers than before, and the British Museum houses a collection of them.
21 The shadow puppet is held at the British Museum; the Registration Number is As1972,13.3.
22 Rajadhyaksha and Willemen 1999, 19.
23 These films include *Maurya Patan* ('Fall of the Mauryas', 1929), a silent black and white film made by Royal Pictures Corporation and written and directed by R. S. Dutta Chowdhury (1903–72). Chowdhury went on to write the script for the famous film *Mughal-e-Azam* ('The Great Mughal'; 1960) (Narwekar 1994, 74). Another famous example is *Chitralekha* (1941), remade in 1964, which is based on the famous novel of the same name written by B. C. Verma (1903–81) and published in 1934. A smaller number of films, such as *Samrat Ashok* ('Emperor Ashok'; 1947), centred on Aśoka, while others, for example *Sikandar* ('Alexander the Great'; 1941) explored the story of Alexander the Great. Phiroze Vasunia (2010) has written a detailed account of the film *Sikandar* within the broader context of colonialism and nationalism in India.
24 Narwekar 1994, 86–7, 142, 190.
25 Kaul 1998, 93–4.
26 Kaul 1998, 98; Randor Guy, 'Mathru Bhoomi (1939)', *The Hindu*, 13 May 2010: https://www.thehindu.com/features/cinema/Mathru-Bhoomi-1939/article16300528.ece (accessed 2 November 2022).
27 J. E. Wilson 2016, 380; Kaul 1998, 91–2.
28 Kaul 1998, 92, 94–5.
29 Randor Guy, 'Mathru Bhoomi (1939)', *The Hindu*, 13 May 2010: https://www.thehindu.com/features/cinema/Mathru-Bhoomi-1939/article16300528.ece (accessed 3 November 2022).
30 Venkatasubramanian 2010, 130.
31 The 1945 film script was written by Mohanlal G. Dave, Shaheed Latif and Sagar Hussain. The 1958 script was written by Indivar, C. K. Mast, Vishwanath Pande, Pandit R. Priyadarshi, Nirupa Roy and Bharat Vyas.
32 Rajadhyaksha and Willemen 1999, 284.
33 https://www.indianfilmhistory.com/movie/samrat-chandragupta (accessed 3 November 2022).
34 https://www.imdb.com/title/tt0242841/ (accessed 3 November 2022).
35 In 1991, a historical drama series titled *Chanakya*, written and directed by C. Dwivedi (b. 1960), first aired on DD National, a state-owned Indian public entertainment television channel. As the title implies, this series focused on the life of Chandragupta's advisor, Cāṇakya, rather than Chandragupta himself. For this reason, it is not discussed further here.
36 https://www.imdb.com/title/tt9261994/mediaviewer/rm3080874496/?ref_=tt_ov_i (accessed 2 November 2022).
37 'OTT' refers to an 'over-the-top' media service that is offered directly to viewers over the internet. Netflix is an example of an OTT service.
38 Aman Rawat, 'Disney launches Hotstar globally, targets South Asian diaspora', *Inc42*, 11 October 1999: https://inc42.com/buzz/disney-launches-hotstar-globally-targets-south-asian-diaspora/; Vikas SN, 'Star India's Hotstar launches in United Kingdom', *Economic Times*, 14 August, 2021: https://economictimes.indiatimes.com/internet/star-indias-hotstar-launches-in-united-kingdom/articleshow/65778058.cms; Poulomi Das, 'The battle for diaspora viewers', *The Juggernaut*, 15 June 2021: https://www.thejuggernaut.com/streaming-wars-the-battle-for-diaspora-viewers; Lata Jha, 'Indian diaspora, subcontinent audiences drive homegrown OTT viewership overseas', *Mint*, 24 May 2020: https://www.livemint.com/news/india/indian-diaspora-subcontinent-audiences-drive-homegrown-ott-viewership-overseas-11590307029562.html (all accessed 2 November 2022).
39 This idea builds on Rachel Dwyer's argument that Indian cinema represents Indian culture (2013, 414).
40 Thanks to Maria Wyke's pioneering research into how the Romans are presented on film and how viewers have experienced that past world, there is a rich and growing literature on the subject. Wyke's publications on this subject include: *Projecting the Past: Ancient Rome, cinema and history*. New York: Routledge, 1997. Over the years, this work has developed and expanded, although the focus has remained on Graeco-Roman antiquity. As this chapter shows, the time is ripe for investigations into the ways ancient India has been portrayed on film.

9
Chandragupta in popular literature

Historical novels by Indian authors

The earliest historical novels by Indian authors were written in Bengali and published in Bengal in the mid-nineteenth century. They were soon followed by books written in other parts of India and in a range of languages, including Tamil, Urdu and Marathi. Many of these historical novels explored the lives of great Indian rulers; one such is *Anguriya Binimoy* (1862), by Bengali teacher and author Bhudev Mukhopadhyay (1827–94). This book focused on Chhatrapati Shivaji's battles against the Mughal emperor Aurangzeb. Other authors, such as Bankim Chandra Chatterjee (also 'Chattopadhyay'; 1838–94), poet, novelist and colonial administrator, explored other themes in the setting of a variety of historical backdrops. Chatterjee's historical romance *Durgeshnandini* (1865) was set during the sixteenth century, while events in *Anandamath* (1882) took place during the Bengal famine in 1700.[1]

As we saw in Part II, Chandragupta and the Mauryans had not yet been 'discovered' as a great Indian dynasty when Mukhopadhyay and Chatterjee were writing, and so did not feature prominently in these early novels. However, Viśākhadatta's play *Mudrārākṣasa* (see Chapter 8) inspired Kempu Narayana to write *Mudra Manjusha* in 1823; it was the first historical novel published in Kannada and the first to include Chandragupta as a character.[2] Narayana's work, in turn, served as the basis for the Amar Chitra Katha comic book *Chandragupta*. Almost a century later, the Marathi author Hari Narayan Apte (1864–1919) wrote *Chandragupta*. Apte was the first well-known novelist to take up this topic, and his focus, like Narayana's before him, was on both Cāṇakya and Chandragupta.[3] However, neither of these novels saw the widespread popularity and acclaim of D. L. Ray's play *Chandragupta* (1911). It wasn't until the mid-twentieth century that Chandragupta featured prominently as a character in his own right.

Chandragupta's arrival in print

The two most popular and influential books of the mid-twentieth century that involved Chandragupta or the early Mauryan period came on either side of independence and Partition. The first, A. S. Panchapakesa Ayyar's *Three Men of Destiny* (1939), written in English, featured Chandragupta as a primary character. The other was Qurratulain Hyder's *Aag Ka Darya* ('River of fire'; 1959) written in Urdu and 'transcreated' into English by the author in 1998.[4] The early part of the latter book is set during Chandragupta's reign, and he is mentioned in it, but does not feature as a character.

In the 1940s and 1950s Ayyar (1899–1963), justice of the Madras High Court and author, wrote a series of historical novels set in the ancient past; they remain his best-known works.[5] A narrative thread designed to appeal to his readers' patriotism runs through all of these books: disunity among Indian rulers encourages foreigners to invade India, but India unites to repulse them and prevails in the end. The story of Chandragupta and Seleucus is a perfect fit here and Ayyar makes the most of it in *Three Men of Destiny*. The three men are Alexander, Chandragupta and Cāṇakya.

In his Introduction, it is the relationship between Chandragupta and Seleucus, and particularly their treaty, that Ayyar emphasises. He interprets a carving from the Sanchi stupa as representing the time after their battle and ensuing treaty, when the two kings became friends. Projecting the East–West relationship forward to the period during which he was writing, Ayyar asks, 'Is it too fanciful to imagine that the Lotus of India and the Grapes of Europe will mingle once more through the Englishman seated on the British Lion and the Indian seated on an Elephant?'[6] Here, Ayyar hopes for a future in which there is cultural parity between India and Britain.[7]

Ayyar's Introduction is lengthy, because it covers the many sources he has consulted. He explains that he has tried 'not to go against proved historical facts of importance', whether from South Asian or Graeco-Roman sources.[8] In this connection, he refers to McCrindle's translations a number of times, particularly highlighting his 'excellent book "Alexander's Invasion of India"'. As we see here, McCrindle's influence has made its way out of the academy into popular culture. Ayyar notes that 'where history is silent, or speaks with no certain voice, I have taken a novelist's liberty'.[9] The outcome of the skirmish between Seleucus and Chandragupta is unquestionably a moment when history 'speaks with no certain voice', so his interpretation of this event is interesting.

In 1939, when Ayyar's book was published, Britain declared war on Germany. The British Indian Army comprised more than two hundred thousand men – a number that was to rise to over two million by 1945 – and they were an integral part of the Allied forces. Over one million men from the British Indian Army had also served in the First World War, playing an important role in this war. The version of ancient events that Ayyar presents in his books must be understood in the context of Indian involvement in both world wars and the rising Indian nationalist clamour for independence.

Ayyar writes that the result of the battle between the Mauryan and Seleucid forces was a 'foregone conclusion'. According to him the Mauryans had 100,000 soldiers and 6,000 elephants compared with 150,000 Seleucid men. The Mauryan infantry 'attacked the Greeks and mercenaries with determination, and massacred whole regiments'. Seleucus is made to respond, '"There is no use fighting any further .... We had better make peace and clear out of this mess"'.[10] Chandragupta accepts Seleucus' terms, which involve taking the provinces of Aria, Arachosia, Paropamisadae and eastern Gedrosia in exchange for 500 elephants. In addition, Chandragupta asks for the hand of Seleucus' daughter, Diophantes, in marriage. So while Ayyar hoped for cultural parity with the British in modernity, it was still important to him that India experienced military supremacy over a European enemy in antiquity.

Hyder's book *Aag Ka Darya* was written in a wholly different context. Hyder (1927–2007), author, academic and translator, was one of the leading writers of fiction in Urdu, Urdu literature having previously focused on poetry. Born in India, Hyder moved to Pakistan with her family in 1947. After publishing *Aag Ka Darya*, she spent some time living in England before returning to India where she spent the rest of her life. Hyder won numerous awards for her work, including the Jnanpith Award (1989), India's highest literary honour, and various honours from the Government of India, including the Sahitya Akademi Fellowship (1994) and the Padma Bhushan (2005).

The Partition of India – a violently tumultuous event in which her family was involved – features prominently in much of Hyder's work, including *Aag Ka Darya*. Unlike Ayyar's novel, this book is not a straightforward fictionalisation of a particular historical period. Instead, it covers a vast sweep of history, from the time of Chandragupta's rule through the Mughal period to the post-independence countries of India and East and West Pakistan. These ages are seen and experienced through the eyes of a handful of characters who are reincarnated into different moments and cultures of the past. The religious differences and difficulties between Hindus and Muslims are a central theme; they are played out cyclically from era to era until the novel comes to a close after Partition.

Given the novel's subject matter, it is interesting to note that Hyder chose to set the beginning of her narrative at the time of the nascent Mauryan empire and with an emphasis on Buddhism. As the story unfolds, the manifold reasons behind this decision become clearer. At first glance, Chandragupta appears to be a tangential character in the book, mentioned on only a handful of occasions, but a closer look reveals the importance of his actions. A short paragraph describes Chandragupta as an ordinary, rather than extraordinary, man who succeeded on his own merits, a 'self-made man', according to Hyder. And it was this self-made man who had 'got up an army and driven out the Greeks from the land of the Five Rivers' after Alexander's invasion.[11] This event sets the scene for the later events of Partition that took place across the same geographical location and sets up the tension: where Chandragupta saw off the Europeans and united India, some two thousand years later other Europeans drew a line across the subcontinent and divided it.

The other reasons for beginning the novel in the early Mauryan period include religion and cultural plurality. Gautam, one of the main protagonists is revealed to be a Brahmin who 'had inherited the prejudices against Buddhist philosophy'.[12] His religious affiliation enables a series of conversations with Buddhists during which common ground and differences between these two groups are uncovered. This region, therefore, is a place where multiple religions have flourished since ancient times. Similarly, it is a place where the world met: Indians, Persians, Greeks and many more. Variety was the norm throughout history until the moment of an unnatural, man-made rupture during Partition.

With the exception of Ayyar's book, Chandragupta remained a peripheral figure in historical novels written between the early nineteenth and mid-twentieth centuries. This situation only changed during the 2010s, and then only briefly.

Chandragupta: hero of historical novels

Since the 2010s in particular, historical fiction has proliferated in India. These books, like those written previously, are artefacts of the period during which they were produced. This period has not seen the violence and upheaval that accompanied the two world wars, agitation for Indian independence and then the Partition of India. However, the period has seen the rise of a new type of Indian nationalism which includes political endorsement of sectarian violence, particularly between Hindus and Muslims, and an emphasis on the country's Hindu past. The country has also experienced a period of significant economic growth which has enabled the proliferation of a large and growing middle class with the financial resources and leisure to buy and read books for pleasure.[13] The writing of historical novels, including those about Chandragupta, must be seen against this backdrop.

There is another point of comparison between the authors and playwrights discussed previously and the three considered here. With the exception of Hyder, the earlier authors were not full-time, professional writers; they had other jobs which meant that they had to write in their spare time. In contrast, Rajat Pillai, Adity Kay and Indrayani Sawkar write professionally.[14] They produce historical fiction for a broad, international readership, albeit one focused on India. Their books are not sold in India alone, but are readily available to audiences in different markets, including the UK and the United States. It is harder to glean their political ideology from their work than it is for the earlier authors of fiction discussed above.

In India, historical novels are published in Hindi and a range of regional Indian languages as well as in English. Prominent publishers, including Bloomsbury India, Pan Macmillan India, Penguin Random House and Hachette India, have expanded into this genre, as have smaller, independent publishing houses such as Pustak Mahal. Cedar Books is a now defunct imprint of Pustak Mahal which focused on publishing new Indian talent in the fiction genre. Most of these books explore the lives and exploits of great rulers of India's ancient, mediaeval and early modern past, and the British colonial period also features prominently. Nandini Sengupta's trilogy about the fourth-to-fifth-century Gupta king Chandragupta II Vikramaditya, published by HarperCollins India, is among the most successful series of historical fiction to be sold in India.[15] While the great and the good remain popular protagonists, a gradual change can be observed: Veena Muthuraman's *The Grand Anicut* (2021), for example, focuses on the adventures of a Roman trader in Puhar, the capital of the Chola dynasty during the first century, not on a Chola ruler.[16]

Despite significant sales of historical fiction books in India, this genre has not seen the popularity it enjoys in countries such as the UK, with books such as Hilary Mantel's Cromwell trilogy. Instead, mythological fiction like Amish Tripati's Shiva trilogy and Ashok K. Banker's Ramayana series are in strong demand, as are non-fiction histories.[17] This latter genre has proliferated over the last thirty years. Books by authors such as William Dalrymple and Manu S. Pillai, set during the colonial period but approached from different angles, have seen growing audiences and enjoy widespread success.[18] This state of affairs is reflected in the roll call of authors and themes of the panels at the Jaipur Literary Festival, India's largest and most significant literary festival. Here, authors of history books aimed at the general public draw large audiences.

Within this broad context, three historical fiction books with Chandragupta as a central character have been released within the last ten years. *Chandragupta: Path of a fallen demigod* (2012) by Rajat Pillai was followed by Adity Kay's *Emperor Chandragupta* (2016) and *Chakravarti Chandragupta Maurya: First sovereign king of India* (2019) by Indrayani Sawkar. All three novels are written in English and published both in paperback and digitally for Kindle.[19]

There are many ways to gauge a book's popularity, from publisher sale figures and bestseller lists to Amazon sales ranks, and reviews. According to the front cover of Pillai's book, it is 'A National Bestseller'. What this means in practice is more difficult to ascertain, because there is no clear definition of what a 'bestseller' is.[20] In Pillai's case, it could be that his novel was one of Cedar Books' bestselling books in India. A more immediately available, although by no means straightforward, point of comparison between the three books is through Amazon India's historical fiction sales ranking.[21] According to this metric, as at 12 April 2022 the Kindle versions of the books are ranked as follows: Kay #3730; Pillai #5648; Sawkar #6892. Of the print versions, Kay's book stands at #461 and Sawkar's at #9690. Ranking details are not provided for Pillai's printed book on Amazon India.[22]

Amazon sales do not give the full story because they are also sold in physical retail shops and through other online retailers. There is also the issue of book piracy. Estimates suggest that many millions of pirated books are sold in India annually, particularly at train stations and in city or town markets, often at a tenth of the publisher's price.[23] It is impossible to gauge how many pirated copies of the Chandragupta novels are in circulation. On the basis of the Amazon figures alone, therefore, the books are moderately popular and Kay's in particular stands out among them.

Notably, there is a strong correlation between the publication dates of the historical novels about Chandragupta and the screening of multiple television series about him. Pillai's book, for example, was published after the release of the successful television series *Chandragupta Maurya* (2011–12). Kay's novel came in the same year as *Chandra Nandini*

(2016–17), and Sawkar's volume was published at the end of the series *Chandragupta Maurya* (2018–19). Of course, correlation is not causation, but it is certainly worth pointing out that since the last of these series ended, no further books about this ruler have been published. So it seems that the television series generated interest in Chandragupta and the books rode this wave.

In addition to the correlation between the release of the television series and publication dates of the books, there are numerous similarities between their narratives. Given the core storylines about Chandragupta's life that have come down to us from the ancient sources, and which have been embellished and codified in popular plays and literature over the last century, many of the parallels are to be expected. In addition, certain events make for good dramatic tension. A striking comparison relates to Chandragupta's marriages to Durdhara and to Seleucus' daughter Helen. This is an aspect that Kay in particular draws out.

Kay is a well-known author of historical books for children and young adults, including the Mythquest series, published by Hachette India and written under the pseudonym 'Anu Kumar'.[24] Her Emperor trilogy was also commissioned by Hachette and is aimed at an adult audience. According to Kay, Hachette wanted a series specifically on ancient emperors along the lines of Alex Rutherford's Mughal Emperor books, and she decided to start with Chandragupta.[25] The other books in the series are *Emperor Vikramaditya* (2019) and *Emperor Harsha* (2020).

Kay studied history at Delhi University, and when she embarked on a literary career she recognised that history is 'so much misunderstood, and so maliciously used as well. It's thus vital to promote, in any small way one can, a better understanding of it.'[26] To this end, she undertook considerable research to prepare for and inform the writing of *Emperor Chandragupta*. Her reading included books by a range of prominent contemporary scholars such as Upinder Singh, Romila Thapar, Nayanjot Lahiri and Paul Kosmin. However, for translations of Graeco-Roman sources pertinent to the early Mauryan period, she turned to the nineteenth-century scholar J. W. McCrindle (Chapter 5). It is fascinating to see that McCrindle's work continues to inform not only academic scholarship, but also the writing of historical fiction for a new and modern audience. Why did Kay use this work instead of more recent translations and interpretations? It was freely and easily accessible on Google Books, which highlights the importance of open-access content.[27]

Given this extensive research and her explicit acknowledgement of the importance of promoting a better understanding of history, it is curious that Kay chose to portray Durdhara and Helen in the way she did.

There is no information whatever about Chandragupta's marriage to Seleucus' daughter in the sources, but it remains a compelling story. In Kay's novel, as in the television series *Chandra Nandini*, Durdhara is presented as the dutiful and loyal Indian wife whom Chandragupta mourns when she dies. In contrast, Helen is an unsympathetic, selfish and sometimes childish character who constantly rails against her situation and so causes problems for those around her.

When asked about this dichotomy in her novel, Kay responded by saying that she wished she 'could have added more complexity to the characters, especially Durdhara and Helen. But I had just so many pages in which to fit in the book. I'd much rather have done a 4 volume series on Chandragupta like the Conn Iggulden books on Caesar and Genghis Khan.'[28] Perhaps developing the characters in more depth over multiple volumes might have led to a less stark and troubling 'Indian good, foreign bad' division between the two women. This contrasting treatment was not mentioned by any of the reviewers on Amazon (India, UK and USA), nor on the Goodreads website. Reviewers on these sites tend to share their opinions freely, so the omission suggests that this aspect of the story was acceptable to them and did not stand out in the narrative.

Different approaches are, of course, possible. In Sawkar's *Chakravarti Chandragupta*, Chandragupta marries Seleucus' daughter Cornelia – a surprisingly anachronistic Roman name for a Hellenistic-era Greek woman – as well as Durdhara. In her book, the women have an idealised relationship, with Cornelia even raising Durdhara's son, Bindusāra, after Durdhara's murder. Pillai sets up the thorny issue of Chandragupta marrying Helen and then neatly sidesteps it. In his novel, Seleucus offers his daughter to Chandragupta as part of their treaty, but Chandragupta rejects the marriage, saying that he is 'well past the age of marriage'.[29]

Overall, the same basic narrative and impression of Chandragupta are shared in these three books, as in most of the previous historical novels written about him. The primary focus is on the lead-up to his gaining the throne and establishing the Mauryan empire. It is only towards the end of the story, usually the last third of the book, that the action climaxes with Chandragupta's battle with Seleucus. At this point, Chandragupta reaches the pinnacle of his success and power, repulsing the foreign invader and agreeing a treaty of peace. Seleucus is invariably cast as the consummate 'baddie' while Chandragupta is the heroic India ruler who fights for his country. So far, so similar. The key difference between these publications and in the earlier novels is the presentation of Seleucus and the Greeks as stand-ins for the British, or other colonising

European powers, and the colonised Indians fighting back for their independence.

For a modern audience, this British versus Indian clash no longer needs to be concealed within an ancient story in case of repercussions from the colonial authorities. Instead, there are now numerous, globally available works of historical fiction, popular histories, and other forms of art, film and popular culture that explicitly and critically deal with all aspects of the colonial period. Artwork by the Singh Twins stands out in this regard. The display of their triptych *Rule Britannia: Legacies of exchange* at Buckingham Palace in 2018 as part of the *Splendours of the Subcontinent* exhibition shows just how much things have changed. After all, it would have been almost unimaginable, even 50 years ago, that a work of art created by members of the South Asian diaspora which vividly, unabashedly and critically explores the themes of trade and empire, and their legacies, could be displayed at the Queen's residence in London.[30]

Chandragupta: repackaging a hero for children

Over the last few decades, the story of Chandragupta's life and achievements has been reshaped and repackaged for children through comic books, cartoons, toys and video games. The first comic book about Chandragupta was published by Amar Chitra Katha (ACK; 'immortal illustrated story') in 1978. It was accompanied by three comics featuring figures associated with him: *Chanakya* (1971), *Ashoka* (1973) and *Megasthenes* (1987).[31]

ACK was founded by Anant Pai (1929–2011), editor and publisher, in 1967. He was inspired to do so after watching a television quiz show in which Indian children were able to answer questions about Greek but not Indian mythology. In response, he created a series of lavishly illustrated comics with child-friendly narratives that told the stories of India's religious epics as well as of its religious and historical figures, and folk tales. The aim was to educate through an entertaining and easily accessible medium, and foster the integration of Indian children through their knowledge of a shared past. The idea is most clearly expressed in one of his most famous quotations: 'Unless you have continuity with the past, you can't easily adjust with the present. An acquaintance with the past is a must. You may not agree with it. You can disagree with it, but be aware of it.'[32] Emphasising the central importance of this principle to the comics are the words 'The route to your roots', which are printed below the ACK logo inside each comic.

The story about Chandragupta fits neatly into Pai's model. The narrative is based on Narayana's *Mudra Manjusha* (see above). Pai not only had editorial oversight of all of the comics produced during his tenure at ACK, but was also closely involved in the development of the narrative and the artwork. His ideas for presenting Chandragupta's story were therefore influential, and either the decision to base it on Narayana's work came directly from him or he agreed to it. This decision is a curious one: apart from Chandragupta's replacing the Nanda empire with his own, and the much later Jain tradition which associated him with Cāṇakya, the story has no basis in the available historical evidence. The contents of this comic thus run counter to Pai's founding vision for ACK publications.

According to the comic, Chandragupta was one of a hundred brothers who were closely related to the ruler of Magadha. In order to neutralise their influence and the competition for power they represented, Nanda, the heir to the throne, murders Chandragupta's father and all of his brothers when they are invited to a banquet. Chandragupta alone survives and is imprisoned by Nanda. Later, he is given permission to solve a riddle to uphold Magadha's honour – which he does – and as a reward he is released from prison and put in charge of the state guesthouse. It is here that he meets Cāṇakya, the Brahmin, whom Nanda insults. This offence leads Cāṇakya to vow to destroy Nanda. At this point, Chandragupta and Cāṇakya join forces and successfully engage in political intrigue against Nanda which involves neighbouring rulers. At the very end, Chandragupta kills Nanda and enters Pataliputra in triumph.

As we saw in Chapter 1, there is very little information about Chandragupta's life, which leaves plenty of room for imaginative improvisation, but there are *some* surviving details. So deciding to set historical information to one side and to present instead a wholly imagined one is bizarre, not least because Pai's stated aim is that ACK comics will provide a 'route to your roots'. In this case, the route was to an ahistorical past, a story devoid of history. A note that accompanies some of the comics states that basing the narrative on Narayana's story is 'only befitting, for Chandragupta, though born in the North, spent his last days at Shravanabelagola, in Karnataka'. Both Narayana and Pai were from the south: Narayana worked in the court of Krishnaraja Wadiyar ('Wodeyar') III, Maharaja of Mysore, and Pai was born in Karkala, in neighbouring Karnataka (formerly Madras Presidency). Pai's personal connection with the region in which Chandragupta was believed to have died may have influenced his decision to base the comic's narrative on the work of an author from south India.

Another reason for using Narayana's story may be a decision to focus on Chandragupta's exploits other than those that involved the Macedonians. Most modern narratives about his life, written before the publication of the ACK comic, peak at the moment he defeats Seleucus by the banks of the Indus. These earlier works were written at a time when India was still under colonial rule and this story enabled Indian authors to make known their opposition to this state of affairs. In contrast, the comic was published in 1978, decades after independence. At this point, there was no longer a need to subsume a subversive, anti-colonial narrative within an ancient story. So the comic provided an opportunity to shape a new image of Chandragupta and share it with a new, youthful audience unfamiliar with previous iterations of the story, or, in fact, with Mauryan history in general.

The *Chandragupta* comic provided a slightly different narrative from that found in the *Chanakya* or *Megasthenes* publications, and there are a number of discrepancies between the three storylines. For example, Chandragupta is presented as the eldest of eight sons of King Nanda in *Chanakya*, but not in the comic that bears his name. While there is no reference to his battle with Seleucus in *Chandragupta*, this story is told at the start of the *Megasthenes* comic and at the end of *Chanakya*.

In *Chanakya*, a page is devoted to this part of Chandragupta's story. After 'building a stronger empire, Chandragupta declared war on the Greek invaders'. He defeated the Greeks and married Seleucus' daughter. This is the only aspect of the Seleucid-Mauryan treaty that is mentioned and the only time Seleucus is mentioned. The rest of the comic is devoted to his rise to power in India with Cāṇakya's help. Overall, Chandragupta is shown to be the victorious defender of India who gains a Macedonian wife upon defeating Seleucus. The contrast between the successful and heroic Chandragupta and the conquered Seleucus is even more marked in the *Megasthenes* comic.

In *Megasthenes*, Chandragupta is presented as a well-established ruler worried about the threat posed by the Greeks on the borders of his kingdom. His response is to invade Greek territory, and in the ensuing war he defeats Seleucus' army. Seleucus is brought before Chandragupta shackled and on his knees. There is no treaty: Seleucus says, 'My forces have been crushed. I am prepared to pay whatever tribute you demand.' Chandragupta requests 'only those areas that belong to India', namely Aria, Arachosia and Paropamisadae. At this point, Chandragupta announces that they are friends and says, 'As a token of this friendship, I give you 500 elephants, as a special gift from India.' The gift exchange continues as Seleucus offers Chandragupta 'what is dearest to my heart': his daughter and Megasthenes.

The details about the exchange of land and elephants and a marriage alliance correspond with information found in the sources, but this is where any similarity to the ancient texts ends. The nature of comics, especially those produced for a younger audience, means that stories need to be condensed down to their essentials. The Seleucid-Mauryan power relations presented by ACK comics follow those established by the Indian historians writing in the period immediately before and during independence (see Chapter 5). In this case, the gaps in the sources have been filled in so as to elevate Chandragupta and demean Seleucus in dramatic fashion. Any nuance in the story has been lost.

ACK comics, like other plays, stories, films and television series, have used artistic licence to share a fictionalised account of Chandragupta's life. But there is a key difference: ACK purports to present accurate historical accounts of the past to its young readership. However, as the dramatically illustrated comics sharing stories of Chandragupta and Megasthenes have shown, it does not always succeed. Scholars and journalists have long written about the discrepancy between historical fact and the sometimes ahistorical stories presented in these comics. They also highlight the nationalist thread that runs through them; this is an important point because Indian nationalism encourages the adoption of a particular viewpoint in the publications. The comics about Chandragupta and Megasthenes exemplify both of these points, and also show the extent of the problem.

The result has been the widespread dissemination of a very partial account of Chandragupta's rise to power and interaction with Seleucus. This is important because these comics are so influential. Their consistently low price means that they are affordable to a large segment of the population in India; in fact ACK leads the children's publishing sector in India. Its publications have proved very popular: the ACK website notes that over one hundred million copies of their comics have been sold to date and they continue to sell over one and a half million every year.[33] ACK has also expanded into the digital arena, with approximately half a million downloads of its app and similarly large numbers of followers across its social media platforms, including YouTube.[34] Whereas its content was previously consumed primarily in India and among the South Asian diaspora, it is now looking to expand globally.[35]

In India, school children are taught the history of early India, including the Mauryans, so there are opportunities to counter the faulty narratives found in the ACK comics. This is not the case elsewhere. In the UK, for example, this period of history is only taught at university level, and then only at a few places, where it is generally a minor part of archaeology courses. Most people with an interest in Mauryan or early Indian history, whether they live in India or elsewhere in the world, look to other sources of information to develop their knowledge independently. These sources include television shows, history books, Wikipedia and, especially for children, ACK comics.[36] The result is that children, and others, who read the comics are presented with faulty historical accounts infused with nationalist ideology.[37] This knowledge is not countered unless they actively seek out other, more carefully argued sources of information. And unfortunately, accessible and well-researched books on ancient Indian history written for a general audience remain few.

Pai aimed to be as exact as possible in the scholarship showcased in his comics, but this aspiration had its limitations. After all, he also said, 'You must tell the truth; you must tell what is pleasant. And that which is unpleasant – just because it is true, you need not say it.'[38] The result was a complex series of tensions that often drew criticism in relation to a range of subjects, including religious stories and figures, gender, and the portrayal of non-Hindus as well as of people of different castes.[39] Pai and his staff responded to these complaints and began to make changes in the way they depicted, for example, different religious and historical figures.[40] Nowadays, ACK editors and artists take care to correct stereotypical representations of characters in their comics.[41] However, the editors, authors and artists have not yet returned to the stories of Chandragupta, Cāṇakya or Megasthenes in order to revise the problematic and ahistorical narratives that they contain. I hope that this book encourages ACK to revisit these comics.

Notes

1 Chatterjee's poem *Vande Mataram* ('I salute you, Mother [India]') was first published in *Anandamath*. The title became a political slogan during the struggle for independence, and was later adopted as the national song (not anthem) of India.

2 Mukherjee 1999, 238; Das 1995, 113. Kempu Narayana's dates are unknown.

3 A Telugu novel, *Vasumati Vasantam* (1911), was written by Venkata Parvatisvara Kavalu. It was set during the period of Chandragupta Maurya (Das 1995, 110), but it has not been possible to find out more about the storyline of this book or about its author.

4 Ayyar later split *Three Men of Destiny* into two parts, one of which, with some revisions, became *Chanakya and Chandragupta* (1951). Because it has already been discussed as part of *Three Men of Destiny*, *Chanakya and Chandragupta* is not included here.
5 Elias, 2005, 91.
6 Ayyar 1939, vii.
7 Vasunia (2013, 113), also emphasised this point about Ayyar's hope for cultural parity.
8 Ayyar 1939, xxii.
9 Ayyar 1939, xxii.
10 Ayyar 1939, 303.
11 Hyder 1998, 42.
12 Hyder 1998, 16.
13 Socio-economic trends in India provide more context for the upsurge in publishing during this period. After economic liberalisation in India from 1991 onwards, the middle class grew significantly and also had more disposable income to spend on non-essentials, including books. During the 2010s, India's GDP increased rapidly, as did the number of Indian households with a disposable income of $10,000+. There are numerous books and articles about the Indian economy and middle class, including Roy 2018.
14 Another book could be added to this list: *Chanakya and Chandragupta: The mentor and the prodigy* (Delhi: Vijay Goel, 2013) by Manoj Kumar. Unfortunately, I was not able to source a copy of this book, so I do not include it here.
15 All three of Sengupta's books are listed among the '28 Best Historical Fiction Books That You Should Read' on the HarperCollins India website: https://harpercollins.co.in/historical-fiction-books/ (accessed 3 November 2022). This list encapsulates the wide range of historical fiction published in India, from the ancient past (represented by Sengupta's trilogy), through Indu Sundaresan's *Shadow Princess* set in seventeenth-century Mughal India, and *Jorasanko* by Aruna Chakravarti, which tells the story of the women in Rabindranath Tagore's family.
16 In an interview for Scroll India, Muthuraman addresses the question of whether there will be a change in the trend for historical fiction to focus primarily on the kings and emperors of north India: Abdullah Khan, MEET THE WRITER:
'I'd like to see historical fiction that talks less about kings and wars and more about people': An interview with Veena Muthuraman, the author of 'The Great Anicut'. 31 October 2021: https://scroll.in/article/1009366/id-like-to-see-historical-fiction-that-talks-less-about-kings-and-wars-and-more-about-people (accessed 3 November 2022).
17 Manimughdha S. Sharma, 'Indian readers prefer fact over fiction', *Times of India*, 14 April 2020: https://timesofindia.indiatimes.com/home/sunday-times/indian-readers-prefer-fact-over-fiction/articleshow/75142266.cms (accessed 3 November 2022).
18 Dalrymple discusses the growth of interest in this genre in India with Nishtha Narayan, 'Writing on historical non-fiction has become mainstream than 3 decades ago', *The Print*, 13 March 2022: https://theprint.in/india/writing-on-historical-non-fiction-has-become-mainstream-than-3-decades-ago-william-dalrymple/871325/. So does Pillai for Scroll India: Sayari Debnath, 'Making history enjoyable is more difficult than people sometimes think', 26 March 2022: https://scroll.in/article/1019563/making-history-enjoyable-is-more-difficult-than-people-sometimes-think-manu-s-pillai (accessed 3 November 2022).
19 Rahul Mitra's *The Boy from Pataliputra* (2017) is set during Chandragupta's rise to power but, as in Muthuraman's book, the protagonist is not one of the great rulers but a minor nobleman from Pataliputra. For this reason, the book is not included here.
20 Amish Raj Mulmi discusses the topic of bestselling books in India in 'How many copies must a book sell to be a bestseller in India (and why are there so many lists?)', Scroll India, 20 August 2017: https://scroll.in/article/847675/how-many-copies-must-a-book-sell-to-be-a-bestseller-in-india-and-why-are-there-so-many-lists (accessed 3 November 2022).
21 At the top of each bestseller list on its website, Amazon states that the lists are 'Our most popular products based on sales. Updated hourly.' For example, this is the list for historical fiction: https://www.amazon.in/gp/bestsellers/books/1318164031/ref=zg_bs_pg_2?ie=UTF8&pg=2 (accessed23 November 2022).
22 It is more difficult to compare these books on Amazon UK, because they are ranked under different headings. The ranking for Sawkar's book in historical fiction (Kindle Store) is #34,853 (#73,894 in printed books) and that for Pillai's is #62,657. Kay's novel is not listed under historical fiction, but is ranked #29,916 in war story fiction. As with Amazon India's listings, it has not been possible to determine how many books are included under each heading. This lack

of information makes it difficult to understand how well the books are selling in comparison with others in the genre. Notably, there are no reviews or ratings for any of these books on Amazon UK. This detail coupled with the low-ranking numbers suggests that the books are not selling particularly well in the UK.

23 Much has been written on the issue of book piracy in India, including Aswin Sekhar, 'Sale of illegally photocopied books on trains: What do authors have to say?', *News Minutes*, 23 January 2018: https://www.thenewsminute.com/article/sale-illegally-photocopied-books-trains-what-do-authors-have-say-75190 (accessed 3 November 2022).

24 The name Adity Kay is also a pseudonym.

25 R. Krithika, 'We don't "trust" ourselves to understand history', interview with Adity Kay [Anu Kumar], *The Hindu*, 10 December 2016: https://www.thehindu.com/books/books-authors/%E2%80%9CWe-don%E2%80%99t-%E2%80%98trust%E2%80%99-ourselves-to-understand-history%E2%80%9D/article16789339.ece#:~:text=Aditi%20Kay%20was%20the%20pseudonym,fiction%20in%20India%20and%20more (accessed 3 November 2022).

26 Interview with Adity Kay in *The Hindu*, as in note 25.

27 Adity Kay (pers. comm., February 2018).

28 Adity Kay (pers. comm., February 2018).

29 Pillai 2012, 284.

30 For a high-resolution image of *Rule Britannia: Legacies of exchange* see https://www.rct.uk/resources/game-splendours-of-the-subcontinent-triptych-by-the-singh-twins (accessed 3 November 2022).

31 This is one of only a handful of ACK comics that focus on a European figure. The others are *Paurava and Alexander* (1978), *Albert Einstein* (1983), *Sea Route to India* (1986; focuses on Vasco da Gama), *Louis Pasteur* (1990), *Napoleon Bonaparte* (1990), *Pierre and Marie Curie* (1991), *Mother Teresa* (2010) and *Jim Corbett* (2012).

32 ACK website: https://www.amarchitrakatha.com/about-us/ (accessed 25 November 2022).

33 ACK website: https://www.amarchitrakatha.com/about-us/ (accessed 3 November 2022).

34 The ACK YouTube channel includes video versions of the *Chandragupta* and *Chanakya* comics in English; they have been viewed over 34,000 and 56,000 times respectively. The Hindi version of the *Chanakya* video has been viewed over 68,000 times.

35 Priti David, 'And now, a dapper Ravana: Amar Chitra Katha undergoes makeover', *The Hindu*, 16 December 2017: https://www.thehindu.com/entertainment/art/and-now-a-dapper-ravana-amar-chitra-katha-undergoes-makeover/article61844885.ece (accessed 3 November 2022).

36 Hawley (1995, 382–4) shares his discussions about ACK comics with members of the Hindu diaspora community in the USA. While the focus is on religion, history and historical figures are mentioned as well.

37 Pritchett (1997, 92ff.) discusses the explicit and more subtle presence of Indian nationalism in the ACK comics that deal with the modern period, particularly in relation to Indian independence. As part of this study, she also explores the negative 'them' and more positive 'us' dichotomy, which is equally relevant to the comics dealing with ancient history.

38 Pritchett 1997, 80. This was Pai's translation of a Sanskrit phrase: 'satyam brūyāt priyam brūyāt mā brūyāt satyam apriyam.'

39 Pritchett 1997, 92–4, 95–6.

40 A prominent example concerned the ACK depiction of Valmiki, the author of the *Rāmāyaṇa*, as a thief. A group named the Valmiki Sabha took offence at this portrayal. See Shahnaz Habib, 'Anant Pai obituary', *The Guardian*, 7 April 2011: https://www.theguardian.com/world/2011/apr/07/anant-pai-obituary (accessed 3 November 2022).

41 See Priti David, 'And now, a dapper Ravana', as in note 35.

Bibliography

Alam, Muzaffar and Sanjay Subrahmanyam. *Writing the Mughal World: Studies on culture and politics*. New York: Columbia University Press, 2011.

Ayyar, A. S. Panchapakesa. *Three Men of Destiny*. Madras: C. Coomarasawmy Naidu & Sons, 1939.

Bagchi, Sanat Kumar (ed.). 'Correspondence between Rabindranath and Radhakrishnan'. *Visva-Bharati Quarterly* NS 1 (1 & 2) (1990): 16–55.

Bailey, Gregory. 'The Purāṇas: A study in the development of Hinduism'. In *The Study of Hinduism*, edited by Arvind Sharma, 139–68. Columbia: University of South Carolina Press, 2003.

Balcerowicz, Piotr. 'Royal patronage of Jainism: The myth of Candragupta Maurya and Bhadrabāhu'. In *The Gift of Knowledge: Patterns of patronage in Jainism: Essays in honour of Hampa Nagarajaiah's promotion of Jain studies*, edited by Christine Chojnacki and Basile Leclère, 33–66. Gandhinagar: Sapna Book House, 2018.

Banerjee, Prathama. 'Chanakya/Kautilya: History, philosophy, theater and the twentieth-century political', *History of the Present* 2 (1) (Spring 2012): 24–51.

Banerjee, Prathama. *Elementary Aspects of the Political: Histories from the Global South*. Durham, NC: Duke University Press, 2021.

Bapu, Prabhu. *Hindu Mahasabha in Colonial North India, 1915–1930: Constructing nation and history*. Abingdon; New York: Routledge, 2013.

Bar-Kochva, Bezalel. *The Seleucid Army: Organization and tactics in the great campaigns*. Cambridge: Cambridge University Press, 1976.

[Barnett, Lionel D.] L. D. B. 'Review: *Chandragupta Maurya and His Times* by Radha Kumud Mookerji: Sir William Meyer Lectures: University of Madras, 1943', *English Historical Review* 59 (235) (Sept. 1944): 416–17.

Barnett, Lionel D. 'Obituary: F. W. Thomas, C.I.E., F.B.A., Ph.D., D. Lit., D.Litt. (1867–1956)', *Journal of the Royal Asiatic Society* 89 (1–2) (April 1957): 142–3. https://doi.org/10.1017/S0035869X00107762.

Baums, Stefan. 'Greek or Indian? The *Questions of Menander* and early onomastic patterns in early Gandhāra'. In *Buddhism and Gandhara: An archaeology of museum collections*, edited by Himanshu Prabha Ray, 33–46. Abingdon; New York: Routledge, 2018.

Bayly, C. A. *Empire and Information: Intelligence gathering and social communication in India, 1780–1870*. Cambridge: Cambridge University Press, 1996.

Bayly, C. A. *Recovering Liberties: Indian thought in the age of liberalism and empire: The Wiles lectures given at the Queen's University of Belfast, 2007*. Cambridge: Cambridge University Press, 2012.

Bedrosian, Robert (trans.). *Eusebius' Chronicle translated from the Classical Armenian*. http://www.attalus.org/armenian/euseb.html (accessed 8 December 2022).

Bhandare, Shailendra. 'From Kauṭilya to Kosambi and beyond: The quest for a Mauryan/Asokan coinage'. In *Reimagining Aśoka: Memory and history*, edited by Patrick Olivelle, Janice Leoshko and Himanshu Prabha Ray, 93–128. New Delhi: Oxford University Press, 2012.

Bhandarkar, Ramkrishna Gopal. *A Peep into the Early History of India: From the foundation of the Maurya dynasty to the downfall of the imperial Gupta dynasty (B.C. 322–circa 500 A.D.)* Bombay: Education Society's Steam Press, 1900.

Bhandarkar, Ramkrishna Gopal. *A Peep into the Early History of India: From the foundation of the Maurya dynasty to the downfall of the imperial Gupta dynasty (B.C. 322–circa 500 A.D.)*, 2nd edn. Bombay: D. B. Taraporevala Sons & Co., 1920.

Bhargava, Manjul. 'Dr. P. L. Bhargava and his contribution to Indology', *Indologica Taurinensia* 36 (2010): 21–35.

Bhargava, Purushottam Lal. *Chandragupta Maurya*. Lucknow: Upper India Publishing House, 1935.
Billows, Richard A. *Antigonos the One-Eyed and the Creation of the Hellenistic State*. Berkeley and Los Angeles: University of California Press, 1990.
Billows, Richard A. *Kings and Colonists: aspects of Macedonian imperialism*. Leiden: E.J. Brill, 1994.
Black, Jonathan. *Power & Beauty: The art of Sir Oswald Birley*. London: Philip Mould, 2017.
Bose, Mihir. *Bollywood: A history*. Stroud: Tempus, 2006.
Bosworth, A. B. *A Historical Commentary on Arrian's History of Alexander. Volume 2: Commentary on books iv–v*. Oxford: Clarendon Press, 1995.
Bosworth, A. B. 'The historical setting of Megasthenes' Indica', *Classical Philology* 91 (2) (1996): 113–27.
Briant, Pierre. 'Alexander the Great and the Enlightenment: William Robertson (1721–1793), the Empire and the road to India', *Cromohs* 10 (2005): 1–9.
Briant, Pierre. *The First European: A history of Alexander in the age of empire*. Trans. Nicholas Elliott. Cambridge, MA: Harvard University Press, 2017.
Brown, Stewart J. 'William Robertson (1721–1793) and the Scottish Enlightenment'. In *William Robertson and the Expansion of Empire*, edited by Stewart J. Brown, 7–35. Cambridge: Cambridge University Press, 1997.
Brown, Truesdell S. 'The merits and weaknesses of Megasthenes', *Phoenix* 11 (1) (1957): 12–24.
Brunt, Peter A. 'On historical fragments and epitomes', *Classical Quarterly* 30 (2) (1980): 477–94. https://doi.org/10.1017/S0009838800042403.
Brunt, Peter A. (trans.). *Arrian. Anabasis of Alexander, volume II: Books 5–7, Indica*. Cambridge, MA: Harvard University Press, 1983.
Burgess, James (ed.). *The Indian Antiquary: A Journal of oriental research in archaeology, history, literature, languages, philosophy, religion, folklore &c., &c., &c.* 4. Bombay: Education Society's Press, 1875.
Capdetrey, Laurent. *Le pouvoir séleucide: Territoire, administration, finances d'un royaume hellénistique (312–129 av. J.-C.)*. Rennes: Presses universitaires de Rennes, 2007.
Chakrabarti, Dilip K. *India: An Archaeological History: Palaeolithic beginnings to early historic foundations*, 2nd edn. New Delhi: Oxford University Press, 2009.
Chatterjee, Sris Chandra. *Magadha Architecture and Culture*. Calcutta: University of Calcutta, 1942.
Chatterjee, S. D., N. N. Ghosh, S. Kisdnasami and K. G. Bandopadhyay, 'Radiocarbon dating of ancient Pāṭaliputra rampart', *Science and Culture* 20 (12) (1955): 615–17.
Chattopadhyay, Jayanti. 'The rise and fall of *Chandragupta*: The Hindi response to Dwijendralal Roy'. In *Comparative Literature: Theory and practice,* edited by Amiya Dev and Sisir Kumar Das, 219–31. New Delhi: Allied Publishers, 1989.
Coloru, Omar. *Da Alessandro a Menandro: Il regno greco di Battriana*. Pisa; Rome: Serra, 2009.
Commins, David and David W. Lesch. *Historical Dictionary of Syria*, 3rd edn. Lanham, MD: Scarecrow Press, 2013.
Coningham, Robin and Ruth Young. *The Archaeology of South Asia: From the Indus to Asoka, c. 6500 BCE–200 CE*. Cambridge: Cambridge University Press, 2015.
Corbridge, Stuart and John Harriss. *Reinventing India: liberalization, Hindu nationalism and popular democracy*. Cambridge: Polity Press, 2000.
Cort, John. Review. '*The Lives of the Jain Elders*. By Hemacandra; translated by R. C. C. Fynes. Oxford World's Classics. Oxford: Oxford University Press, 1998', *Journal of Asian Studies* 58 (4) (1999): 1166–7. https://doi.org/10.2307/2658552.
Coulson, Michael (ed. and trans.). *Rākṣasa's Ring by Viśākhadatta*. New York: New York University Press, 2005.
Cribb, Joe. 'The Greek contacts of Chandragupta Maurya and Ashoka and their relevance to Mauryan and Buddhist chronology'. In *From Local to Global: Papers in Asian history and culture, Prof. A.K. Narain Commemoration Volume*, edited by Kamal Sheel, Charles Willemen and Kenneth Zysk, 3–27. Delhi: Buddhist World Press, 2017.
Cunningham, Alexander. *The Bhilsa Topes; or, Buddhist Monuments of Central India: Comprising a brief historical sketch of the rise, progress, and decline of Buddhism; with an account of the opening and examination of the various groups of topes around Bhilsa*. London: Smith, Elder, 1854.
Cunningham, Alexander. *The Ancient Geography of India. I. The Buddhist period, including the campaigns of Alexander, and the travels of Hwen-Thsang*. London: Trübner and Co., 1871.
Das, Sisir Kumar. *A History of Indian Literature 1911–1956: Struggle for freedom: Triumph and tragedy*. New Delhi: Sahitya Akademi, 1995, repr. 2005.
David, Saul. *The Indian Mutiny: 1857*. London: Viking, 2002.

De Casparis, Johannes G. Review. '*The Classical Accounts of India*. By R. C. Majumdar, ... K. L. Mukhopadhyay, Calcutta, 1960', *Journal of the Royal Asiatic Society* 94 (304) (1962): 152. https://doi.org/10.1017/S0035869X00120714.

Desai, Mahadev. *The Gospel of Selfless Action: or, The Gita according to Gandhi* (translation of the original in Gujarati). Ahmedabad: Navajivan Publishing House, 1946.

Dihle, Albrecht. *Antike und Orient: gesammelte Aufsätze* (ed. Viktor Pöschl and Hubert Petersmann). Heidelberg: Winter, 1984.

Dimmitt, Cornelia and J. A. B. van Buitenen (eds and trans). *Classical Hindu Mythology: A reader in the Sanskrit Purāṇas*. Philadelphia, PA: Temple University Press, 1978; repr. New Delhi: Rupa, 1983.

Dutt, Romesh C. *The Civilization of India*. London: J.M. Dent, 1900.

Dwyer, Rachel. 'Bollywood's empire: Indian cinema and the diaspora'. In *Routledge Handbook of the South Asian Diaspora*, edited by Joya Chatterji and David Washbrook, 409–18. Abingdon; New York: Routledge, 2013.

Elias, Mohamed. 'Ayyar, A. S. Panchpakesa (1899–1963)'. In *Encyclopedia of Post-Colonial Literatures in English*, 2nd edn, edited by Eugene Benson and Leonard W. Conolly, vol. 1, 91–2. Abingdon; New York: Routledge, 2005.

Errington, Elizabeth and Vesta Sarkhosh Curtis. *From Persepolis to the Punjab: Exploring ancient Iran, Afghanistan and Pakistan*. London: British Museum Press, 2007.

Errington, R. Malcolm. *A History of the Hellenistic World, 323–30 bc*. Malden, MA; Oxford: Blackwell Publishing, 2008.

Falk, Harry. *Aśokan Sites and Artefacts: A source-book with bibliography*. Mainz am Rhein: Verlag Philipp von Zabern, 2006.

Ferguson, John (ed. and trans.). *Clement of Alexandria. Stromateis: Books one to three*. Washington, D.C.: Catholic University of America Press, 1991.

Fitzgerald, James L. (trans. and ed.). *The Mahābhārata. Book 11: The Book of the Women; Book 12: The Book of Peace, Part One*. Chicago: University of Chicago Press, 2004.

Fouracre, Paul. *The Age of Charles Martel*. Harlow: Longman, 2000.

Franklin, Michael J. *'Orientalist Jones': Sir William Jones, Poet, Lawyer, and Linguist, 1746–1794*. Oxford: Oxford University Press, 2011.

Fraser, Peter M. *Cities of Alexander the Great*. Oxford: Clarendon Press, 1996.

Frey, James. *The Indian Rebellion, 1857–1859: A short history with documents*. Indianapolis: Hackett, 2020.

Fussman, Gérard. 'L'Indo-Grec Ménandre ou Paul Demiéville revisité', *Journal asiatique* 281 (1–2) (1993): 61–138. https://doi.org/10.2143/JA.281.1.2006132.

Fynes, R. C. C. (trans.). *The Lives of the Jain Elders*. By Hemacandra. Oxford: Oxford University Press, 1998.

Geiger, Wilhelm. *The Dīpavamsa and Mahāvaṃsa and their historical development in Ceylon* (trans. Ethel M. Coomaraswamy). Colombo: H. C. Cottle, Government Printer, Ceylon 1908.

Geiger, Wilhelm and Mabel H. Bode. *The Mahāvaṃsa or the great chronicle of Ceylon*. London: Oxford University Press for the Pali Text Society, 1912.

Gillies, John. *The History of the World, from the Reign of Alexander to that of Augustus*, vol. 1. London: Printed for A. Strahan; and T. Cadell and W. Davies, 1807.

Gombrich, Richard. 'Dating the Buddha: A red herring revealed'. In *The Dating of the Historical Buddha/Die Datierung des historischen Buddha*, 3 vols, edited by Heinz Bechert, vol. 2, 237–59. Göttingen: Vandenhoeck & Ruprecht, 1992.

The Government Regulations for the Examination of Candidates for Appointments to the Civil Service of the East India Company. London: Edward Stanford, 1855.

Grainger, John D. *A Seleukid Prosopography and Gazetteer*. Leiden: Brill, 1997.

Grainger, John D. *Alexander the Great Failure: the Collapse of the Macedonian Empire*. London: Hambledon Continuum, 2007.

Grainger, John D. *Seleukos Nikator: Constructing a Hellenistic kingdom*. London: Routledge, 1990; repr. Abingdon; New York: Routledge, 2014.

Grayson, A. K. *Babylonian Historical-Literary Texts*. Toronto: University of Toronto Press, 1975.

Gruen, Erich S. 'Greeks and non-Greeks'. In *The Cambridge Companion to the Hellenistic World*, edited by Glenn R. Bugh, 295–314. Cambridge: Cambridge University Press, 2006.

Gupta, Samita. 'Sris Chandra Chatterjee: The quest for a national architecture', *Indian Economic and Social History Review* 28 (2) (1991): 187–201. https://doi.org/10.1177/001946469102800204.

Guruge, Ananda W. P. *Mahāvaṃsa, the Great Chronicle of Sri Lanka: Chapters one to thirty-seven: An annotated new translation with prolegomena*. Colombo: Associated Newspapers of Ceylon, 1989.

Habib, Irfan and Vivekanand Jha. *Mauryan India*. New Delhi: Tulika Books, 2004.

Hall, Catherine. *Macaulay and Son: Architects of imperial Britain*. New Haven, CT; London: Yale University Press, 2012.
Hamilton, Hans C. and William Falconer. *The Geography of Strabo*. Literally translated, with notes, in three volumes. London: George Bell & Sons, 1854–7.
Harris, Peter. *Income Tax in Common Law Jurisdictions: From the origins to 1820*. Cambridge: Cambridge University Press, 2006.
Harrison, Brian (ed.). *The History of the University of Oxford. Volume 8: The Twentieth Century*. Gen. ed. Trevor H. Aston. Oxford: Clarendon Press, 1994.
Harvey, Peter. *An Introduction to Buddhism. Teachings, History and Practices*, 2nd edn. Cambridge: Cambridge University Press, 2013.
Haubold, Johannes, Giovanni B. Lanfranchi, Robert Rollinger and John M. Steele (eds.). *The World of Berossos: Proceedings of the 4th International Colloquium on 'The Ancient Near East between Classical and Ancient Oriental Traditions', Hatfield College, Durham 7th–9th July 2010*. Wiesbaden: Harrassowitz, 2013.
Hawley, John S. 'The saints subdued: Domestic virtue and national integration in *Amar Chitra Katha*'. In *Media and the Transformation of Religion in South Asia*, edited by Lawrence A. Babb and Susan S. Wadley, 107–36. Philadelphia: University of Pennsylvania Press, 1995.
Heckel, Waldemar. *Who's Who in the Age of Alexander the Great: Prosopography of Alexander's empire*. Malden, MA: Blackwell, 2006.
Hercher, Rudolf and Alfred Eberhard (eds). *Arriani Nicomediensis Scripta Minora*. Leipzig: Teubner, 1885.
Hinüber, Oskar von. *A Handbook of Pāli Literature*. Berlin; New York: Walter de Gruyter, 1996.
[Holdich, Thomas H.] T. H. H. Review. 'Dr. McCrindle's "*Ancient India*"', *Geographical Journal* 18 (6) (Dec. 1901): 609–11. https://doi.org/10.2307/1775364.
Holt, Frank L. *Alexander the Great and Bactria: The formation of a Greek frontier in central Asia*. Leiden; New York: Brill, 1988.
Hornblower, Jane. *Hieronymus of Cardia*. Oxford: Oxford University Press, 1981.
Horner, I. B. (trans.). *Milinda's Questions*, vol. 2. London: Luzac, 1964.
Hyder, Qurratulain. *River of Fire (Aag Ka Darya)*. New Delhi: Kali for Women, 1998 [1959].
Inden, Ronald. *Imagining India*. Oxford: Basil Blackwell, 1990.
Jacobs, Bruno. 'Achaemenid Satrapies'. *Encyclopaedia Iranica, online edition* (2011). http://www.iranicaonline.org/articles/achaemenid-satrapies.
Jaffrelot, Christophe. *The Hindu Nationalist Movement and Indian Politics: 1925 to the 1990s: Strategies of identity-building, implantation and mobilisation (with special reference to Central India)*. New Delhi: Penguin Books, 1999.
Jaffrelot, Christophe (ed.). *Hindu Nationalism: A Reader*. Princeton; Oxford: Princeton University Press, 2009.
Jaffrelot, Christophe. *Religion, Caste and Politics in India*. Delhi: Primus Books, 2010.
Jaffrelot, Christophe. *Modi's India: Hindu nationalism and the rise of ethnic democracy*. Princeton, NJ: Princeton University Press, 2021.
Jain, H. and A. Upādhāya (eds.). *Śrī Yativṛṣabhācārya-viracita Tiloya-paṇṇattī*, 2 vols. Solapur: Jaina Saṃskṛti Saṃrakṣaka Saṅgha, 1951; repr. 2007 = TiP.
Jansari, Sushma. 'From geography to paradoxography: The use, transmission and survival of Megasthenes' *Indica*', *Journal of Ancient History* 8 (1) (2020): 26–49. https://doi.org/10.1515/jah-2019-0013.
Jansari, Sushma. 'South Asia'. In *The Graeco-Bactrian and Indo-Greek World*, edited by Rachel Mairs, 38–55. Abingdon: Routledge, 2021.
Jhabwala, M. S. H. 'Report of the Village Mobile Health Van Committee (A.I.W.C. Skippo)', *The All-India Women's Conference* (1953): 51–54.
Johnson, Rachel E. and Shirin M. Rai. 'Imagining pasts and futures: South Africa's Keiskamma Tapestry and the Indian Parliament murals'. In *Political Aesthetics: Culture, critique and the everyday*, edited by Arundhati Virmani, 13–29. Abingdon; New York: Routledge, 2016.
Jones, William. 'The third anniversary discourse, delivered 2 February 1786. By the President', *Asiatick Researches* 1 (1798): 415–31.
Jones, William. 'The tenth anniversary discourse, delivered 28 February, 1793, by the President, On Asiatic history, civil and natural', *Asiatick Researches* 4 (1799; rpt. 1801): xiii–xxxv.
Kalota, Narain Singh. *India as Described by Megasthenes*. Delhi: Concept Publishing Company, 1978.
Kapila, Shruti. 'Race matters: Orientalism and religion, India and beyond c. 1770–1880', *Modern Asian Studies* 41 (3) (2007): 471–513. https://doi.org/10.1017/S0026749X06002526.

Karttunen, Klaus. *India in Early Greek Literature*. Helsinki: Finnish Oriental Society, 1989.
Karttunen, Klaus. *India and the Hellenistic World*, Helsinki: Finnish Oriental Society, 1997.
Kaul, Gautam. *Cinema and the Indian Freedom Struggle*. New Delhi: Sterling Publishers, 1998.
Kay, Adity. *Emperor Chandragupta*. Gurgaon: Hachette India, 2016.
Kesavan, B. S. and V. Y. Kulkarni (gen. eds). *The National Bibliography of Indian Literature 1901–1953. Volume 1: Assamese, Bengali, English, Gujarati*. New Delhi: Sahitya Akademi, 1962.
Kirk-Greene, Anthony. *Britain's Imperial Administrators, 1858–1966*. Basingstoke: Macmillan, 2000.
Kosmin, Paul J. 'Seleucid ethnography and indigenous kingship: The Babylonian education of Antiochus I'. In *The World of Berossos*, edited by Johannes Haubold, Giovanni B. Lanfranchi, Robert Rollinger and John M. Steele, 199–212. Wiesbaden: Harrassowitz, 2013a.
Kosmin, Paul J. 'Apologetic ethnography: Megasthenes' *Indica* and the Seleucid elephant'. In *Ancient Ethnography: New approaches*, edited by Eran Almagor and Joseph Skinner, 97–115. New York: Bloomsbury Academic, 2013b.
Kosmin, Paul J. *The Land of the Elephant Kings: Space, territory, and ideology in the Seleucid empire*. Cambridge, MA; London: Harvard University Press, 2014.
Kudelska, Marta, Dorota Kamińska-Jones, Agnieszka Staszczyk and Agata Świerzowska. *The Temple Road Towards a Great India: Birla Mandirs as a strategy for reconstructing nation and tradition* (trans. Steven Jones). Krakow: Jagiellonian University Press, 2021.
Kuracina, William F. *The State and Governance in India: The Congress ideal*. Abingdon: Routledge, 2010.
Lassen, Christian. *Commentatio geographica atque historica de Pentapotamia Indica*. Bonn: Weber, 1827.
Lahiri, Nayanjot. *Ashoka in Ancient India*. Cambridge, MA: Harvard University Press, 2015.
Lal, Vinay. *The History of History: Politics and scholarship in modern India*. New Delhi: Oxford University Press, 2003.
Lang, Jon T., Madhavi Desai and Miki Desai. *Architecture and Independence: The search for identity: India 1880 to 1980*. Delhi; New York: Oxford University Press, 1997.
Langford, Paul. *A Polite and Commercial People: England 1727–1783*. Oxford; New York: Clarendon Press, 1989.
Liddell, Henry George, Robert Scott, Henry Stuart Jones and Roderick McKenzie. *A Greek-English Lexicon*. Oxford: Clarendon Press, rev. ed. 1953.
Macaulay, Thomas Babington. 'Minute on Indian education'. In *Selected Writings*, edited by John Clive and Thomas Pinney, 237–51. Chicago; London: University of Chicago Press, 1972.
Macaulay, Thomas Babington, Lord Ashburton, Henry Melvill, Benjamin Jowett and John George Shaw Lefevre. *The Indian Civil Service. Report to the Right Hon. Sir Charles Wood*. London: W. Thacker and Co., 1855.
Macdonald, George. 'The Hellenic kingdoms of Syria, Bactria, and Parthia'. In *The Cambridge History of India. Volume 1: Ancient India*, edited by Edward J. Rapson, 427–66. Cambridge: Cambridge University Press, 1922.
MacGregor, Arthur. *Company Curiosities: Nature, culture and the East India Company, 1600–1874*. London: Reaktion Books, 2018.
Mairs, Rachel. 'Ethnic identity in the Hellenistic Far East', PhD thesis, University of Cambridge, 2006.
Majeed, Javed. *Ungoverned Imaginings: James Mill's 'The History of British India' and orientalism*. Oxford: Clarendon Press, 1992.
Majumdar, Ramesh C. *Outline of Ancient Indian History and Civilisation*. Calcutta: Chuckervetty, Chatterjee & Co., 1927.
Majumdar, R. C. *Ancient India*. Delhi: Motilal Banarsidass, 1952.
Malalasekera, G. P. *Vaṃsatthappakāsinī: Commentary on the Mahāvaṃsa*, 2 vols. London: Published for the Pali Text Society by H. Milford, Oxford University Press, 1935.
Masselos, Jim. *Indian Nationalism: A history*, 5th rev. edn. New Delhi: New Dawn Press, 2005.
Matthews, Peter. *London's Statues and Monuments*. Oxford: Shire Publications, 2018.
McClish, Mark. *The History of the Arthaśāstra: Sovereignty and sacred law in ancient India*. Cambridge: Cambridge University Press, 2019.
McCrindle, J. W. *Ancient India as Described by Megasthenês and Arrian; Being a translation of the fragments of the Indika of Megasthenês collected by Dr. Schwanbeck, and of the first part of the Indika of Arrian*. Reprinted (with additions) from the 'Indian Antiquary', 1876–77. Calcutta: Thacker, Spink; Bombay: Thacker; London: Trübner, 1877.

McCrindle, John W. *The Invasion of India by Alexander the Great: As described by Arrian, Q. Curtius, Diodoros, Plutarch and Justin*, 2nd edn. Westminster: Archibald Constable & Co., 1896.
Mehl, Andreas. *Seleukos Nikator und sein Reich*. Leuven: Peeters Publishers, 1986.
Metcalf, Thomas R. *Ideologies of the Raj*, The New Cambridge History of India III.4. Cambridge: University of Cambridge Press, 2008.
Mill, James. *The History of British India*, vol. I. London: Baldwin, Cradock, and Joy, 1817.
Montesquieu, Charles de Secondat. *De l'esprit de loix*. Geneva: Barrillot et fils, 1748.
Mookerji, Radha Kumud. *Chandragupta Maurya and His Times. Sir William Meyer Lectures, 1940–1941*. Madras: University of Madras, 1943.
Mookerji, Radha Kumud. 'Chandragupta and the Maurya empire'. In *The History and Culture of the Indian People. Volume 2: The Age of Imperial Unity*, edited by R. C. Majumdar, 54–70. Bombay: Bharatiya Vidya Bhavan, 1960 [1951].
Moore, R. J. 'The abolition of patronage in the Indian Civil Service and the closure of Haileybury College', *Historical Journal* 7 (2) (1964): 246–57. https://doi.org/10.1017/S0018246X00025450.
Mukharji, P. C. *A Report on the Excavations on the Ancient Sites of Pátaliputra (Patna-Bankipur) in 1896–97*. Calcutta: Bengal Secretariat Press, 1898.
Mukherjee, Sujit. *A Dictionary of Indian Literature: One: Beginnings–1850*. Hyderabad: Orient Longman, 1999.
Müller, F. Max. *A History of Ancient Sanskrit Literature so far as It Illustrates the Primitive Religion of the Brahmans*. London: Williams and Norgate, 1859.
Munshi, K. M. 'Foreword'. In *The History and Culture of the Indian People. Volume 1: The Vedic Age*, edited by R. C. Majumdar, vii–xii. Bombay: Bharatiya Vidya Bhavan, 1951.
Munson, Rosaria Vignolo (ed.). *Herodotus. Volume 2: Herodotus and the World*. Oxford: Oxford University Press, 2013.
Narasimhachar, R. *Epigraphia Carnatica. Volume II: Inscriptions at Sravana Belgola*, rev. edn, Mysore Archaeological Series. Bangalore: Mysore Government Central Press, 1923.
Narwekar, Sanjit. *Directory of Indian Film-Makers and Films*. Trowbridge: Flicks Books, 1994.
Nehru, Jawaharlal. *Glimpses of World History: Being further letters to his daughter, written in prison, and containing a rambling account of history for young people*. First published in India in 1934; second edition follows the 1949 printing of the third British edition, repr. New York: Asia Publishing House, 1975.
Nehru, Jawaharlal. *The Discovery of India*. Calcutta: Signet Press, 1946; Delhi: Oxford University Press, repr. 1994.
Neujahr, Matthew. 'When Darius defeated Alexander: Composition and redaction in the Dynastic Prophecy', *Journal of Near Eastern Studies* 64 (2) (2005): 101–7. https://doi.org/10.1086/431685.
Nichols, Andrew (intro., trans. and commentary). *Ctesias, on India, and fragments of his minor works*. London: Bristol Classical Press, 2011.
Ogden, Daniel. *Polygamy, Prostitutes and Death: The Hellenistic dynasties*. London: Duckworth with the Classical Press of Wales, 1999.
Ogden, Daniel. *The Legend of Seleucus: Kingship, narrative and mythmaking in the ancient world*. Cambridge: Cambridge University Press, 2017.
[Oldham, Charles E. A. W.] C. E. A. W. O. 'Review: *Political History of Ancient India from the Accession of Parikshit to the Extinction of the Gupta Dynasty*. By Hemchandra Raychaudhuri .... 2nd edition. ... University of Calcutta, 1927', *Journal of the Royal Asiatic Society of Great Britain and Ireland* 3 (Jul.) (1928): 689–92.
Olivelle, Patrick (trans.). *The Law Code of Manu*. Oxford: Oxford University Press, 2004.
Olivelle, Patrick. *Manu's Code of Law: A critical edition and translation of the 'Mānava-Dharmásāstra'*. New York: Oxford University Press, 2005.
Osborn, Eric. *Clement of Alexandria*. Cambridge; New York: Cambridge University Press, 2005.
Page, J. A. 'Bulandi Bagh, near Patna'. In *Annual Report of the Archæological Survey of India Annual Report 1926–27*, edited by John Marshall, 135–40. Calcutta: Government of India Central Publication Branch, 1930.
Panda, Harihar. *Prof. H. C. Raychaudhuri as a historian*. New Delhi: Northern Book Centre, 2007.
[Pargiter, Frederick E.] F. E. P. Obituary notice: 'Vincent Arthur Smith', *Journal of the Royal Asiatic Society of Great Britain and Ireland* 3 (Jul. 1920): 391–5.
Pargiter, Frederick E. Review. '*The Cambridge History of India* edited by E.J. Rapson'. *Journal of the Royal Asiatic Society of Great Britain and Ireland* 4 (October, 1922): 633–635.

Patel, Dinyar. *Naoroji: Pioneer of Indian nationalism*. Cambridge, MA: Harvard University Press, 2020.
Petech, L. Review. '*Age of the Nandas and Mauryas* by K. A. Nilakanta Sastra'. *East and West* 4 (4) (January, 1954): 300–1.
Pillai, Rajat. *Chandragupta: Path of a fallen demigod*. Delhi: Cedar Books, 2012.
Prasad, Rajendra. *Autobiography*. Bombay: Asia Publishing House, 1957 [1946].
Primo, Andrea. *La storiografia sui Seleucidi: Da Megastene a Eusebio di Cesarea*. Pisa: Serra, 2009.
Pritchett, Frances W. 'The world of *Amar Chitra Katha*'. In *Media and the Transformation of Religion in South Asia*, edited by Lawrence A. Babb and Susan S. Wadley, 76–106. Delhi: Motilal Banarsidass, 1997.
Rai, Shirin M. 'Political aesthetics of the nation', *Interventions* 16 (6) (2014): 898–915. https://doi.org/10.1080/1369801X.2014.882147.
Rajadhyaksha, Ashish and Paul Willemen. *Encyclopaedia of Indian Cinema*, new rev. edn. London: Fitzroy Dearborn, 1999.
Rankin, David Ivan. *From Clement to Origen: The social and historical context of the Church Fathers*. Aldershot: Ashgate, 2006.
Rapson, E. J. *Ancient India: From the earliest times to the first century A.D.* Cambridge: Cambridge University Press, 1914.
Rapson, E. J. *The Cambridge History of India. Volume 1: Ancient India*. Cambridge: Cambridge University Press, 1922.
Rama Rau, D. 'Introduction', *The All-India Women's Conference* (1946): 25.
Ray, Himanshu Prabha. *The Return of the Buddha: Ancient symbols for a new nation*. New Delhi; Abingdon: Routledge, 2014.
Ray, Himanshu Prabha. *Archaeology and Buddhism in South Asia*. Abingdon; New York: Routledge, 2018.
Ray, Himanshu Prabha (ed.). *Buddhism and Gandhara: An archaeology of museum collections*. Abingdon; New York: Routledge, 2018.
Raychaudhuri, Hemchandra. *Political History of Ancient India: From the accession of Parikshit to the extinction of the Gupta dynasty*. [Calcutta]: University of Calcutta, 1923.
Raychaudhuri, H. C. 'Chandragupta and Bindusara'. In *Age of the Nandas and Mauryas*, edited by K. A. N. Sastri, 132–70. Delhi: Motilal Banarsidass, 1952.
Renold, Leah. *A Hindu Education: Early years of the Banaras Hindu University*. New Delhi; Oxford: Oxford University Press, 2005.
[Rhys Davids, Caroline A. F.] C. A. F. R. D. Review. '*Political History of Ancient India. From the Accession of Parikshit to the Extinction of the Gupta Dynasty*. By Hemchandra Raychaudhuri, ... 2nd edition .... University of Calcutta, 1927', *Bulletin of the School of Oriental Studies, University of London* 4 (4) (1928): 855–7. https://doi.org/10.1017/S0041977X0012378X.
Rice, B. Lewis. *Inscriptions at Śravaṇa Beḷgoḷa, a Chief Seat of the Jains*. Bangalore: Mysore Government Central Press, 1889.
Robert, Jeanne and Louis Robert. 'Bulletin épigraphique'. *Revue des Études Grecques* 97 (Juillet–décembre, 1984): 419–522.
Robertson, William. *The History of America*, vol. 1. Dublin: Messrs. Whitestone, W. Watson et al., 1777.
Robertson, William. *An Historical Disquisition Concerning the Knowledge which the Ancients had of India; And the progress of trade with that country prior to the discovery of the passage to it by the Cape of Good Hope*. Dublin: Messrs. G. Burnet, L. White et al., 1791.
Roos, A G. and Gerhard Wirth, *Flavii Arriani quae exstant omnia. Volume 2: Scripta Minora et Fragmenta*, rev. edn. Leipzig: Teubner, 1967.
Roy, Abhijit. 'The middle class in India: From 1947 to the present and beyond'. *Education about Asia*, 23 (1) (2018): 32–7. https://www.asianstudies.org/publications/eaa/archives/the-middle-class-in-india-from-1947-to-the-present-and-beyond/ (accessed 3 November 2022).
Sack, Ronald H. *Images of Nebuchadnezzar: The emergence of a legend*. Selinsgrove, PA: Susquehanna University Press; London and Toronto: Associated University Presses, 1991.
Salomon, Richard. *Indian Epigraphy: A guide to the study of inscriptions in Sanskrit, Prakrit, and the other Indo-Aryan languages*. New York; Oxford: Oxford University Press, 1998.
Sangave, Vilas Adinath. *The Sacred Śravaṇa-Beḷagoḷa: A socio-religious study*. New Delhi: Bharatiya Jnanpith, 1981.

Sastri, Isvara Chandra. (ed.). *Cāṇakya-Rājanītī-Śāstram*, 2nd edn. Calcutta: Baidya Nath Dutt, 1926.
Sastri, K. A. N. Review. '*The Oxford History of India*. By the late Vincent A. Smith, C.I.E. Third edition, edited by Percival Spear. Oxford: Clarendon Press, 1958', *Journal of Asian Studies*, 19 (1) (November, 1959): 94–6. https://doi.org/10.2307/2943468.
Sastri, K. A. N. *Age of the Nandas and Mauryas*. Banaras: Motilal Banarsidass for the Bharatiya Itihas Parishad, 1952.
Sawkar, Indrayani. *Chakravarti Chandragupta Maurya: First sovereign king of India*. Independently published, 2019.
Schober, Ludwig. *Untersuchungen zur Geschichte Babyloniens und der Oberen Satrapien von 323–303 v. Chr.* Frankfurt am Main: Lang, 1981.
Schwanbeck, E. A. *Megasthenis Indica: Fragmenta*. Bonn: Pleimes, 1846.
Sebastiani, Silvia. *The Scottish Enlightenment: Race, gender, and the limits of progress* (trans. Jeremy Carden). New York: Palgrave Macmillan, 2013.
Secord, James A. 'Knowledge in transit', *Isis* 95 (4) (2004): 654–72. https://doi.org/10.1086/430657.
Seligman, Hilda. *When Peacocks Called*. London: John Lane, Bodley Head, 1940.
Seligman, Hilda. *Skippo of Nonesuch*. Wimbledon: Edwin Trim, 1943.
Seligman, Hilda. *Asoka, Emperor of India*. London: Arthur Probsthain, 1947.
Sen, Abhijit. *Rabindranath Tagore's Theatre: From page to stage*. Abingdon; New York: Routledge, 2022.
Seymour, Michael. *Babylon: Legend, history and the ancient city*. London; New York: I.B. Tauris, 2014.
Sher, Richard B. *The Enlightenment and the Book: Scottish authors and their publishers in eighteenth-century Britain, Ireland, and America*. Chicago; London: University of Chicago Press, 2006.
Sherwin-White, Susan and Amélie Kuhrt. *From Samarkhand to Sardis: A new approach to the Seleucid empire*. Berkeley and Los Angeles: University of California Press, 1993.
Shipley, Graham. *The Greek World after Alexander, 323–30 bc*. Abingdon: Routledge, 2000.
Singh, Upinder. *The Discovery of Ancient India: Early archaeologists and the beginnings of archaeology*. Delhi: Permanent Black, 2004.
Singh, Upinder. *A History of Ancient and Early Medieval India: From the Stone Age to the 12th Century*. New Delhi: Pearson Education India, 2008.
Singh, Upinder. *Political Violence in Ancient India*. Cambridge, MA; London: Harvard University Press, 2017.
Smith, V. A. 'A classified and detailed catalogue of the gold coins of the imperial Gupta dynasty of Northern India, with an introductory essay', *Journal of the Asiatic Society of Bengal* 53 (1) (1884): 119–206.
Smith, Vincent Arthur. 'The coinage of the early or imperial Gupta dynasty of Northern India', *Journal of the Royal Asiatic Society of Great Britain and Ireland* 21 (1) (1889): 1–158.
Smith, Vincent Arthur. 'Observations on the Gupta coinage', *Journal of the Royal Asiatic Society of Great Britain and Ireland* 25 (1) (1893): 71–148. https://doi.org/10.1017/S0035869X00022188.
Smith, Vincent A. *The Remains near Kasiā, in the Gōrakhpur District, the reputed site of Kuçanagara or Kuçināra, the scene of Buddha's death*. Allahabad: North-Western Provinces and Oudh Government Press, 1896.
Smith, Vincent A. *The Jain Stûpa and other Antiquities of Mathurâ*. Allahabad: Government Press, North-Western Provinces and Oudh, 1901a.
Smith, Vincent A. *Asoka, the Buddhist Emperor of India*. Oxford: Clarendon Press, 1901b.
Smith, Vincent A. *Asoka, the Buddhist Emperor of India*, 3rd edn. Oxford: Clarendon Press, 1920.
Smith, Vincent A. *The Indian Civil Service as a Profession: A lecture delivered at Trinity College, Dublin, on June 10th, 1903*. Dublin: Hodges, Figgis, 1903.
Smith, Vincent A. *The Early History of India: From 600 B.C. to the Muhammad Conquest, including the invasion of Alexander the Great*. Oxford: Clarendon Press, 1904.
Smith, Vincent A. *The Early History of India: From 600 B.C. to the Muhammadan Conquest including the invasion of Alexander the Great*, 2nd edn. Oxford: Clarendon Press, 1908.
Smith, Vincent A. *Catalogue of the Coins in the Indian Museum, including the Cabinet of the Asiatic Society of Bengal, Calcutta*. Vol. I. Oxford: Clarendon Press, 1906.

Smith, Vincent A. *A History of Fine Art in India and Ceylon: From the earliest times to the present day*. Oxford: Clarendon Press, 1911.

Smith, Vincent A. *The Oxford History of India: From the earliest times to the end of 1911*. Oxford: Clarendon Press, 1919.

Smitten, Jeffrey R. 'Robertson's letters and the life of writing'. In *William Robertson and the Expansion of Empire*, edited by Stewart J. Brown, 36–54. Cambridge: Cambridge University Press, 1997.

Smitten, Jeffrey R. *Life of William Robertson: Minister, historian, and principal*. Edinburgh: Edinburgh University Press, 2016.

Spooner, D. B. 'Mr. Ratan Tata's excavations at Pāṭaliputra'. In *Archæological Survey of India: Annual Report 1912–13*, edited by John Marshall, 53–86. Calcutta: Superintendent Government Printing, 1916

Stein, Otto. 'Megasthenes 2'. In *Paulys Realencyclopädie der classischen Altertumswissenschaft*, vol. 15.1, edited by Georg Wissowa and Wilhelm Kroll, cols. 230–326. Stuttgart: Druckenmüller Verlag, 1931.

Sternbach, Ludwik (ed.). *Cāṇakya-Rāja-Nīti: Maxims on Rāja-Nīti compiled from various collections of maxims attributed to Cāṇakya*. Madras: Adyar Library and Research Centre, 1963.

Stoneman, Richard. *The Greek Experience of India: From Alexander to the Indo-Greeks*. Princeton, NJ; Oxford: Princeton University Press, 2019.

Stoneman, Richard. *Megasthenes' Indica: A new translation of the fragments with commentary*. Abingdon; New York: Routledge, 2022.

Strong, John S. *The Legend of King Aśoka: A study and translation of the 'Aśokāvadāna'*, 1st Indian edn. Delhi: Motilal Banarsidass, 1989.

Strong, John S. *Relics of the Buddha*. Princeton, NJ: Princeton University Press, 2004.

Tarn, W. W. *The Greeks in Bactria and India*. Cambridge: Cambridge University Press, 1938.

Tarn, William W. 'Two notes on Seleucid history: I. Seleucus' 500 elephants, 2. Tarmita', *Journal of Hellenic Studies* 60 (1940): 84–94. https://doi.org/10.2307/626263.

Tarn, William W. *Alexander the Great. Volume 1: Narrative*. Cambridge: Cambridge University Press, 1948a.

Tarn, William W. *Alexander the Great. Volume 2: Sources and studies*. Cambridge: Cambridge University Press, 1948b.

Thapar, Romila. *Aśoka and the Decline of the Mauryas*. [London]: Oxford University Press, 1961.

Thapar, Romila. *A History of India*, vol. 1. London: Penguin Books, 1990.

Thapar, Romila. *Early India: From the origins to AD 1300*. Berkeley and Los Angeles: University of California Press, 2004.

Thomas, F. W. 'Chandragupta, the founder of the Maurya empire'. In *The Cambridge History of India. Volume 1: Ancient India*, edited by E. J. Rapson, 467–73. Cambridge: Cambridge University Press, 1922.

Timmer, B. C. J. *Megasthenes en de Indische Maatschappij*. Amsterdam: H. J. Paris, 1930.

Trautmann, Thomas R. *Kauṭilya and the Arthaśāstra: A statistical investigation of the authorship and evolution of the text*. Leiden: E. J. Brill, 1971.

Trautmann, Thomas R. 'Elephants and the Mauryas'. In *India: History and thought: Essays in honour of A. L. Basham*, edited by S. N. Mukherjee, 254–81. Calcutta: Subarnarekha, 1982.

Trautmann, Thomas R. *Aryans and British India*. Berkeley and Los Angeles: University of California Press, 1997.

Trautmann Thomas R. (ed.). *The Aryan Debate*. New Delhi: Oxford University Press, 2005.

Trautmann, Thomas R. *Elephants and Kings: An environmental history*. Chicago: University of Chicago Press, 2015.

Tucci, Giuseppe. Review. '*Chandragupta Maurya and His Times* by Radha Kumud Mookerji: Delhi, Motilal Banarsidass, Benares University, Sir William Meyer Lectures 3rd edition. 1960', *East and West* 14 (3/4) (Sept.–Dec. 1963): 248.

Turner, R. L. and R. Burn. Obituary notice. 'Professor E. J. Rapson', *Journal of the Royal Asiatic Society* 70 (4) (October 1938): 639–43.

Turnour, George. *The Mahâwanso in Roman characters, with the Translation Subjoined; and an introductory essay on Pâli Buddhistical literature, in two volumes. Vol I containing the first thirty eight chapters*. Ceylon: Cotta Church Mission Press, 1837.

Van der Spek, Bert. 'Multi-ethnicity and ethnic segregation in Hellenistic Babylon'. In *Ethnic Constructs in Antiquity: The role of power and tradition*, edited by Ton Derks and Nico Roymans, 101–16. Amsterdam: Amsterdam University Press, 2009.

Vasunia, Phiroze. 'Alexander Sikandar'. In *Classics and National Cultures*, edited by Susan A. Stephens and Phiroze Vasunia, 302–24. Oxford: Oxford University Press, 2010.
Vasunia, Phiroze. *The Classics and Colonial India*. Oxford: Oxford University Press, 2013.
Venkatasubramanian, T. K. *Music as History in Tamilnadu*. Delhi: Primus Books, 2010.
Verbrugghe, Gerald P. and John M. Wickersham. *Berossus and Manetho, Introduced and Translated: Native traditions in ancient Mesopotamia and Egypt*. Ann Arbor: University of Michigan Press, 2001.
Waddell, Laurence A. *Report on the Excavations at Pāṭaliputra (Patna). The Palibothra of the Greeks*. Calcutta: Bengal Secretariat Press, 1903.
Wagner, Kim A. *The Skull of Alum Bheg: The life and death of a rebel of 1857*. London: Hurst and Company, 2017.
Walbank, F. W. *The Hellenistic World*. Cambridge, MA: Harvard University Press, 1981.
Watson, John Selby. *Justin, Cornelius Nepos, and Eutropius: Literally translated, with notes and a general index*. London: George Bell and Sons, 1886.
Weerakkody, D. P. M. *Taprobanê: Ancient Sri Lanka as known to Greeks and Romans*. Turnhout: Brepols, 1997.
Welles, C. Bradford. *Royal Correspondence in the Hellenistic Period*. New Haven CT: Yale University Press, 1934.
Wells, Peter S. *The Battle that Stopped Rome: Emperor Augustus, Arminius, and the slaughter of the legions in the Teutoburg Forest*. New York; London: W. W. Norton & Company, 2004.
Wheatley, Pat. 'Antigonus Monophthalmus in Babylonia, 310–308 B.C.', *Journal of Near Eastern Studies* 61 (1) (2002): 39–47.
Whitehead, Clive. *Colonial Educators: The British India and Colonial Education Service 1858–1983*. London: I.B. Tauris, 2003.
Wiley, Kristi L. *The A to Z of Jainism*. Lanham, MD: Scarecrow Press, 2009.
Wilford, Francis. 'On the chronology of the Hindus', *Asiatick Researches; or, Transactions of the Society Instituted in Bengal, for Inquiring into the History and Antiquities, the Arts, Sciences, and Literature, of Asia*, vol. 5 (1799): 241–95.
Willis, Michael. *Buddhist Reliquaries from Ancient India*. London: British Museum Press, 2000.
Wilson, H. H. (trans.), ed. Fitzedward Hall. *The Vishńu Puráńa: A system of Hindu mythology and tradition*, vol. 4. London: Trübner & Co., 1868.
Wilson, Jon E. *India Conquered: Britain's Raj and the chaos of empire*. London: Simon & Schuster, 2016.
Winkler, Martin M. *Arminius the Liberator: Myth and Ideology*. Oxford: Oxford University Press, 2015.
Yardley, John C. (trans. & appendices) and Waldemar Heckel (commentary). *Justin: Epitome of the Philippic History of Pompeius Trogus. Vol. I, Books 11–12: Alexander the Great*. Oxford: Clarendon Press, 1997.
Yardley, John C. (trans. & appendices), Pat Wheatley and Waldemar Heckel (commentary). *Justin: Epitome of the Philippic History of Pompeius Trogus. Vol. II, Books 13–15: The Successors to Alexander the Great*. Oxford: Oxford University Press, 2011.

Index

A New History of the Indian People: Age of the Nandas and Mauryas 118, 119, 120
Aag Ka Darya 11, 200–201
Alexander III, of Macedon ('Alexander the Great') 15–17, 29, 40, 48, 51, 76, 78, 80, 115, 182–183, 191, 193
All India Women's Conference (AIWC) 162, 171–173, 189
Amar Chitra Katha 7, 11, 128, 176, 199, 207, 208–211
Antigonus I Monophthalmus 32, 33, 48, 52, 74, 77, 79, 98, 116
Apama 31, 32, 194
Appian 2, 33–34, 54, 75, 114–116
Archaeological Survey of India 55, 89
Arrian 16, 43–45, 46–50, 52–53, 55, 57, 59, 105, 164
Arthaśāstra 140, 168, 183, 194
Asiatic Society of Bengal (also known as The Royal Asiatic Society of Bengal) 3, 69, 70, 72, 86
Aśoka 28, 90, 135–136, 159, 162–163
  Edicts 28, 90–91
Athenaeus 41, 46
Aṭṭhakathā 24, 25
Ayyar, A. S. P. 11, 184, 200–202

Bhadrabāhu 19–21, 23
Bhandarkar, Sir R. G. 104, 105–108, 163
Bhāratīya Itihās Prasad 119
Bharatiya Vidya Bhavan 109, 121, 126n76
Bindusāra 27, 61n2, 67, 119, 125n49, 193, 195, 206
Birla (family and Mandirs) 10, 121, 127, 129–131, 133–143, 146, 148, 150, 154, 156, 179, 184
Birley, Sir Oswald H. J. 160, 161, 165, 168, 176n1

Cambridge History of India 9, 82, 93, 96–98, 118
Cāṇakya 5, 19, 23–24, 29, 35, 141, 146–148, 151, 153, 154, 155, 168, 179, 182, 191, 194–195, 208
Cāṇakya Nīti 140–142, 148, 150, 152
Chakravarti Chandragupta Maurya: First sovereign king of India (novel) 204, 206
Chandra Nandini (tv series) 6, 193–195, 204
Chandragupta (also: Androcottus; Candagutta; Sandracottus; Sandrocottus)
  comic book 7, 11, 128, 176, 199, 208–211
  film (director unknown) 187; (directed by A. R. Kardar) 187
  mural (Lakshmi Narayan mandir, Delhi) 10, 129, 143–146, 168,
  painting (Birla Mandirs) 146–155,
  play (by N.C. Kelkar) 184; (by Badrinath Bhatia) 184; (by Balkrishna Kar) 184; (by Jaishankar Prasad) 184.
  postage stamp 174–176
  sculpture (Birla Mandir) 10, 127, 130, 135, 137–143, 176; (Indian parliament) 10, 127, 159, 162, 165, 166, 170, 174, 176
Chandragupta: Path of a fallen demigod (novel) 204
Chandragupta Chanakya (film) 184, 188
Chandragupta Maurya (tv series) 193, 194, 195
Chandraguptha Chanakya (film) 188
Chatterjee, Sris Chandra 10, 130, 131–134, 139
Clement of Alexandria 46, 49, 51, 52
Ctesias 41, 60

daughter of Seleucus and wife of Chandragupta (variously: Helena, Cornelia) 6, 7, 128, 139, 140, 144, 145, 146, 182, 183, 184, 193, 194, 195, 197, 206
Desai, Jayant 128, 188, 189, 190–191, 195
Diodorus 43, 44–45, 46–47, 55, 57
Dīpavaṃsa 24, 27–28, 165
Dutt, R. C. 4, 9, 68, 104–108, 118, 123, 163

East India Company 3, 9, 67, 71, 72, 79, 80, 85, 180
Emperor Chandragupta (novel) 6, 204, 205

film posters 128, 190, 191–192, 195

Gandhi, Mohandas Karamchand 5, 108, 131, 135, 143, 160–161, 186
Gillies, John 71, 75, 77–80, 81–82

Hemacandra 19, 23, 24
History and Culture of the Indian People: The age of imperial unity 118, 122
Hyder, Qurratulain 11, 200, 201–203

Indian Civil Service 4, 67, 71, 82, 85, 86, 87, 88, 92, 105
Indian National Congress 103, 109, 119, 189
Indian parliament 10, 112, 127, 159, 162, 166, 168, 169, 170, 173, 174, 176, 187

Jones, Sir William 3, 9, 67, 69–71, 78, 81, 86
Justin 2, 17, 24–25, 29–31, 33, 53, 110, 113, 114

Kay, Adity 6, 11, 203, 204–205, 213n24

Macaulay, Thomas Babington 87–88, 104, 123
Macdonald, Sir George William 98, 99, 116, 120, 123
Magadha 10, 31, 130, 132, 133, 182, 183
Mahāvaṃsa 13, 24, 27, 28, 164, 165
Mahāvaṃsa-ṭīkā 19, 23, 24, 25, 26, 29, 164, 166, 193
Majumdar, R. C. 4, 68, 104, 105, 108, 109, 111–112, 113, 116, 121, 123
Mathru Bhoomi 6, 128, 187, 188–189
Mavalankar, G. V. 166–167
McCrindle, J. W. 10, 105, 107, 110, 112,114, 117, 119, 122, 124n5, 164, 200, 205
Mill, James 3, 9, 67, 71–75, 76, 77–78, 81–82, 99
Minute on Indian Education 87, 104
Mistry, Babubhai 128, 188, 190, 191, 192, 195
Modern Indian Architecture 10, 139
Montesquieu 72, 76, 77
Mookerji, R. K. 4, 29, 68, 104, 108, 109, 111, 113–116, 121–122, 123, 163
Mudrārākṣasa ('*Rākṣasa's* ring') 13, 71, 179, 199
Munshi, K. M. 121, 157n23

Nanda dynasty and empire 7, 17, 18, 19, 24, 25, 26, 29, 30, 110, 179, 182, 191, 193, 194

Oxford History of India 9, 82, 93, 96–99, 118

Pataliputra (Palibothra, Palimbothra) 5, 19, 29, 44–45, 46, 49, 52, 53, 55, 56–58, 59, 70, 91, 92, 104, 105, 132, 152, 164, 208
Patna *see* Pataliputra
Pattani, Sir Prabhashankar 160, 176n1
Pillai, Rajat 11, 203–204, 206
Plutarch 2, 28–29, 33, 34, 78, 110, 114
Pompeius Trogus 17, 24–25, 110, 113
Porus 8, 16–17, 29, 40, 42, 48–51, 52, 53, 54, 168, 194
Purāṇas 27–28

Rama Rau, Lady Dhanvanthi 172–173
Rapson, E. J. 9, 68, 82, 85, 86, 92–94, 96–99, 103, 123, 163–164
Ray, Dwijendralal (also Dvijendralal Ray/Roy) 6, 128, 181–184, 188, 190
Raychaudhuri, H. C. 104, 108, 109, 110–111, 118, 119–121
Reddy, H. M. 6, 127, 187, 188
Robertson, Rev. W. 71, 75–77, 78, 80, 81–82

Samanta, Sankha 174–176
Samrat Chandragupt 128, 188–190, 192
Samrat Chandragupta 128, 188–189, 190, 192
Sastri, K. A. N. 119, 121
Sawkar, Indrayani 11, 203–206,
Scylax of Caryanda 41
Seligman, Hilda 10, 127, 139, 159, 162, 164–166, 170–174, 176, 193
Sibyrtius 8, 40, 42, 48, 49, 51, 53–54, 61n3, 61n18, 61n21, 62n49, 63n62
Skippo Fund 162, 163, 171, 172, 173, 177n8
Smith, V. A. 4, 9, 67, 68, 71, 76, 82, 85–86, 87, 88, 92–96, 97, 99, 103, 110–112, 118, 120, 122
Sophytes 16, 17
Śravaṇa Beḷgoḷa 20, 21, 23,
Sri Lanka (Palaisimundu, Taprobane) 13, 23, 24, 27, 28, 58, 59, 80, 91, 164, 189, 193,
Sthavirāvalīcaritra 18, 19, 24, 25, 26, 27, 31, 37n60
Strabo 2, 25, 33, 34, 43, 44–45, 46, 47, 52, 53, 54, 55, 61n2, 64n80, 75, 110, 114, 115, 116, 120
Swadeshi Movement 10, 108, 130, 131, 160, 176n2, 188, 189

Tagore, Rabindranath 10, 171, 189, 212n15
Thomas, F. W. 98, 99, 123,

Viśākhadatta 26, 179, 180, 182, 197n1, 199

Milton Keynes UK
Ingram Content Group UK Ltd.
UKHW050025200224
438105UK00030B/509

9 781800 083899